"*A New Kind of Diversity* gives stirring reflections of the past generations and a glimpse into future generations. Dr. Elmore provides sound advice for what leaders must do to build strong, collaborative, inter-generational teams at work. This wonderfully written book captures his leadership experiences, expertise, and wisdom as he identifies the characteristics and contributions of each generation, lessons learned from each generation, and steps for connecting the various generations in an organization. He points out that each generation brings their differences in personal opinions, personal assumptions, and personal demands, and effective leaders must identify these differences within each team member. While this work is hard, it is important that seasoned, experienced leaders must pass wisdom on to the young so that they can then surpass us by standing on our shoulders. Dr. Elmore is an inspirational leader and mentor to many, helping us to think about this new kind of diversity. Learning how we can work with the many generations in our organizations will make us more effective leaders and will help us build leaders within each generation. I highly recommend this book to all leaders and their teams. It is not only about generations, memories, and experiences but also how we can use these experiences to build a better future in our workplaces."

—PAM DEERING, Executive Director, CCOSA

"Tim Elmore has done it again! I found myself thinking deeply about how the various generations—from our student-athletes, coaches, staff, and administrators—could benefit from understanding one another better. This book has ideas and strategies to achieve just that and can be a game changer if you share this same goal."

—JOSEPH R. CASTIGLIONE, Sr., Vice President and Director of Athletics, University of Oklahoma

"*A New Kind of Diversity* is a must-read! Tim Elmore has so eloquently addressed an issue that so often gets neglected. As a Chief People and DEI Officer, I believe we need to focus on all dimensions of diversity and inclusion, including the various generations that make up today's workforce. Tim Elmore has an innate way of cutting through theories about generations to get to the core of what helps a leader empower all team members to operate at their best."

—**CAMYE MACKEY,** Chief People Officer,
Diversity, Equity and Inclusion,
Atlanta Hawks

"Many from my generation have retired. Those of us who continue working need to focus our attention on helping younger generations stand on our shoulders to gain perspective and learn from our mistakes and successes. The book you're holding in your hands will give you a jump-start on this goal. Tim Elmore has given his life to helping generations connect."

—**DR. JOHN C. MAXWELL,** #1 *New York Times*
Bestselling Author, Founder of Maxwell
Leadership

A NEW KIND OF
DIVERSITY

A NEW KIND OF
DIVERSITY

MAKING THE
DIFFERENT
GENERATIONS
ON YOUR TEAM
A COMPETITIVE
ADVANTAGE

TIM ELMORE

FOREWORD BY **JOHN C. MAXWELL**

MAXWELL
LEADERSHIP.

A New Kind of Diversity
Making the Different Generations on Your Team a Competitive Advantage

© 2022 Tim Elmore

Library of Congress Control Number: 2022910780

Published by Maxwell Leadership, an imprint of Forefront Books.

Cover Design by Bruce Gore, Gore Studio, Inc.
Interior Design by Bill Kersey, KerseyGraphics

ISBN: 979-8-88710-000-5 print
ISBN: 979-8-88710-001-2 e-book

TABLE OF CONTENTS

What's behind the creation of a book like this? It was the
data supporting the fact that the generation gap, which
was first noticed in the 1960s, has widened today, making
collaboration and synergy on a team more challenging

Part One
MIND THE GAP

Interactions among people from differing generations can
resemble a cross-cultural relationship. Generations can
possess different values, customs, and languages. While
the generation gap was spotted more than fifty years ago,

Just like concrete is moldable when it's first poured,
so do our brains establish unique neural pathways in our
earliest years. Likewise, recognizing generations enables us to
connect with others distinctively. The goal is not to stereotype

Part Three
BRIDGE THE GAP

"If you think you're smarter than the

previous generation, consider this:

Fifty years ago, the owner's manual of a

car showed you how to adjust

the valves. Today, it warns you not to drink

the contents of the battery."

~Derric Johnson

FOREWORD

John C. Maxwell

OVER THE LAST FIVE YEARS, SOME QUESTIONS I'VE BEEN ASKED OFTEN are: "How do I manage my youngest team members? They join our team with very different attitudes and work ethics than our veteran team members do, and they're affecting our culture. What should I do?"

On the other hand, younger audiences are asking similar questions from their perspectives: "How do I show respect for my boss when I know there are better ways to manage our team? He doesn't seem to get me, and sometimes I wonder if I really fit in here. What should I do?"

As I speak across the country and around the world, I've noticed this is a global challenge. Older and younger generations working on a team can feel like a tug-of-war. Lines are drawn in the sand on how to get things done, and working together can be difficult. That's why I'm so glad my friend Tim Elmore wrote *A New Kind of Diversity*.

The leadership environment we are in today is more polarizing than ever, at least in my lifetime. We have a choice: will we allow the environment to determine our leadership, or will we intentionally change the environment? The good news is—there are strengths in our differences. It's a leader's job to find those strengths and maximize them.

Let's consider some strengths that can be found in an intergenerational team:

- · The wisdom of the Builder generation.
- · The stories of the Baby Boomer generation.
- · The pragmatism of Generation X.
- · The idealism of Millennials.
- · The innovative mindset of Generation Z.

Are you maximizing the strengths of the individuals on your team? It all starts with your perspective on others. Anybody can see weaknesses, mistakes, and shortcomings. Seeing good things is harder, but that's the difference between *anybody* and a great leader.

A New Kind of Diversity will accomplish a few goals.

First, it will enable you to understand your younger and older colleagues working alongside you. In these pages you'll read insights that are both personal and sociological about what shaped each of the last five generations. You'll pick up cues that you might never gain by talking to someone from each of these populations. While everyone has a unique personality and no one wants to be stereotyped, Tim Elmore reminds us: our goal is not to stereotype but to understand. This book helps you recognize the narrative each generation tends to possess.

Second, it will provide ideas on how to connect with other generations. The best leaders understand that for communication to be effective, they must be people-centric and other-focused. We must *read* our people before we *lead* our people. One of the things I love most about what Tim does in this book is the way he challenges you to see strengths in the differences of others. It's impossible to empathize with a team member or colleague if you don't see them as valuable. I've often said, valuing other people and adding value to them is the foundation of relationships. Applying the insights in this book will make you a better leader, teammate, mentor, and coach as you learn to connect with people who are different from you.

Third, it will enable you to get the very most out of each generation on your team. Effective leaders understand that each person on a team has something unique to add to the mission, and they learn how to capitalize on it. They bring out the best in their people, regardless of a person's experience. They find ways to get diverse age groups to collaborate to make the team better. Those irritating traits that, at one point, caused friction can now bear fruit. Good leaders demonstrate that while diversity may not make interactions smoother, they almost always make them more productive. Differences can be a beautiful thing.

This Book Is a First

I am proud to introduce you to a brand-new department in the Maxwell Leadership Enterprise—*Maxwell Publishing*. This book is the first of many we plan to publish in the years ahead. I am excited to have Tim Elmore as our first author and this book as our first resource. Our goal is to deliver outstanding resources that are values-based and that can transform teams, families, organizations, and even nations. Tim and I discussed this book at my home in 2021 and when he told me it was a project he was working on, I immediately resonated with the topic. I knew this book would be relevant and helpful.

I've known Tim for forty years. He was a young leader when I first invited him to join my staff, and he served alongside me for twenty years. During that time, I saw him bloom not only into an effective leader but, an effective communicator and author as well.

Tim has been studying, speaking, and writing on this topic since 2001. He's put in his 10,000 hours and has drawn some helpful conclusions on how to manage multiple generations, how to lead each one, and how to pull out their strengths.

Much of my generation has retired. Those of us who continue working need to focus our attention on helping younger generations stand on our shoulders to gain perspective and learn from our mistakes and successes. The book you're holding in your hands will give you a jump-start on this goal.

John C. Maxwell
Founder, Maxwell Leadership

BEFORE YOU READ
ANYTHING ELSE
An Introduction

IN THE SUMMER OF 2020, EVERY AMERICAN WHO OWNED A TELEVIsion was reminded of the racial divide that still exists in this country. George Floyd's life had been taken at the hands of Derek Chauvin following other African American deaths in the previous weeks. In almost every major city, marches and protests took place against police brutality and for racial equality.

But this was only the most recent in a long line of painful realizations in the American consciousness. In 2006, we were all reminded of the need to address gender inequality as story after story was broadcast of sexual harassment and assault on women in the workplace as well as on young female gymnasts. The #MeToo movement continues as a reminder of the gender gap that still exists and the need for equal respect and remuneration for females at work.

In 2011, news reports surfaced once again about income inequality in America. Certain job salaries paid to workers in specific demographics had not kept up with inflation. Regardless of whether it was hourly wages or salary packages, the divide existed and protest groups such as Occupy Wall Street (while it was terribly disorganized) attempted to raise the issue.

Regardless of how you might feel about these protests, each symbolizes a gap. Each one also illustrates a group of people who feel misrepresented or underrepresented. Those who protested wanted to raise awareness of an issue. Although I understand that each situation I've listed has complex details and varying angles, a legitimate issue remains. There is a gap that people need to be aware of and do something about:

There is a gap between generations on teams.

This book is my attempt to bring awareness to this new and different kind of diversity. I am not diminishing the importance of ethnic, gender, or income diversity. I am only saying there is a tangible diversity that's often missed or misrepresented by bosses and employees, by coaches and young athletes, by teachers and students, and among family members. I am speaking of generational diversity, the widening gap between the five generations that still influence our world yet don't seem to understand one another. This became evident over the last several years on social media as hashtags like these surfaced:

#HowToConfuseAMillennial (Boomers and Gen Xers making fun of Millennials)

#OKBoomer (Millennials making fun of Boomers)

#OKNancy (Generation Z making fun of Generation X)

#Doggo (Generation Z making fun of Millennials)

#BoomerRemover (Millennials and Gen Z making fun of Boomers)

This last one was used in especially poor taste, citing COVID-19 as the cause of death for many Boomers.

In 2020, I heard a nineteen-year-old member of Generation Z using the word *cheugy* as he made fun of someone he'd seen who was trying too hard to be "hip" and trendy. When I asked what older person he was poking fun at, he explained it was a twenty-nine-year old Millennial. I laughed in disbelief. The gaps surface so quickly. Yet instead of bridging the gap we feel between older and younger people, we've allowed the chasm to widen. At lunch breaks, water cooler conversations, or even in text message threads, we find it easier to talk to "our own kind." When we don't understand someone, it's easier to make fun of them. It's like different demographics living in different zip codes. It often feels like too much work to get to know a twenty-two-year-old at work when we are fifty-nine.

But what if we could resolve this dilemma and even *benefit* from our age differences?

What Prompted This Book

For the last twenty-eight years, I've been both an organizational leader and have taught leadership in every US state and around the world in fifty countries. I've met more than a few leaders over the years. During this time, I have observed four to five generations working together in a variety of contexts. As time marched onward, I noticed the generation gap widening. In fact, I have two reasons for writing this book. First, this is the number one topic I'm asked to speak on by businesses and the second most-requested topic by athletic departments and schools. I believe the subject is growing because more managers have identified divided teams that communicate differently, value different priorities, and have different definitions of work ethic and excellence.

Second, professionals have always assumed that kids are lazy or disrespectful (dating back to Socrates), but the generation gap is more distinct because new technology creates subcultures. Hence, generations often don't have to connect to survive. We need insight in order to bridge these subcultures in workplaces and among families. As an American population, young adults are taking longer to grow up, middle-aged adults are taking longer to grow old, and the elderly are taking longer to depart this earth. It's created generational gaps we've never seen before. According to Paul Taylor at the Pew Research Center, "As a people, we're growing older, more unequal, more diverse, more mixed race, more digitally linked, less married, less fertile, less religious, less mobile and less confident."[1]

Because I work with emerging generations, I've watched this for forty years.

Around 1980 I began noticing the emergence of a relational "gap" that existed in the marketplace. Baby Boomers were coming of age in large numbers, joining the workforce and starting families. I was one of them. A growing number of employers began saying they didn't quite understand their young employees. A growing number of coaches identified communication gaps with their young athletes. And a growing number of parents hinted that they didn't understand their teenager at home. This gap wasn't a fluke. By the late 1980s, Generation X had become the hot topic. This youth population represented everything alternative: they were unplugged, grunge, and commonly called the "MTV generation." The gap grew wider. Within a decade or so, the Millennials had become a topic of conversation. Neil Howe and William Strauss published a book in 2000 called *Millennials Rising*, a definitive work on the newest population of kids who were quite different than their predecessors. It was at that point that I began publishing my own studies and conclusions about the different populations influencing the world. I wrote a book in 2001 called *Nurturing the Leader within Your Child* that included my first "generational chart." It illustrated how the current generations both influenced and were influenced by the others. By 2003, I launched a nonprofit organization called Growing Leaders, which focused on preparing the emerging generations to be leaders. Seven years later, I wrote a book called *Generation iY*, detailing how the second half of the Millennials (Generation Y) was noticeably different than the first half. That book sold well and drew media attention from the *Wall Street Journal*, *Forbes*, the *Washington Post*, and *Psychology Today* as well as CNN's *Headline News* and Fox News's *Fox and Friends*. Clearly, others had noticed an issue at hand. This gap was a thing.

Before we jump in, allow me to share one caveat. I don't believe every problem on your team will be solved if you understand the information in this book. Not every challenge is caused by a generation gap. There are differences in:

- personalities
- socioeconomics
- gender perspectives

- ethnic and cultural background
- geographical history
- family origin

On top of that, if you were born within five years of the beginning or end of a generation, you'll likely adopt characteristics from both the previous and the upcoming one. Sociologists call you a "tweener." I am one of those as a late Baby Boomer.

Establishing when one generation ends and another begins is not an exact science, but it is a social science. The Pew Research Center places value on understanding generations: "It is a way of understanding how global events and technological, economic and social changes interact to define the way a set of people see the world."[2]

This book is more about sociology than psychology. It is about how growing up in different time periods and experiencing different realities can affect a person's mindset on a team. Our first two decades of life shape us based on shared music, tragedies, economies, heroes, milestones, technology, television shows, and events. Each person tends to bring their personal mindset with them to work, which is why an employer can say one thing and a teammate from a different generation can hear something else entirely. Yet this is not another book on managing or enduring Millennials or Generation Z at work. It is different in three ways: First, it includes the benefits of each generation in the workforce, including Generations Y and Z. Second, it offers ideas on how to leverage each generation's benefits to a team, making the most of what each demographic has to offer. Third, it furnishes a plan to practice principles on social and emotional intelligence among all team members.

My hope is that this content enables you to better understand, empathize, and connect with people who are different from you. In the end, I believe you will lead them better.

PART
ONE

MIND
THE GAP

1

WHO ARE TODAY'S CLASHING GENERATIONS?

THREE YEARS AGO I WAS IN CHICAGO SPEAKING AT A CONFERENCE about resolving conflict. After my session, a CEO approached me with a comment. I could tell he was frustrated at his inability to "mend some fences" between employees on his team. His team was divided on a go-to-market strategy for a new offering. Some felt they should focus on their new social media platforms and utilize a more personal approach, interacting with potential customers via social media. Others felt they should go with their proven methods that had worked well over the years. He suspected the factions represented conflicts between labor and management. After digging deeper, however, he recognized the issue was not that simple. He then wondered if the friction was about problems between departments, but it was more than that too. As we bantered, he had an epiphany. The lines his employees had drawn in the sand were about demographics. With few exceptions, the two younger generations perceived the issue one way, while the older two generations saw it another way. Interestingly, five other executives entered our conversation, verbalizing their agreement that there was a generational problem. They, too, were experiencing divisions—even chasms—on their teams along generational lines.

This conversation is not an isolated event. It happens thousands of times every year among people in the workforce. With the introduction of four to five generations in the workplace and with the rapid pace of change, we can predict we'll see friction on an increasing level. Paul Taylor, executive vice president at Pew Research Center, says, "Demographic transformations are dramas in slow motion. They unfold incrementally, almost imperceptibly, tick by tock, without trumpets or press conferences. But every so often, as the weight of change builds, a society takes a hard look at itself and notices that things are different. These 'aha' moments are rare and revealing."[3] Sadly, according to researcher Megan Gerhardt at Miami University, only 8 percent of companies recognize different generations as a category of "diversity."[4]

Today I interface with a growing number of managers who struggle to assimilate the younger age groups joining their teams. Their attempts to communicate company values or approaches to work receive varying reactions, depending on the generation and background. While these differences have been around for decades, the times have changed. When I began my career, the mantra of most bosses was, "Leave your personal problems at the door. You are here to work." Today the mantra seems to be, "Bring your whole selves to work." This means bringing their opinions, styles, posts, anxieties, and the desire to weigh in on issues, as if it were a democracy. Too often the old and the young dig their heels in and reach an impasse.

Allow me to provide two case studies.

Tony Piloseno was an Ohio University student who took a part-time job working at a nationally known paint retailer a few years ago. Unlike many employed college students, he actually enjoyed his work. In fact, he loved it so much, he started a TikTok account just to show off all the amazing colors that could be made by mixing the store's paint.

People were so attracted to Tony's posts that he rapidly grew a massive following. As of late 2020, his @tonesterpaints account had over 1.4 million followers and 24 million "likes." As his "tribe" mushroomed, Tony realized he was on to something and told his employers his viral account was an example of what the retailer's brand could do on social media. He felt it would be a great way to attract a new, younger audience the store chain was not currently reaching. Tony pitched the idea for months, complete with a slide deck, but alas, no one was interested— no curious inquiries, no positive responses.

What he did get was something he never expected. He got fired.

"They first accused me of stealing—I told them I purchased all my paint," Tony told reporters. "They made me answer a bunch of questions like when was I doing this and where, if there was anyone in the store while I filmed. There was never anyone with me while I was doing it."

After the corporate offices investigated his TikTok account, they showed him to the door. A brand spokesperson told *BuzzFeed* that "a customer's concerns" led to an investigation and ultimately led to their decision to fire Tony Piloseno.

Why This Paint Store Missed Out on an Opportunity

This story is a sort of case study on "old school" and "new wave" thinking. Here are three common reasons why we stumble into mistakes like the one Tony's employer made.

1. **When we're comfortable, we default to, "It's not the way we did it before."**

   While TikTok is among the newest social media platforms users are leveraging to market and tell their stories, the paint retailer had no official account. Tony was current on TikTok and saw what corporate failed to see. Instead of embracing his viral approach, they dismissed him. Why? Despite the smoke screens the paint store hid behind, it's clear to me they just couldn't see beyond their familiar methods. Their current models were safe and predictable, and that's what preoccupied their minds.

2. **When we're scared, we become more concerned with protocol than progress.**

   In the aftershock of a pandemic, it's easy to shift into survival mode. Many organizations relied on employee handbooks and bylaws to determine how to lead in this period of disruption. But when we do this, we can unwittingly become consumed with protocol. We miss opportunities to adapt and turn *interruptions* into *introductions* to new paths toward progress. No doubt that's what happened to the paint retailer. Tony is now building his own brand.

3. **When we're experienced, we assume the young don't know much.**

   When seasoned leaders talk to a twenty-one-year-old student, they can instantly assume their young ideas stem from naivete. We think they don't know what they're talking about. Sadly, "reverse mentoring" is one of the best gifts a seasoned veteran can receive, allowing a young person who recognizes the new world of communication to pass their intuition along. This mutual value can be exchanged only if their leader is humble and hungry.

There are likely more details to this story that we'll never know. Perhaps these would explain the leadership decisions at the paint store. Nonetheless, I still believe the company missed an opportunity when it fired Tony Piloseno instead of promoting him. He later moved to Florida, started his own company, and is staying in touch with his 1.8 million potential customers.

The challenge between generations, however, can go both ways.

THE OTHER SIDE OF THE COIN

I know a number of employers who are ready to welcome a new generation of team members into their workplaces, but the recent graduates are not prepared for a full-time job. Their schools did not get them "career-ready."

While older generations can benefit from the intuition of the newest population entering the workforce, it's clear the young ones often need input from seasoned veterans. Some graduates entering their careers have never had a job at all, neither part-time nor full-time. They only know the classroom, not the workroom or the boardroom. Millions need to be "coached up" by someone with experience who cares about them and their future.

For example, Laura is a senior human resources executive who had just finished her fourteenth interview in a single week with prospective job candidates when we spoke by phone. She told me she was exhausted, but it wasn't the volume of candidates she'd met that had worn her out; it was their readiness for a job. Or I should say, their *lack* of readiness.

Laura is a "fan" of Generation Z. She always reminds me of the immense potential recent graduates have, how much energy they bring to the workplace, and how much she loves coaching them as a human resource officer. This round of grads, however, was not prepared for much except more schooling. Her interviews were almost unbelievable:

- One potential employee could not look up from his phone. He was preoccupied with social media feeds—perhaps other job opportunities—and chose to multitask. There was no eye contact in the interview, poor listening skills, and very poor communication.
- Another interviewee told her he wanted lots of free time every day. When she said full-time employees work eight hours a day, he said he wasn't ready for that kind of commitment. He left after learning this information!
- Yet another candidate received a phone call right in the middle of the interview—and took the call. After a moment, she requested her caller to wait a moment, then asked Laura to leave the room (Laura's office), so she could finish the call in private.

Laura's reaction to these mishaps was revealing. She didn't blame the young people. She said, "I just wish schools and parents prepared these graduates for what was coming. I wish the schools operated more like a workplace. I wish moms and dads required their teens to work jobs during high school and college and discussed what they were learning along the way." Sadly, this is rare today, at least when you compare it to my teen years. My dad encouraged me to get a job (a paper route) when I was twelve years old. On rainy days, I didn't like it at all, but my parents reminded me how much I was growing from it, how much I loved making money, and how it was preparing me for an adult, full-time job. I ended up working all through middle school, high school, and college in fast-food restaurants, ice cream shops, country clubs, and nonprofits. While I recognize some parents still encourage this, millions actually *discourage* their teens from working, wanting them to focus completely on academics.

After graduation, however, those parents often realize their kid is unprepared for the marketplace and begin to compensate. Some even join their adult child on job interviews! In 2017, 26 percent of employers said parents had contacted them to convince them to hire their twenty-two-year-old son or daughter.[5] One in eight parents attended the job interview (as a sort of agent) with their adult child. This kind of thing would have been mortifying for a young adult in my generation, but it's becoming shockingly common today.

In any case, when the newest generation shows up at work having never had a full-time job nor worked alongside professionals, it can be frustrating. What's more, it can burn up all sorts of energy—call it *sideways energy*—that distracts everyone from pursuing their objectives.

What makes this issue even tougher is that the marketplace is changing rapidly. We've all heard the statistics about how today's kids will likely graduate into a career or a job that doesn't even exist today. According to the World Economic Forum, 65 percent of children in primary school today will be employed in jobs that do not yet exist.[6] The world of work is changing.

One reason is that many current jobs will become automated by artificial intelligence in the future. McKinsey Global predicts that almost half of all workplace activities could be automated in the future. Once again, the world of work is changing.

Employers must remember that younger generations of workers tend to adapt to such changes more quickly than older generations do. Generation Z will be especially at home with such shifts because of the experience they had in 2020. When the COVID-19 pandemic spread globally, Generation Z was sent home and adjusted to online learning better than their teachers did. In fact, I heard countless stories of students who actually helped their teachers navigate Zoom and Google Hangouts. The adjustments young people had to make in a year of protests, pandemics, political polarization, pay cuts, and panic attacks were stunning. While Gen Z suffers from mental health issues far more than previous generations, much of that was happening long before the COVID-19 outbreak. If we can help them navigate that issue, we'll find them intuitive when it comes to the future. They'll likely be the quickest to alter methods and will be your fastest learners.

> Pause and reflect. Do you see any divide between veterans and rookies on your team?

UNDERSTANDING EACH GENERATION

Recognizing how to interact with other generations is both an art and a science; it is a social science. According to historian Neil Howe, each generation tends to intuitively pursue three outcomes as they come of age. This isn't necessarily a conscious pursuit but rather an organic one as each age group responds to older populations. Years ago, Howe and William Strauss recognized that each new generation tends to

1. **Break with the previous generation.** Generation Z says to the Millennials, "You're cool, but we are cooler. You're into Beyoncé. We're into Billie Eilish."

2. **Correct two generations ahead of them.** Generation Z says to their parents, "I love you, but I will never do that to my kids when I'm a parent. I see your mistakes."

3. **Replace three generations older.** Generation Z becomes aware of their aging grandparents who will be gone soon, so they value retro: "I want a record player to listen to Sinatra."[7]

Having as many as four or five generations working on a team is enough to exhaust any leader who's attempting to connect with each of them. The following is an updated chart I included in my 2019 book *Generation Z Unfiltered: Facing Nine Hidden Challenges of the Most Anxious Generation* (the entire chart includes several more categories). I attempt to illustrate the different paradigms of each generation as they entered their careers and why they see things uniquely. Take a look at the big picture.

Reflect for a moment about what shaped each generation:

• **Builders:** They grew up during the Great Depression and World War II. They're frugal, resourceful, grateful, conservative—and they save the wrapping paper at Christmas.

• **Baby Boomers:** There was a "boom" of babies after World War II. These kids grew up in a time of expansion, not depression; the economy swelled, and they questioned everything.

• **Baby Busters:** This generation began with the birth control pill. It was a bust, not a boom. Generation X grew up jaded—raised by parents during the Vietnam War and Watergate.

• **Millennials:** They were raised by parents preoccupied with their safety, self-esteem, and status. Life was customized. Entitlement naturally grows with participation trophies.

• **Coronials (Gen Z):** Today's kids grow up in the wake of three recessions, mass shootings, a pandemic, political polarization, and lots of anxiety. Mental health is their top problem.

These summaries explain each generation's "life paradigm" as they joined the workforce. Now, consider each one's "attitude toward authority." My parents were Builders who taught me to respect all authority, from police to presidents. Baby Boomers like me felt we could solve the problem of authority just by taking over. Busters (Gen X) unplugged and simply endured authority as young professionals. Millennials choose their authorities. Since life is a big cafeteria, they are picking who they'll genuinely follow. The emerging Gen Z population feels empowered by those smartphones in their hands; they ask Google questions we used to ask our parents. If they were honest, millions of them would acknowledge, "I am not sure I even need an older person to guide me. What do they know about my future?"

It's a new day.

WHAT IT TAKES TO CONNECT THE GENERATIONS

Lieutenant Colonel Christopher Hughes led a troop of soldiers in Iraq during the second US invasion. When a shipment of food, clothes, and blankets arrived from the United States for refugees, Hughes felt the best place to distribute them was the local mosque. When he led his troop through the streets to meet with the cleric, people saw them and assumed the worst. They believed the soldiers were heading to their mosque to bomb it. When Hughes and his soldiers arrived, the mosque was surrounded by locals with stones and sticks ready for a street fight. It was a huge misunderstanding. Fortunately, Hughes was a master leader. He first ordered his soldiers to halt. Then, he asked them to point their weapons toward the ground. Next, he told them to take a knee, a most vulnerable position for anyone in public. Finally, he had his soldiers look up into the faces of the Iraqis and smile.

One by one, the local people dropped their rocks and sticks. Slowly they became calm and began to smile back, long enough for Hughes to locate a soldier who spoke Kurdish and Iraqi Arabic to explain to them what they had in their packages and what their intent was.

Disaster averted.

Lt. Col. Hughes displayed what psychologists call *social intelligence*. It is a subset of emotional intelligence. It's the capacity to navigate

Generational Issue	Builders Silent Generation	Boomers Pig in Python Gen
Birth years	1929–1945	1946–1964
Life paradigm	Be grateful you have a job	I want better
Technology	Hope to outlive it	Master it
Market	Goods	Services
Ethics	Conservative	Self-based
View of authority	Respect them	Replace them
Pandemic's effects	We've seen tough times before	My retirement is disappearing
Role of work	Means for a living	Central focus
Role of relationships	Significant	Limited, useful
Sense of identity	I am humble	I am valuable
View of future	Seek to stabilize	Create it

Busters Generation X	Millennials Generation Y	Coronials Generation Z
1965–1982	1983–2000	2001–2015
Keep it real	Life is a cafeteria	I'm coping and hoping
Employ it	Enjoy it	Hack it
Experiences	Transformations	Reinventions
Media-based	Shop around	Elastic
Endure them	Choose them	Not sure I need them
See, I told you life was hard	What will this do to my dreams?	I feel postponed and penalized
Irritant	Place to serve	It's my hobby
Central, caring	Unlimited, global	Utilitarian
I am self-sufficient	I am awesome	I am fluid
Skeptical	YOLO	FOMO

complex social relationships or environments. It's the very ingredient leaders desperately need today. As I mentioned, relationships between generations at work can feel like "cross-cultural" relationships. When a Baby Boomer speaks to someone from Generation Z, it may be like a conversation with someone from another country who has different values, different customs, and a different language. The effort that's needed not only to avoid damage but to collaborate is the same effort we must put into a relationship with someone from a foreign land. And far too often, we're not ready to put in that effort.

But if we did, what kind of advantages could we enjoy?

What If Each Generation Could See the Value the Others Bring to the Table?

Each of the four generations still at work offers a variety of gifts to the others. For instance:

1. **Baby Boomers:** Life experiences, awareness of pitfalls, life coaching for younger generations
2. **Baby Busters (Gen X):** Realistic perspective and pragmatic wisdom, resourcefulness, balance
3. **Millennials:** Energy and confidence, tech savviness, optimism, social connections
4. **Generation Z:** Entrepreneurial, "hacker" mindset, cause-oriented, social media savvy, fresh view

What if your organization had all four generations contributing from their strengths? What if each generation actually listened to the others? It might just be astonishing. We'll discuss this later in the book.

Every leader and team should be in the business of building strong, collaborative generations at work. When each of us can identify the strength of the others, everyone becomes stronger. In my humble opinion, our problem is that we live in a time where this is very difficult. Listening and understanding each other is not what we currently see in our culture. In fact, I think ours becomes a polarized cancel culture far too quickly. What's more, with the conveniences of an on-demand, instant-access society, we are vulnerable to becoming more fragile and less patient as a nation.

Executive producer Michael Hoff summarized the issue well. I have taken his thoughts and broadened the language for our purposes here. As each generation comes of age, they have the option to develop into a strong or weak population of adults. They can become known more for *consuming* or *contributing*, to become *victors* or *victims* of their era. Following is the cycle of history that demonstrates these sobering outcomes:

The Reality	The Result
1. Hard times create a strong generation.	1. Likely resilience
2. A strong generation creates good times.	2. Likely opportunity
3. Good times create a weak generation.	3. Likely entitlement
4. A weak generation creates hard times.	4. Likely passivity

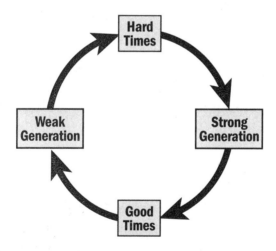

Where are we in this wheel of history?

Both my parents and my grandparents played vital roles in raising me as a child. They each experienced strong marriages and families; they demonstrated strong work ethics and wanted to build one in me. They volunteered their time in the community and donated much of their money. My grandparents' generation survived the Spanish Flu pandemic and fought in World War II. My parents' generation grew up during the Great Depression and World War II. From my experience, both of these generations became strong from it. *They became resourceful because they had fewer resources.* While they didn't have some of the knowledge we have today, they led the best they could from what they possessed.

As times got easier, however, the succeeding generations became susceptible to abundance; the data reveals that our grit levels and our resiliency declined (more on that later). But we can recover if we learn to benefit *from* one another and to benefit to one another. Our only hope is that we learn from each generation, both old and young. Regardless of what we think of younger generations, we must acknowledge they are our future. They represent what's coming ahead, not what's behind us. If we care about the future, we must care about connecting with and equipping the generations behind us to lead well.

Cross-Cultural Connection

I'm not sure if you've ever traveled overseas, but I have noticed in my international travel that once I land in Paris, Cairo, or Hong Kong, I am mentally prepared to work harder than usual at making a connection with locals. Why? In their country, they have different customs and values and likely speak a different language. I have arrived in a different culture.

Bingo.

Even now, Millennials no longer hold the "cool" spot on the team. Generation Z has arrived, and they are intimidating to anyone older who thinks they've kept up on what's trending. In late 2021 the *New York Times* posted at article titled "The 37-Year-Olds Are Afraid of the 23-Year-Olds Who Work for Them." It was all about the pace of change and how quickly team members who were once intuitive about markets and consumer culture are now lagging behind. "Twenty-somethings rolling their eyes at the habits of their elders is a longstanding trend, but many employers said there's a new boldness in the way Gen Z dictates taste."[8] And those employers who are not even forty years old are learning to listen to the input from a twenty-something. Buying habits and customs go extinct quickly, and the youngest teammates seem to know those customs naturally. Believe it or not, there is a gap between twenty-somethings and thirty-somethings.

Allow me to say it again: interactions among people from differing generations can resemble a cross-cultural relationship. Generations can possess different values, customs, and language. The generation gap is wider today, and leaders must commit to work harder at these relationships than, perhaps, ones from within their own generation. Awareness and tolerance, though important, are not enough. In the workplace, we must move beyond the baseline of mere tolerance of each other and toward having each other's backs; we must move from awareness to integration. Once we grasp *diversity* training, we must move on to *unity* training.

The people from different generations on the team have moved past colliding and are now collaborating. That's what this book is about. My question is, Are you willing to invest the necessary effort to connecting with different generations on your team or in your family?

Talk It Over

(1) Where do you see evidence of generational differences on your team or in your office?

(2) What do you think are some of the dangers of this, if left unchecked?

(3) Do you see any positive elements in the various generations where you work?

WHY IT'S IMPORTANT TO UNDERSTAND THE GENERATIONS NEXT TO YOU

BELIEVE IT OR NOT, THE MOST POPULAR TOPIC ORGANIZATIONS ASK me to speak on today is this one: How do we manage *generational diversity*? How can supervisors inspire teams made up of three to four generations, including Baby Boomers, Gen Xers, Millennials, and Generation Z? This year I spoke to two organizations that actually had *five* generations on staff. Today's workplace is more multi-generational than ever.

I recently spoke to the coaching staff at an NCAA university's athletic department and later met with several administrators to discuss the challenges they faced in their department. The year was 2019, and an argument had surfaced over the issue of allowing college athletes to be paid for their "image and likeness." Many students felt that since the sale of their jersey generated revenue for the school, they should get a piece of the action. It was a controversial issue at the time, and millions were divided over whether it was right or wrong. What's most interesting to me was that this school—which will remain nameless—split over the controversy right down *generational* lines. Their debate was almost stereotypical as staff shared their point of view with me in a predictable fashion.

Let me summarize their viewpoints:

Baby Boomers (who were mostly athletic administrators) did not like the idea. They felt the student athletes were already "paid" through scholarships, and furthermore, if they were paid more, they may have ulterior motives since the most popular players would make more money than the majority. Richard Burr, a North Carolina senator, had recently increased the divide, stating that athletes who make money for endorsements should be taxed on their scholarships. "If college athletes are going to make money off their likenesses while in school, their scholarships should be treated like income," he wrote. "I'll be introducing legislation that subjects scholarships given to athletes who choose to 'cash in' to income taxes."

Gen Xers (who were mostly head coaches) sided with their Boomer counterparts, wanting to keep the game "pure" so that athletes performed for the genuine love of the game, not for a "bonus." At the same time, the Xers were conflicted because they'd always been quietly suspicious of the administration, who seemed to hoard money and retain power over the purse strings. *Can they be trusted?* they wondered. Furthermore, perhaps allowing student athletes the chance to get paid might incentivize them to display more effort on the field. Who knows? It might be a good experiment to try out. In short, Gen X staff and coaches were a little skeptical of both sides.

Millennials (who were mostly assistant coaches) tended to side with the student athletes. They were still young and witnessed how much universities capitalized on players to make more money for the schools. It felt unethical not to give a "cut" to athletes who busted their butts each week. Most of these assistant coaches were former athletes themselves who remembered how it felt to spend an extra forty hours a week in practice and competition on top of a full load of classes. The only Millennials I met who didn't like the new idea were those who felt resentful that it didn't happen during their own playing days. They had missed their chance at endorsement deals and licensing contracts with companies such as Nike, Adidas, Under Armour, and PUMA.

Generation Z (which were all student athletes) generally liked the idea of being paid for their names and likenesses. Their debate was merely how to make the ruling fair to athletes who played less popular sports that didn't generate as much income through ticket sales and television. Fairness and equality were top of mind. They agreed with me when I summarized their view: If coaches push college athletes like professionals are pushed, then we also ought to be able to enjoy some of the perks the pros enjoy. Just make sure each athlete gets a fair shake at the money. Some told me they felt "triggered" by the "microaggressions" of the school administrators who were treating them like "slaves." In response, some of the staff felt the athletes needed to "grow up," to stop being "snowflakes," and to build a little grit.

Much like our nation at the time, this department was divided.

This isn't a new or novel issue, however. Almost two centuries ago, Alexis de Tocqueville was amazed at the different generations in America. He stated that in the United States "each generation is a new people." Because our country was built by adventurous entrepreneurs, we have always embraced change, making it a hothouse for young adults who have different worldviews from their parents and grandparents. According to a 2010 Pew Research Center poll, most members of each of the last four age groups say their generation has a distinctive and unique identity.[9] An earlier Pew Research Center poll asked Americans of all ages whether they saw a generation gap between young and old. About eight in ten said yes—almost the same number that reported a gap in 1969, forty years earlier.

Nevertheless, when I address generational diversity, I often hear a common complaint. Some people wonder why folks make such a big deal of these generations. Is it really a science? Aren't people merely different because of personalities? And doesn't this conversation merely stereotype whole groups of people? To the contrary, I believe it doesn't have to pigeonhole anyone; in fact, it can be extremely helpful. It's all about recognizing what factors shaped each generation. The goal is not to *stereotype* but to *understand*.

EACH GENERATION HAS A PERSONALITY

When I was eight years old, my friend Steve and I were goofing around outside when we discovered a patch of repaired sidewalk. Workers had just finished setting the concrete, and it was still wet.

I am sure you can imagine what a temptation this was for two kids.

Being more adventurous than I was, Steve suggested we press our hands into the wet cement and leave a print that would forever let people know we had been there. In fact, we decided to sign our handprints. It seemed brilliant at the time. We recognized later what a mistake it was. Steve and I both told our sisters who, in turn, told our parents what we'd done. Mom and Dad immediately reminded us that concrete hardens and that the neighbors would likely be upset that our handprints were now onstage forever in front of their house.

> The goal is not to *stereotype* but to *understand*.

Our parents were right.

Two days later, the neighbors knocked on our front door complaining. By that time, however, it was too late to fix what we had done. Everything had hardened and could not be smoothed over. Trust me, Steve and I tried our best to undo our work, but alas, cement workers had to return to lay a fresh sidewalk square.

So it is with our brains.

Just as concrete is moldable when it's first set, our brains establish unique neural pathways in our earliest years. Neural pathways, comprising neurons connected by dendrites, are created in the brain based on our habits and behaviors, especially in the earliest years of our life. As young people, those pathways are very pliable. As we age, they become less so. Dr. Britt Andreatta, an internationally recognized expert on leadership and learning and author of *Wired to Resist* recently presented her brain research at our National Leadership Forum. She says we are biologically wired to resist change after we become adults. This resistance is the key to our survival and yet the obstacle that gets in the way of us fulfilling our potential and connecting with others.

"When the brain is young and still forming, there's a lot of flexibility and plasticity, which explains why kids learn so quickly," adds MIT professor Deborah Ancona. After twenty-five years, we're less flexible. It isn't that we can't change; it's simply that it requires harder work to do so. It's the reason people say you can't teach an old dog new tricks. "The more we use our neural pathways over years and years and years, they become stuck and deeply embedded, moving into deeper portions of the brain," Ancona says. By the time we reach age twenty-five, we have so many existing pathways that our brain relies on, it's hard to break free of them.[10]

As a result, major milestones and events affect adults and youth differently. These important events influence behavior and can guide the narrative of emerging populations.

- **Life cycle effects:** Young people might act differently from older people, but they may become more like them later as those young people age.
- **Period effects:** Significant historical occasions (movements, wars, technology breakthroughs) impact all age groups differently based on where people are located in their life cycles.
- **Cohort effects:** Important period events often leave a specific mark on the young because they are still forming their worldview and values.

I believe each of these effects should be considered, but *cohort effects* seem to linger longer because they represent "wet cement."

Factors That Foster the Personality of a Generation

The social science of understanding different generations is all about recognizing the personality of a population of people. What shapes their comprehensive values, sense of humor, fears, and hopes? Generations, just like individuals, have unique personalities. In many ways, any study of the personality of a generation compares well to the study of an individual's personality. Perhaps you've taken a personality or temperament assessment such as the Myers-Briggs Type Indicator, the DISC Profile, or even the Enneagram. While each is meant to help you and others understand your personality, it's easy to fall into the trap of stereotyping others. For example, have you ever heard someone who failed to keep track of details excuse their behavior by saying, "Oh well, I am a Sanguine. We just don't do details very well!" Or have you observed someone grow impatient and frustrated with a colleague or family member and excuse it by saying, "I guess that's just to be expected. I am a 3 on the Enneagram." In time, we begin to excuse behavior by conforming people into a stereotype. We allow them to be less than they're capable of, or we stop expecting mature behavior. That, of course, was never the point of the personality assessment. Once again, the goal is to understand, not to stereotype.

The elements that make up a generation include:

Their Time in History

When a person spends their first couple of decades helps determine what the "brain concrete" looks and feels like. My mother and father, for instance, grew up in the midst of the Great Depression and World War II. Virtues such as gratitude, humility, and resourcefulness were firmly drilled into their mindsets. Think about how that must have shaped their neural pathways.

In contrast, I am a Baby Boomer who grew up in the 1960s and 1970s. I'm shaped by the Civil Rights protests, the Vietnam War, and Watergate. My children are Millennials who grew up in the 1990s and 2000s, and they are shaped by computers, cell phones, and technology.

This issue isn't black-and-white since there are so many other factors that play into shaping each human being, but there is both a biological and a social science at play here that we must consider.

Shared Economies

As we'll examine later in this chapter, bear markets and bull markets affect the positivity or negativity of consumers, many of whom happen to be parents. Even though children may not be aware of the state of the economy or the stock market, they see the faces and watch the caution or risks taken by adults and tend to reflect the times. As I mentioned, my parents grew up during the Great Depression and clearly reflected a "Depression mindset" throughout their adult years.

Technology

Technology is considered *new* only if it was introduced during your childhood. No one today calls a dishwasher "technology," but we do consider our latest portable device technology. Since new technology is introduced in each generation, it tends to define the youngest population. While Generation Z isn't the only group using TikTok, they'll always remember it was introduced when they were kids. For Boomers it was television; for Generation X it is was the Walkman and cassette tapes; for Millennials it was the cell phone and the Internet; for Generation Z it has been smart technology and social media.

Entertainment

The last four generations have been deeply influenced by the entertainment industry. Americans have more discretionary income to spend on entertainment than past generations, and media production has improved exponentially. Entertainment *topics* have also changed dramatically. For example, music has moved from topics that revolved around love and romance (eighty years ago) to social protest and personal feelings. In the 1960s, the word *love* was used in song lyrics twice as much as it is today. The word *hate* wasn't introduced in the *Billboard* Top 100 until the 1990s. And today the word *me* has taken center stage in pop music.

Tragedies, Heroes, and Villains

Each generation has its own heartbreaks that shape its persona and emotions. The Great Depression, World War II, the Vietnam War, the Cold War, assassinations, Watergate, the Space Shuttle *Challenger* explosion, the Rodney King beating, the Columbine High School massacre, the terrorist attack on September 11, the frequent mass shootings we see today—tragedies shape our risk aversion. Public figures surface such as Adolf Hitler, Dr. Martin Luther King Jr., Malcolm X, Richard Nixon, Princess Diana, Sadaam Hussein, Osama bin Laden, Barack Obama, George Floyd, and Donald Trump, each one taking on a public persona as hero or villain and shaping our emotional responses.

Shared Culture

A second cousin to the preceding list is how culture itself forges our character, for better or worse. For example, as shootings and abductions climbed over the last forty years, society's obsession with safety also climbed. As social media became ubiquitous, we began to experience FOMO (Fear of Missing Out), and our status assumed an even greater role in our lives. Data shows that culture grew more narcissistic as people became preoccupied with sharing photos of their meals, their trips, and themselves.[11] Thanks to our private, portable devices, culture plays a larger role in our lives than ever.

Family Environments

Families have always played a big role in how people turn out as adults, yet family has morphed over the last fifty years as society experienced higher divorce rates, more single-parent homes, and same-sex marriages and partners raising kids outside the traditional family definition. Over time, the definition of *family* has broadened and is now seen by millions as any cluster or community living under one roof that shares life in common. Society's understanding of gender is also morphing, moving from a binary issue (male or female) to over seventy-two gender identifications according to *Medical News Today*.[12]

With change happening more rapidly than ever, populations born within a time period are now perceived as "microgenerations." Within the Millennials and Generation Z, social scientists have spotted at least two if not three microgenerations within them. I wrote a book in 2010 called *Generation iY*, which focused on the second half of the Millennial generation and how different they were from the first half. In short, the '80s kids were different than the '90s kids. Indeed, almost every element above is changing more rapidly than in the past. For example, a Generation Z member born in 2001 has lived through three economic downturns; they watched portable devices shift from cell phones to smartphones; they've seen movies and television upgrade the complexity of their plots, computer graphics, and production; they've seen tragedies such as mass shootings and terrorism more than any generation over the last seventy years; they've seen culture shift rapidly during the COVID-19 pandemic, during which quarantines, massive protests for racial equality, and online commerce morphed in a matter of weeks.

Further, the influence of the world around us has increased exponentially. Consider kids growing up a century ago. Parents and family were, far and away, the number one influence on how a child perceived the world as they became adults. Today, thanks to social media, culture "seeps" into every home. Children and teens have their worldview shaped as much by the larger society as by their parents—often more so. And it happens quickly. As we shall see later, once our screens went from public (a TV in the family room) to private (a portable device in our hands), the generation gap increased. One vivid example of this is the Black Lives Matter movement. The term has been around since July 2013, a year after the death of Trayvon Martin. Yet the hashtag #BlackLivesMatter was used only about six hundred times prior to the death of Michael Brown in Ferguson, Missouri. After this, messaging on social media took off. By 2019, the hashtag was being used seventeen thousand times a day—millions of times since the death of George Floyd in 2020.

I'm not saying movements didn't take off prior to social media, just that social media accelerates ideas. And it has increased the gap. While everyone I know believes in the sentiment that Black lives matter, the divide between parents who use social media less than their young adult children has expanded measurably on the issue. Some wonder: does the Black Lives Matter (BLM) movement express a belief in equality for African Americans, or does it mean you support the organization? And does being pro-Black mean we're anti-white? Even schools have participated in this divide. In Minnesota, elementary school students were given an "equity survey" and instructed not to tell their parents about the questions. Fourth grader Hayley Yasgar said the questions were confusing and got concerned she couldn't tell her mom.[13]

It's a new day.

TIMING AND TITLES

Before we go any further, let's examine what shaped each generation and why they are named the way they are. Recognizing generations enables us to connect with others distinctively. It enables us to understand one another and helps us adapt to others and tailor our approach. Let's take a look at the shaping factors in each of the last five.

The Builder Generation (1929–1945)

This generation started with the stock market crash in November 1929. There was a run on the banks as people feared they wouldn't have access to their own money and banks shut down. The ensuing years were called the Great Depression and lasted, according to many economists, about a decade. One reality that shook us out of this depression was our participation in World War II, which ended in 1945. This group is called "Builders" as they had to be resourceful and build their adult lives from very few resources.

The Baby Boomer Generation (1946–1964)

This generation launched with the return of soldiers and sailors from the war. Babies were born as civilians and service members began to focus on starting a family. The 1950s were called the age of "normalcy." We wanted life to get back to normal, with a spouse, some kids, a dog, and a home mortgage. The "boom" of babies turned out to be 76.4 million, the largest number born in one generation up to that point. Some called them the "Pig in the Python Gen" since they were a large bump in the population curve. Life felt good during most of this period.

The Baby Buster Generation (1965–1982)

This generation didn't want to be tagged with a nickname, so the term *Gen X* stuck with them in time. At first, however, they were called "Busters" since their generation began with the public introduction of the birth control pill as a contraceptive. Add to that the *Roe v. Wade* legislation and you have a shrinking population—a bust rather than a boom. They grew up during darker times in the shadow of a much larger Baby Boomer population ahead of them. They held a more skeptical, even cynical, point of view. Naive optimism had diminished in America.

The Millennial Generation (1983–2000)

While some researchers start this generation earlier, it was marked by a shift in culture and parenting. In the 1980s and 1990s, America recalibrated herself, recovering from Vietnam, Watergate, an OPEC gas crisis, and a failed rescue of hostages. Campaigns focusing on child safety, self-esteem, and status became factors on how parents raised kids. They were called Millennials as they'd spend their entire adult life in the new millennium. As children became a top priority, Millennials grew into the largest generation in US history, about 80 million.

Generation Z (2001–2015)

Most of Generation Z will spend their entire lives in the twenty-first century. I mark this generation as launching at the turn of the century because society pivoted again with the dot-com bubble burst and the troubled economy; corporate scandals; the 9/11 attack, which ignited an era of terrorism; racial unrest; mass shootings; and smart technology, which both *connects* and *disconnects* us and fosters mental health issues. We live in a new normal. Some call them the "Coronials" as they're now marked by the coronavirus pandemic.

Millennials are also called Gen Y, following Gen X. Consequently, as sociologists jockeyed to decide the title of the next generation, Gen Z was natural. With a new century, this generation is marked by the dawn of both wonderful and horrible realities. One historian, Neil Howe, calls them the "Homelanders" because they launched about the same time as the Department of Homeland Security. The term currently used to describe the newest population of children following Gen Z is the "Alpha Generation," although at this time it is too early to define their characteristics in any meaningful way. You might say the cement is still wet.

That being said, consider the early memories of children born since 2016. They will assuredly recall adult populations that were divided, diseased, and depressed. Their early years launched alongside the Trump administration and are marked by a pandemic, political polarization, and panic attacks. We'll need to guide their narrative into a hopeful one as they mature.

The Peer Ghetto

One big step we must all take is to break out of our "generational ghettos." We tend to stay with peers, folks who are like us, instead of putting in the work of building bridges to others.

I just met Melanie and discovered she was job hunting. She graduated from college ten months ago and still has not found a career "match." When I asked if she'd ever had a full-time job, she relayed this story. I got her permission to tell it.

Melanie got her first job the summer following graduation and was excited to show her supervisor her skill set. Unfortunately, she got in her own way. She brought her cell phone to orientation and kept checking incoming texts during the training. This bugged her manager. In addition, when she was criticized for getting a project done late, she got defensive in an email. (She broke rule communication number one by sending emotionally charged messages electronically.) During the course of any day, she was checking Instagram to catch up with friends. When team members began growing distant, her supervisor met with her and asked if she had any idea why. She did not. After three months of conversations with her supervisor, she was finally let go.

Something dawned on me as Melanie told her story. One of the biggest reasons recent college grads are struggling to "onboard" at their new full-time job is something we may not have considered: for the first time in their life, the majority of their time is now spent with older adults, not with peers.

Consider this. The average adolescent spends fifty-five hours a week interacting with peers (much of it digital) and only sixteen hours interacting with adults. Further, a full 30 percent of a young teen's life is spent with no adult supervision. Emory University professor Mark Bauerlein predicted the dire consequences of the intellectual condition of young adults who've embraced the trappings of our digital age and disregarded their civic heritage of previous generations. He documents the decline of reading and the unprecedented contact teens have with one another through social media. While we all see the potential that technology makes possible, Bauerlein notes that research shows teens are much more likely to go to sites such as YouTube, TikTok, and Snapchat to see what their friends are up to than to spend time browsing the Library of Congress. What especially worries Bauerlein is how this focus on peer-to-peer interaction reduces the opportunity for vertical modeling—developing relationships with older people who can provide life experience or perspective to really understand an issue. Teen mentors are not Socrates, Augustine, or Moses—they're Tyler and Jessica on Instagram.

Consequently, when they do enter the workforce, it's often a clash or false start. They represent a new generation, likely the third or fourth generation mixing it up in the company. What's this doing to the team members on the job?

First, almost 90 percent of people say that conflict between generations results in wasted time and lost productivity within their organizations, according to a survey of 1,350 employees and managers by the American Society for Training and Development's (ASTD) Workforce Development Community.

Some experts reported unusual friction between Generation X and Millennials in the so-called war of generations. However, the ASTD survey found the greatest frictions to be between Boomers and Millennials. The study suggests that, on that front, conflict usually involves one side dismissing the value of the other side's experience, disagreements over the need to innovate, or a lack of respect.

More than 45 percent of respondents said Boomers and Millennials have the most trouble working together in their organization. About 21 percent said Boomers and Generation Xers were having the most conflict. Just 13 percent reported that the most conflict was between Gen X and Millennials.

Now, here's the kicker—despite the prevalence of such conflict, only about 20 percent of those surveyed said their organization has created a program or strategy for intergenerational relationships.[14]

You Need a Plan

Why does this issue deserve your attention as a leader? As we'll see in this book, the rapid growth of technology has created a greater distinction between how generations connect, what they value, and how they prefer to work. Changes to parenting styles over the years have resulted in a different kind of graduate—one that older staff members feel is "entitled." In fact, due to cultural changes, young team members increasingly expect to move up the career ladder quickly and often have unrealistic expectations of the workplace according to employers. In working with businesses, nonprofits, and universities, I've observed the following:

1. With each new generation, time becomes more valuable.
2. With each new generation, expectations of convenience and service rise.
3. With each new generation, the demand for work to have meaning intensifies.
4. With each new generation, the hunger for options grows.
5. With each new generation, the sense of entitlement increases.
6. With each new generation, the need for speed and space goes up.
7. With each new generation, the desire for customization expands.

It's going to take work, but we must bridge this generation gap.

To accomplish this, we're going to need a plan. Our future depends on it. Our youngest teammates are our future. The US Department of Labor published a graph of the generations that will fill our workplaces in 2025, which is right around the corner. The case is made for understanding different generations and for building a bridge to the young. The future belongs to them.

The Workforce in 2025

Projected size of labor force (in millions) by age for the year 2025

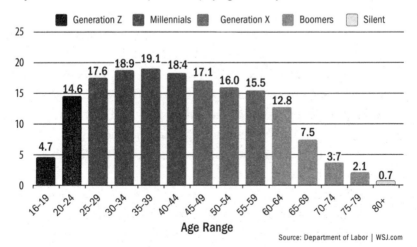

Source: Department of Labor | WSJ.com

Sadly, one nationwide survey reveals only 8 percent of American companies recognize that differing generations represent a category of diversity. My objective in this book is to offer "diversity training," and then follow it with "unity training." The preceding graph explains why this is so essential.

THREE ESSENTIALS TO LEADING SOMEONE FROM A DIFFERENT GENERATION

I continue to hear stories of Boomer or Gen X managers who become frustrated at the audacity of Generation Z or Millennial team members. One manager said a young job candidate told him in her interview: "I'm gonna have your job in eighteen months." Similarly, young professionals tell me about their consternation with older managers whom they call "dinosaurs." One twenty-three-year-old resigned when his boss told him, "I own you."

One of the top five questions I'm asked when I speak on leading multigenerational teams is this: How do you lead a person who is *much older* or *much younger* than you?

Over the past few years, our department managers have hired people who are young and we learned some valuable lessons along the way. Some of them were wrong hires. They weren't bad people, they just were not a good fit for our organization. Others were a good fit, but leaders had to learn how to effectively communicate with them. Conversely, I often hear Millennial managers share how awkward it can feel to lead someone who is twenty or thirty years older. Communication can be clunky, full of nuances, hidden messages, and ego. Based on our life station, we bring different norms and assumptions with us to the workplace. Most respondents to a *MarketWatch* survey said they're unlikely to get along with a team member from another generation.

So what do we need to connect with someone who's from a very different generation?

1. **Humility**

Gavin bluntly corrected one of our senior leaders in front of the entire team on a Zoom call. Regardless of the accuracy of

Gavin's comment, it divided folks because it was made in an arrogant way. Everyone noticed it but him. The irony is, he expected humility from others—but seemed unable to show it. I met with Gavin and attempted to explain the disconnect. The problem wasn't his information; it was his delivery. When people approach a difficult topic or a different generation with humility it communicates an openness to input, a recognition that they're human and flawed. This means I offer ideas, then listen to gain helpful insight myself. Listening screams humility! *I try to speak as if I believe I'm right but listen as if I believe I'm wrong.* Our team practices this too. Gavin never got this and is no longer with our team.

2. **Respect.**

Charlotte had a chip on her shoulder. She was smart and talented enough but began most of her interactions with distrust instead of belief. This twenty-four-year-old even told me when she meets people, she assigns them a grade. They start with an "F" and must earn an "A." She questions everything, which is fine if it's done in a respectful way. I recognize the majority of Gen Z does not trust traditional institutions but if they hope to make improvements on those institutions, respect can accelerate their progress. Once again, Charlotte demanded respect but didn't offer it to others. We live in a very uncivil, disrespectful era yet everyone wants to feel respected. Respect communicates you esteem the other person. Even if you feel you have a better idea, it's good to recall that current ideas were implemented as solutions to problems at one point.

3. **Curiosity**

If we enter conversations curious to learn and to see new perspectives, it enables connection between two points of view. When teammates from two generations embody curiosity, they can naturally smooth over rough spots and differences in style. Curiosity trumps conflict and builds a bridge where there might have been a wall. It communicates openness to new ideas and a hunger to grow and improve. Rachel is forty-six and Sam is twenty-two. At first, they butted heads during ideation meetings, but once the need to improve on methods was obvious, both switched gears and became more curious. Those teammates sharpen each other today, and now they not only overlook their differences but welcome them as an impetus for growth.

When we embody these qualities, we can say almost anything and connect with almost anyone.

We've created a free assessment to enable you to evaluate your generational fluency. It's called the GQ. It will reveal how well you understand the different generations on your team. You can find it here, along with my new book: NewDiversityBook.com.

THE RIGHT SIDE OF HISTORY

This university I spoke of in the beginning of this chapter never resolved its debate until people from all four generations resigned or transferred. Staff and coaches quit their jobs and student athletes left for other schools because the leadership was unable to convene civil conversations about a tough issue. They reached an impasse and lost some of their best people and students. It was so unnecessary.

This type of split over perspectives on significant issues is one big reason I believe we must figure out our differences and learn to benefit from them. Civil discourse is essential today, and multi-generational workplaces (even athletic departments) are incredible places to begin.

From time to time I hear the phrase "the right side of history." It's usually connected to a desire to see ahead and make decisions in light of where society is going, or at least where we believe it should be going. It means making decisions that, in retrospect, you don't look back on with regret. I've heard speakers encourage audiences to stay on the right side of history regarding civil rights or women's rights. It's about taking the long view and seeing beyond our own noses.

I believe this issue requires us to look ahead and choose to be on the right side of history. Young generations generally provide us a preview of where our society and marketplace are going. I encourage you to avoid neglecting to address the issue of the multiple generations. Pew Research Center's Paul Taylor remarks, "If ever there was a moment to gird for a generation war, now would seem to be it. The unsparing arithmetic of a graying population is about to force political leaders to rewrite the social contract between young and old."[15]

Here's the key: if we can understand each generation's story, we can likely connect with them better. We must *read* them before we *lead* them. My hope is that leaders can capitalize on what each generation has to offer the team and leverage it as a competitive advantage.

Talk It Over

(1) Who and what were your greatest influences during your teen years? Did certain "cohort effects" leave a lasting impression on you and affect you to this day?

(2) This chapter lists several factors that make up the personality and experience of each generation. How have you seen these factors play out? What other factors would you add?

(3) What are your thoughts regarding generations having "personalities?" How have you seen this?

3

IS THERE REALLY A GENERATION GAP TODAY?

I CHUCKLED AT A ONE-FRAME COMIC THAT SHOWED A YOUNG, LONG-haired college student sporting a beard, several tattoos, and flip-flops, speaking to his father who was seated in an easy chair in the living room. The student explained his lifestyle to his dad by saying, "But Dad, I gotta be a nonconformist if I'm gonna be like everyone else!"

Such are the sentiments of each generation of young adults over the last sixty years. We all wanted to be different, and we all wanted to fit in. We all felt we were unique, and we all felt as if we were discovering realities no one had discovered before. In some ways, history does repeat itself due to the cycles that our culture experiences as each new iteration of humans matures into adulthood. Perhaps Rafiki was right in *The Lion King* when he talked about a "circle of life."

EXAMINING THE GENERATION GAP

People often ask me why I make an issue of the different generations in the workforce today. Is there really a disparity between them, or are the differences merely about life stage? In other words, isn't every generation of teenagers basically the same, just growing up in different times? Earlier, I shared the logic behind life cycle effects, period effects, and cohort effects and how they can all play a role in influencing our outlooks. But questioning the reality of a generation gap is still legitimate, and it deserves a response.

Certainly, adolescents in every generation share common characteristics. Their brains are still maturing, which introduces multiple challenges. Consequently, a "gap" has always existed between the old and the young—and the elders usually complain about the immaturity of the kids. One old grump complained,

> Children now love luxury; they have bad manners, contempt for authority; they show disrespect for elders and love chatter in place of exercise. Children are now tyrants, not the servants of their households. They no longer rise when elders enter the room. They contradict their parents, chatter before company, gobble up dainties at the table, cross their legs, and tyrannize their teachers.

Some of the language is a bit dated, but this sounds like something anyone over age forty might say these days. But guess what? This complaint was sighed by Socrates twenty-four hundred years ago!

Likewise, the Roman playwright Plautus reportedly quipped, "Manners are always declining." Much later, poet and playwright T. S. Eliot noted, "We can assert with some confidence that our own period is one of decline; that the standards of culture are lower than they were fifty years ago; and that the evidence of this decline are visible in every department of human activity."

The term *generation gap* was coined by *Look* magazine editor John Poppy in the 1960s. He noticed there was a substantial divide in politics, tastes, morals, and virtually everything else between the young and the old—with the "old" including everyone over thirty.

Clearly, then, the generation gap is something that's been evidenced and bemoaned by each generation for thousands of years. The gap today, however, is wider and expanding more rapidly than ever.

Change Over My Lifetime

If you're like me, you never appreciated hearing your dad (or grandpa) reminisce about how he walked to school, fourteen miles, in the snow, without shoes, uphill... both ways. Few kids I know want to return to those "good, ol' days"—even in their memories.

On the other hand, I think we'd all agree we *can* learn from the past. Those "old days" included elements that embedded some time-less virtues in the people who lived during that time. The past is both horrible and wonderful.

Let's have some fun walking down memory lane. Allow me to reflect on some of the biggest ways our world is different for kids today—and how it may affect all of us in the future. Journalist Amber Dusick inspired me to do this when she wrote about being a mom in a very different world than the one she grew up in thirty years ago. So I did some reminiscing myself. Here is a short list of changes since my childhood days, fifty years ago.

1. Seat Belts

In my early years, cars didn't even *have* seat belts. I remember riding in the back of my grandpa's pickup on trips to Dairy Queen in Danville, Indiana. He'd purposely hit bumps so we'd experience the thrill and laughter of bouncing around back there. I don't remember ever sitting up straight in a car or truck. Instead, I managed to be in just about every other imaginable position—at least until the "Buckle Up, It's the Law" signs emerged. It's obviously a good law, but *boy* are we safety-obsessed now. My kids have never been able to ride in the bed of a pickup truck. It's far too scary.

2. Childproofing

Oh, my gosh. Hazardous cleaning products were all over the house—and often were left open. They had those scary skull stickers slapped onto them, however, so it was fine. That was childproofing in the 1960s and 1970s. Mom would tell us not to go into certain rooms or touch certain bottles; she might even place a box in front of something. It's so different for my children. These days, kids would need a ladder and have to navigate force fields, lasers, electric eyes, locks, and secret codes to reach a jug of bleach!

3. Helmets

I didn't even know what a bike helmet was when I was young. The only people I knew who wore helmets were football players and soldiers. Yet we did crazy things. We climbed huge trees, rode our bikes over a ravine, or used them to pull skateboards or wagons at full speed down a hill. (I had a huge accident where I fell over the top of my handlebars. It was ugly—and it was awesome.) The only way to stop was to wipe out. Incredible. But my kids today? No way. In the words of some parents, "Our kids wear helmets at the dinner table."

4. Screens

I liked screens when I was a kid. Except the only screen I had was a black-and-white TV—at least until I was nine. Then we finally got a color TV. It was amazing. But this screen was an auxiliary form of entertainment. Most of my time was spent making up stuff to do—games, competitions, sports, imaginary school classrooms, you name it. It was easier to be healthy with all the running around we did. We were creative because we had to be (we had to make our own fun). Today . . . not so much. It's all prescribed, structured, organized, and supervised by an adult. No creativity needed.

5. Cell Phones

As a kid, I only saw portable, wireless communication devices in science-fiction movies. Those were gadgets for the distant future.

Then in the 1980s, the cell phone emerged seemingly from the pages of a comic book. We saw them in cars at first. They were like bricks. Now everyone has them—most certainly every teen. Why? Two reasons: worrying and wandering. Parents worry where their kids are and what they're doing so the device is a sort of tether to keep them "on the line." Not a bad idea, except we became paranoid. The average college student is on their cell phone with Mom eleven times a day. And for kids today, the cell phone morphed into a smartphone. We can track everything.

6. Indoors vs. Outdoors

This one's big. My entire life, until I was seventeen, was spent outside the house. No adult "prescribed" our games either. We'd walk somewhere and mess around—outside. I lived much of my childhood in Ohio; it was cold in the winter and fall, but that was OK with me. Outside meant freedom, risk, the unknown, autonomy. The most striking contrast to today was the freedom I'd have on summer break. I'd eat breakfast and then leave; I'd be gone until Mom called for us to come home when it was dark. My kids growing up? Yeah, right. Freedom to wander around at night? No way—at least not until they are older. Like thirty-five.

7. Trouble at School

I remember when I got in trouble at school growing up. Once I got home, Mom and Dad would find out about it, and I'd get in trouble a second time. They supported the discipline of my teachers. The adults were aligned. Today if a kid gets in trouble or makes a bad grade, Mom and Dad might march down to the classroom and confront the teacher. They side with their child. It's quite funny to me; parents are "buddies" with their kids and tend to believe a child over an adult. Sadly, millions of moms and dads are *pals* more than *parents*.

This list, of course, is simply about fun memories of a world that's gone. As we examine today's cultural landscape, it's vital we recognize the largest distinction between yesterday and today.

8. Technology and the Generation Gap

The greatest difference between populations of youth has to do with the way technology has evolved over the last sixty years. For example, consider how we consume our music. In 1877, the public was introduced to the phonograph, thanks to Thomas Edison. Next, radio became popular about a century ago, later morphing into a portable transistor radio. Then in 1949, vinyl 45s were introduced containing one song on each side. Later we bought LPs, or long-playing records that included several songs. Then in 1963, you could buy cassette tapes that contained the same songs you could get on an LP. Some years later, eight-track tapes emerged that played albums and protected the tape. In 1979, we saw our first Walkman that allowed consumers to use both a radio and tape player. By the 1980s, compact discs became available and were used until MP3 players came along in the 1990s. Now most consumers receive their music via Spotify or iTunes; we're streaming today. These are vivid illustrations of generational change.

Identifying the Generation Gap

A Global Demographic Report prepared in 2018 by the Insights Research Team involved people from four generations (Generation Z, Millennials, Generation X, and Baby Boomers) and included over a half-million individuals (561,507 to be exact) from over sixty countries or regions around the world. These researchers concluded that generations do, indeed, possess personalities. For example, the two younger generations (Gen Z and Millennials) are significantly more social than Baby Boomers.

The study used the "color schema" developed from psychologist Carl Jung and ancient Greek physician Hippocrates. It is built around the four fundamental personalities:

- Fiery Red (Choleric)
- Sunshine Yellow (Sanguine)
- Cool Blue (Melancholy)
- Earth Green (Phlegmatic)

One might assume that globally there would be an even distribution of different personalities among each generation. This isn't the case, however, according to the data. Whether due to nature or nurture (or both), personality types vary depending on which generation someone comes from.

People under twenty-five years old are almost twice as likely to be "Sunshine Yellow" (Sanguine) as those who are over sixty years old, according to the study. Sanguines are social creatures, which makes sense as the study also revealed a tendency toward extroversion in young adults. Twentysomethings—thanks to their smartphones—are prone to be connected to others far more often than Generation X or Boomers. This may explain why I consistently hear remarks from senior managers that their young team members can't seem to stop talking and start working on the task in front of them.

Another finding: those over forty-five years old are more likely to be "Fiery Red" (directive and task-oriented) than those who are younger. In fact, that likelihood tends to climb with age up until age sixty. While there are clearly different personalities in each generation, younger adults tend to favor social relationships and older adults tend to favor task orientation.[16] In other words, while younger team members tend to lean toward extroversion, introversion is more prominent in older age groups.

This gap may explain what's happening on your team right now.

WHY IS THE GAP WIDENING?

There are actually six different generations living today. From my perspective, generation gaps between them are caused by at least five factors:

- Rapid changes in culture
- Increased life expectancy
- The mobility of society
- Shifting economies
- New technologies and media

Let's examine these factors.

First, one huge factor that has influenced generation gaps is the accelerating rate of change in society. Two hundred years ago, cultural developments were slow. As a result, two or three generations lived lifestyles that were very similar to each other. As technological and social advances took place in the twentieth and twenty-first centuries, however, the lifestyles of people even one generation apart became measurably different from each other. One college senior recently asked me, "What's up with the freshmen? They're so weird!"

Second, life spans have increased over the centuries. As people live longer and babies continue to be born, we now have more generations alive at one time than at any other time in modern history. Different paradigms emerge as our minds are exposed to different realities at different ages. Furthermore, because our neural pathways are set in different time periods, we tend to lock into a perspective that's different than what a younger person has. Increasing life spans can actually create more gaps in any population by enabling more generations to cohabitate than ever before.

Third, society has become far more mobile than ever. In earlier time periods, most people stayed in the same area or country with little contact with people outside their general area. Access to information from other cultures was limited. Today, all of us have at least watched a show about different cultures and nations if we've not visited other countries ourselves.

Fourth, young people are impacted by the shifting economy while they're growing up and preparing for adulthood. Even though they're young and only indirectly impacted, they watch the adults react or respond to the marketplace with caution or confidence in their spending and investments. Notice how the economy correlates with the size and spirit (tone) of each generation. Consider the narrative of the last five in the following chart.

Generation	Tone	Economy	Population
1. Builders	1. Caution	1. Mostly bear market	1. Smaller
2. Boomers	2. Confidence	2. Mostly bull market	2. Larger
3. Busters (Gen X)	3. Caution	3. Mostly bear market	3. Smaller
4. Millennials (Gen Y)	4. Confidence	4. Mostly bull market	4. Larger
5. Coronials (Gen Z)	5. Caution	5. Mostly bear market	5. Smaller

Fifth, with the increased advances of technology, people are introduced to new information and media. Just think about all the changes in technology that have occurred in the past twenty years. For example, a young man will choose to spend his time on public transportation texting or watching YouTube, while an older man passes the time reading a physical book or even a newspaper. It's a picture of the times in which we live.

As I ponder today's widening generation gap, the chief cause appears to be reduced to a single word: *exposure*. Life expectancy, travel, media, and technology all increase exposure to new information and experiences, which allows for different perspectives. My team members Sara and Noah are case studies of this astonishing reality. The Great Recession of 2008–2010 caused some despair on our team, but we were all seasoned veterans in our careers. Sara and Noah, however, were young teens who had just received a smartphone. Suddenly, at fourteen years old, they had the world—and all of its bad news—at their fingertips. It was overwhelming. Like millions of their generational cohort, they slipped into anxiety attacks. Mom lost her job. Dad said they could not afford some of the amenities they had once enjoyed. If you look at the data, it was about this time (just over a decade ago) that anxiety and panic attacks in young people began to skyrocket.

The Touchscreen Generation

In a recent publication of the journal *Pediatrics*, researchers found "almost universal exposure" to tablets and the use of smartphones (mobile devices) among young children.[17] A 2013 report said that "72 percent of children age 8 and under have used a mobile device for some type of media activity."[18] A 2015 survey showed "nearly 97 percent of parents said their children used mobile devices of some sort."[19] Additionally, using a device no longer required someone to know an individual's phone number, because we now manipulated it by touching the screen, not with a keypad.

Here are the most surprising findings in *Pediatrics*:

- Nearly 97 percent of parents said their children used mobile devices of some sort.
- The survey found that at age four, 75 percent of kids used their own mobile device.
- Of those children, about half multitasked on more than one screen at a time.
- Twenty percent of one-year-olds use a tablet computer.
- Twenty-eight percent of two-year-olds can navigate a mobile device with no help.
- Twenty-eight percent of parents use the device to put their kids to bed.

Most surprising to lead researcher Matilde Irigoyen was how quickly children as young as three years old use such devices on their own. As futurist Leonard Sweet says, "Gutenberg has given way to Google."

We can't do much about most of the causes for a gap, nor do we want to. There is one cause, however, that we *can* influence, and I'd like to reflect on it now.

Screens Went from Public to Private

Eighty years ago, there were no screens in the average American home. Families enjoyed radio programs and often listened to broadcasts together. In the 1950s, TVs entered the scene. By 1960, we reached a tipping point with television. According to the *World Book Encyclopedia*, "By 1960, there were 52 million sets in American homes, which meant a TV in almost nine out of ten households."[20]

Originally, however, TV programs were designed like radios, where the entire family could gather in front of the television set and watch shows together, such as *I Love Lucy* or *The Andy Griffith Show*. By the late 1960s, however, niche marketing began to happen as shows found specific audiences to target. *Sesame Street* was a show for preschool children. *Rowan & Martin's Laugh-In* was a prime time show designed for adults who enjoyed satire. *Never Too Young* aired in 1965 as the first soap opera geared toward a teen audience. You get the idea. Niche programming began to divide adults from kids. In time, media messaging began to inform each demographic differently. While there may have been just one television in the home and everyone knew what everyone else was watching, the information was segmented. Later, there were multiple television sets in homes, allowing further segmenting in a family.

When personal computing became more commonplace in the 1990s, families became even more segmented. It acted like the television in that there was usually one desktop machine (often in the kitchen) where everyone knew what the others were viewing. This time, however, users could search for content based on their interests. Life became more niched for each generation. Consumption became "on demand."

As the twenty-first century dawned, life changed even more. Our screens moved from public to private. Instead of one screen shared by everyone, it became the norm for each person to have their own screen—a smartphone, tablet, or a laptop. Today, parents may not even know what their teens are consuming. The platforms are in our individual hands and content is targeted toward different audiences. Everything is niched.

Portable devices not only allow a more personalized experience but also create virtual communities for anyone using them. Social media allows millions of teens, for instance, to create an

Instagram account, and perhaps several other "Finsta" accounts, which allow fake Instagram personas. Mom and Dad often have no idea they exist.

Author and Emory University professor Mark Bauerlein writes that teens now network with one another in unique ways. They have never lived a life so wholly unto themselves. A hundred years ago, a teen might have spent as much time with parents, uncles, aunts, and other adults as they did with peers. The gap was widened as:

- education migrated from a one-room schoolhouse to graded classrooms where students spend time with only their age group, not with multiple age groups.
- media programming evolved into niche markets, usually based on demographic interests, which foster homogenous communities.
- faith communities and churches split attendees into age groups so families seldom learn or worship together but rather are in age-targeted audiences.
- consumers now expect content to be customized for them, and they don't want to work as hard at translating concepts for their application (we've grown lazy).

Minimally, this explains why connecting with others is harder work today. We may have so little in common with that older person because their personal niche is so different. Connecting requires greater work to find any overlap or common ground.

If we fail to do this work, the result is almost always stereotyping. Kelly Pledger Weeks released the results of a multigenerational study in 2021. Her conclusion was that every generation wants meaningful work but thinks other age groups are in it for the money. She writes,

> We used a forced-choice survey that asked 298 participants to compare pairs of items and pick the one closest to their definition of meaningful work. Although there were a few differences among generations, when they were forced to choose what is most meaningful, generational

cohorts mostly agreed on their definitions. All generations chose items that revolved around intrinsic motivation first and foremost. They also all chose items related to having good relationships with coworkers as least important to their definition.

These results beg a question: If generational cohorts mostly agree on definitions of meaningful work, why was I getting so many requests for consulting?

The answer may lie in the results of the second part of our interview study: negative stereotypes. One of the most striking findings was that every generation perceived that the other generations are only in it for the money, don't work as hard, and do not care about meaning. If each generation thinks this way, it's not surprising that they treat each other differently than if they believe they are all striving for intrinsic meaning in their jobs. Stereotypes like these likely cause conflict among generational cohorts, which may affect performance, commitment, and job satisfaction.[21]

In short, stereotypes divide us, but understanding builds a bridge to others.

BRIDGING THE GAP

Herein lies our need for action steps to bring generations together. Here are the four steps I think are most urgent as we take on this important challenge.

1. **Find ways to group up and put multigenerational events on the calendar.**

   What if we got intentional about spending time with people unlike us, especially those from different generations? What if we found a spot on the calendar regularly to serve a need in the community, watch sports games, play cards or games, or just have conversations for the purpose of understanding each generation's story? While this may feel awkward at first, these regular meetings have become highlights for people who've chosen to participate.

2. **When in debate, start by acknowledging where both generations agree.**

   Before entering a discussion, those from different generations will profit from identifying all the concepts they agree on before debating their differences. We may be surprised with how often we share the same goals but just prefer different methods to reach those goals. Note where you're similar before you spot where you separate. In fact, the very word *communication* is taken from the Latin root *common*. Communication, then, should start with what you have in common and then expand from there.

3. **Explain your temperament and style when you offer feedback.**

   When interacting, people from different generations can benefit from acknowledging how they typically filter and relay information. For example, you may say, "Before I reply, it might be helpful to know I usually like to ask a lot of questions about what I just heard. It doesn't mean I'm against an idea; it's just how I process new information." This could be a game changer for a person from a different generation who suspects you don't like them.

4. **Express the "story you are telling yourself."**

   Research psychologist Brené Brown encourages us to use the phrase "This is the story I am telling myself" when feeling conflict or confusion over a situation. We often create narratives about ourselves or others that are inaccurate. We overcome these distortions in our heads by candidly admitting them to others. For example, one might reveal, "I feel inadequate right now, and the story I'm telling myself is 'I'm a failure at work.'" This enables vulnerable conversation as the disclosure invites transparency from others.

Are these things easy? No, they are not. But we must step *up* to the challenge, not step *back*.

A few years ago, I found myself in a greenroom before speaking at a conference. I was among a group comprising sixteen CEOs from various industries, male and female, old and young. I decided to turn these leaders into an instant focus group. I asked them, "Do you think leading teams today is harder than it was when you first learned to lead?" Every one of them, to the person, replied, "Yes!" One said, "Absolutely!" Another replied, "A hundred and ten percent!" I smiled as I countered that it was odd we'd all think this way; we might assume leading would be tougher when we were younger and didn't know as much about leadership. But, alas, everyone stuck to their guns.

As 2019 closed out and we entered the first quarter of 2020, there was a "great CEO exodus" according to *Fortune* magazine. As the pandemic hit our world, many workers got pink slips as companies had to lay off employees. Then in 2021, we read about the "Great Resignation," when millions of employees resigned from their jobs to seek better places to work. It felt almost like revenge on their part. The pace of "quitting" was record-setting.

Certainly, there were many reasons for this disruption, including shortages in shipping, strikes, boycotts, and labor disputes. I believe at least part of the reason, though, are the various assumptions of each generation in the workforce. Each generation brings tailored expectations with them into the marketplace. Each of them brings opinions with them. We are leading in complex times. Armchair quarterbacks are everywhere.

But this is doable.

It has been said, "We often meet someone and think they are different, but people are not inherently different: our differences lie between us, not within us."

Let's get started.

PART
TWO

MANAGE
THE GAP

4

THE CONTRIBUTION OF THE BUILDER GENERATION

HENRY STROUD, OR "HANK" AS HIS FRIENDS CALL HIM, IS EIGHTY-four years old and still in relatively good health. Hank enjoys watching Fox News and playing cards with his friends each week. Once in a while, he'll play golf, although it's becoming less of a joy and more of a chore these days. He says he gives all new meaning to the term *handicap*. I smiled as he told me his version of golf is a cross between bumper cars and an Easter egg hunt.

Hank told me recently that he wanted to go back to work, which he hoped would give him a sense of purpose again. When I asked him what he was waiting for, he replied that he had tried . . . but had given up. This is strange because Hank is not a quitter. He explained, however, that he didn't fit in. He was only looking to do handyman work at a local company, including repairs, lawn care, and the like, but he just felt out of place. In fact, he even used the term *foreigner*. He told me the people there (all of whom were younger) were using a different language for their everyday tasks, had a different sense of humor, and valued different priorities. It was like he was from a different country than they were.

Hank wishes he could be more useful, but he feels like a misfit. He is a Builder.

The Builder generation—often called the Silent generation—was born into the Great Depression and World War II. While they may not have been aware it was a global economic calamity then, they learned to live frugally, humbly, and gratefully while serving their fellow man. Not a bad model. In this chapter, we'll examine their chief contribution, how we can benefit from them, and what they'll need to do to adapt to our current times.

Their greatest challenge is to mind the gap.

MINDING THE GAP

During the COVID-19 quarantine, most employees hunkered down in their homes. For many organizations, it was a time to learn how to leverage technology better. For others, it was a time for team members from various age groups to discover how different they were.

I consulted with one company and on a single day heard a Builder generation founder say, "I think it's time to retire. I am just so different than the team members I hired." I could hear the frustration in his voice. He then continued, "I don't think that young man understands me or the core values we embrace here." One hour later, I met with that young man (a Millennial) and heard him say, "I don't think our founder gets me or my values."

Herein lies the problem.

As we've seen, many of us work in an organization that employs up to five generations. Each generation represents a different paradigm as a colleague, supervisor, team member, intern, client, neighbor, friend, or family member. These paradigms don't all stem from the time period in which we grew up, but many of them do. During the first two decades of our lives, we are shaped not only by family but by loads of other factors. Baby Boomers and Millennials both grew up as a large generation in a growing economy; Gen X and Gen Z grew up as smaller generations in a sour economy. So each pair shares some similarities. But Boomers and Xers are very aware of the different paradigm Millennials and Gen Zers brought with them into the workplace, right? Culture and technology had shifted. These shared experiences form a narrative we possess as we enter adulthood, and they're the source of either a unique *contribution* to teammates or a unique *conflict*.

The good news? We get to choose.

A Map for the Gap

I mentioned earlier that the term *generation gap* became popular in the 1960s as the Baby Boomer generation was coming of age. Parents, bosses, and coaches from the Builder generation all recognized their children were growing up in a different world than the one they'd grown up in years earlier. Change was happening faster. World War II was over and rock music hit the music charts. Long hair, illegal drugs, extramarital sex, and anti-war protests were shaping emerging adults, and millions of young Boomers wanted nothing to do with the "establishment."

Sound familiar?

Each generation of young people appears "disrespectful" to their older generations of parents and grandparents, but as the Boomers grew up, they brought with them an entirely new outlook that questioned authority. Boomers were free thinkers, and Builders weren't quite sure what to do with it. Traditions were receiving pushback as young Baby Boomers developed their own subculture with their own language, using phrases such as:

- Totally groovy, man.
- That's a gas!
- What's your bag?
- You're a drip!

Today the terms are even more varied.

Recently, I've had several folks from the Builder and Boomer generations inquire about today's "codes." One asked me what the term *woke* means. Another asked about the term *rent free* and even *cheugy*. Hmmm. What goes around, comes around, right? Generation Z not only has a new language but uses it on platforms their parents don't even know about. Kids have an Instagram account but also several "Finsta" accounts, fake Instagram personas that allow them to post and communicate private messages to friends or strangers. Young adults from Generation Z have told me they possess five or six identities. (How could someone from an older generation even keep up with all of this?) Generation Z is also exposed to adult information younger than ever, often as early as elementary school age, if they've been on social media sites, YouTube, or *BuzzFeed*. In short, because our worlds are more customized and personalized today thanks to smart technology, different generations can experience a unique niche and remain ignorant of those outside it.

The wider gap merely makes our work tougher and more important.

THE BUILDERS BECAME A SILENT GENERATION

Beginning in late 1929, a new population of kids began to be born, kids who would grow up learning life's hardest lessons earlier than most generations did because they would endure an economic depression—officially called the Great Depression—such as our nation had not seen before. It began with a stock market crash in November 1929 that led thousands of Americans to make a run on their bank to withdraw their cash. Because this was before any regulations existed on insurance, the banks were unprepared for such a withdraw. Many closed their doors. As the economy spiraled downward, hard times rose. Companies let employees go, and many went out of business. Folks learned to get by on less and share resources with each other. While the economic downturn hit hardest between 1929 and 1933, unemployment remained high for the entire decade. Many historians and economists believe the Great Depression didn't officially end until we entered World War II in 1941.

Like many industrialized nations in the early twentieth century, the United States experienced a gradual decline in its birth rate. "As more Americans moved off the farm and into the city, having a large family slowly transformed from a good labor investment to a poor economic choice. Consequently, in the midst of the Great Depression, the American birthrate fell to its lowest point yet, to just 18.4 live births per thousand population."[22]

The generation before them fought through World War I and the Spanish Flu pandemic. In his book by the same title, Tom Brokaw called them "the Greatest Generation." They were heroes for what they'd done for our country, for how they'd sacrificed to save Western civilization. Coming along behind them was a generation of kids who struggled in silence, having no famous war to fight and no well-known pandemic to overcome. They were silent "builders" who grew up during tough economic times and frightening political times during the reign of Adolf Hitler.

My parents are part of this generation. My mother passed away at sixty-five years old, far too early in my opinion. I still miss her to this day. My father passed away at ninety in November 2020. He was born in 1930 so the first fifteen years of his life were marked by the Great Depression and World War II. He learned to be frugal and grateful. He carried a "waste not, want not" attitude into the twenty-first century. Some of the daily signals of this attitude for me as a child were the same that many with Great Depression parents will remember:

- "Turn the lights off when you leave the room. It'll save electricity."
- "Shut the door when you leave the house. We're not air-conditioning the neighborhood."
- "Keep that paper bag and rubber band. We may need it someday."
- "Why not just have leftovers tonight? There's no need to go out."
- "You can wear hand-me-downs one more year, can't you?"
- "Remember, enjoying a Coca-Cola is a special treat!"

- "Save that wrapping paper [at Christmas], we can use it
  next year!"

These sentiments are a subtle aftereffect of growing up as a
child during the Great Depression. When I spoke to my dad about
this period of his life, he confirms that those years were tough times
financially. At the same time, however, he believes they were the best
years of his life. Often he told stories of how everyone looked out for
one another in his neighborhood, sharing milk and cheese and meat
and offering others jobs when they had any to give.

In fact, I interviewed two dozen Great Depression kids, all in their
eighties and nineties now, to discover if there were commonalities in
their earliest experiences. I wondered what pattern may have existed
that informs how we lead people today, during this deep economic
downturn. My interviews included my in-laws, Jay (90) and Jackie
(88) Hobson, and my dad, Skip Elmore (89). Here is what I found:

1. **The majority were not aware they were living in the Great
   Depression.**
   Because there was no social media or 24/7 news cycle in the
   1930s, most kids could tell life was tough but did not feel as if
   they were *victims* of horrible times. They saw Mom and Dad
   struggling to provide food, clothes, and necessities, but that
   seemed *normal*. When asked if they even knew about the
   Great Depression when they were kids, many replied, "Oh,
   heavens no." By and large, adults helped their children retain
   an innocence in the midst of hardship. One suggested that
   enduring those tough times may have prepared Americans
   mentally for World War II.

2. **Everyone felt they were all the same and were in this thing
   together.**
   There didn't seem to be a "comparison trap" among families
   in the 1930s, at least not like we have today. Today we might
   be very aware of the vacations others enjoy, the clothes they
   own, or the food they consume thanks to posts on social

media, but ninety years ago, that didn't happen. Not surprisingly, not knowing seemed to have helped them emotionally handle their lack. Think about it this way: if you were to grow up impoverished in a wealthy city like Los Angeles, you'd be much more likely to feel like a victim than if you had grown up with the same level of wealth on a farm in the middle of Nowheresville, a mile from your nearest neighbor. Why? In Los Angeles, an income discrepancy is more obvious with the wealthy population there, while on an Iowa farm, it would be harder to notice. So much of the way we feel about our wealth is relative; our opinion of our own status is often determined by how we compare ourselves to others.

3. **People maintained simplicity, gratitude, and contentment.**
   I was struck by how many Great Depression kids spoke of how little it took to make them happy. One recalled that Saturday night entertainment was walking through town after the stores closed to "window shop." No buying, just looking. That was a highlight from their weekend that they still remember to this day. Another noted that, while more people lived in town, they retained their "farm habits," enabling them to grow gardens for food and trim their grocery bill. One mentioned that church members all grew vegetables, then brought what they grew to the church basement to share with others. They all recalled saving everything, from rubber bands to plastic bags.

4. **Adults raised kids collectively and worked to build morals and work ethic.**
   Yesteryear, an entire neighborhood of parents raised the kids. One child from the Great Depression recalled a neighbor marching him down to the store when he won a free candy bar in a contest, believing he may have stolen or gambled for it. Adults tended to back one another up in such times to ensure kids learned ethics. Several said they had moms who always saw the positive side of life—singing songs, reading books to

neighbor kids, and rarely, if ever, complaining. It was common to borrow flour or butter from neighbors. They recalled adults talking on the porch over a glass of lemonade, discussing how to raise children who were humble but not hungry. Kids learned to be self-sufficient yet interdependent, frugal yet charitable—an interesting mix of traits often missing today.

5. **Good attitudes and virtues seemed to be paramount.**
Every adult reinforced maintaining a positive attitude. There was a sense of *community responsibility*, and complainers were frowned on. There was a collective sense that you were not to feel entitled to special perks nor embrace a victim mindset. Unlike us in 2020, nobody hoarded toilet paper even though it was relatively new. They lived by the mindset "only take what you need." In fact, if you had extra, you gave it to someone who needed it. Families often shared one bike. Hand-me-downs were common. Selfishness was a no-no. Kids were taught to think in "the long term." Planning, frugality, and conservatism were celebrated virtues: saving more than spending; generosity, not hoarding; humility, not cockiness; service over selfishness; what's mine is yours.

As I reflect on how differently this generation handled their lack, it strikes me that these are the same life lessons we must pass on to Generation Z in a post-pandemic world.

LESSONS LEARNED FROM THIS GENERATION

If you're like me, you've had numerous, "Do you recall where you were when this happened?" conversations in your life. I'm always astonished when I discuss past events in a group full of different generations. The oldest in the room learn less from history books and more from firsthand experience. For example, do you remember where you were when these happened?

- The Pearl Harbor attack
- The John or Robert Kennedy assassination

- The Watergate scandal
- The *Challenger* Space Shuttle explosion
- The O. J. Simpson trial
- The 9/11 terrorist attacks
- Kanye West taking the mic from Taylor Swift at the Grammys
- The coronavirus pandemic breaking out

Probably the chief reason I enjoyed interacting with people from the Builder generation is they are walking history books. They usually remember details surrounding each of these events as well as how it made people feel and how it affected others when those events happened. My parents, for instance, remember how it felt when they heard Adolf Hitler was attacking and conquering Europe at will or when Pearl Harbor was bombed.

> Have you noticed any other life lessons from members of the Silent generation you know?

There is so much to learn from our elders.

Since millions among the Silent generation lived long lives and became good citizens decades later (my parents included), we can especially learn a lot from them about leading Generation Z, who is growing up in similar times. Consider for a moment some similarities:

The Silent Generation	Generation Z
Two economic slumps (1929-1939)	Three economic slumps (2001-2020)
Suicide rates increased	Suicide rates increased sharply
Food became scarce for millions	Meat became scarce for millions
Unemployment rose to 25 percent	Unemployment rose to nearly 19 percent

After listening to a focus group of elders (all over eighty years old) and interviewing senior citizens at Mount Miguel Covenant Village (a retirement center near San Diego), I noticed three negative and six positive outcomes from their recollection of the Great Depression that I want to unpack here.

Negative Outcomes of the Builder Generation

The negative results were

1. Increase in suicide rates
2. Risk aversion
3. Lower expectations

Let's break these down a bit.

First, of the six primary causes of death a hundred years ago, only suicides increased during the Great Depression. Suicide mortality peaked (along with unemployment) during the worst years of the depression: 1932 and 1938. In other words, we learned that *economic* depression can and often does trigger *emotional* depression.

Second, risk aversion showed up in the daily habits of everyday Americans for years following the Great Depression. It took decades for people to regain consumer confidence, plan without fear of another period of scarcity, and take risks in their careers. Many retained the outlook of "just be grateful you have a job." And understandably, children of the Great Depression were wary of the stock market for their entire lives.

Third, it became natural for this generation who grew up with fewer material possessions and luxuries to enter adulthood with lower expectations. When people are formed by living simply, it's quite natural for them to be minimalists and have fewer demands even when times are economically better. Standards of living certainly went up for my parents' generation, but they tended to remain satisfied with a simple life. Although I grew up in an upper-middle-class neighborhood, I recall my mother hanging paper towels on the clothesline for them to dry so we could use them again. We didn't expect fresh paper towels or new napkins for every meal.

Positive Outcomes of the Builder Generation

Fortunately, there were a larger number of positive effects, even virtues, that continue to show up in our oldest population who were raised in the Great Depression. Whether the connection between these virtues and the times they were raised in is a causality or a correlation, I find it interesting how often these characteristics appear in our senior citizens. I believe we could and should target these same outcomes as we lead Generation Z.

We must remember: the Silent generation was also called the Builder generation, primarily because they were in charge of reconstruction after the war. They learned to build something out of very little or nothing at all. As I interviewed members of the Builder generation, I began to see predictable patterns. There are at least six beliefs I spotted in my case sample:

1. **Be humble.** One of the consistent virtues of these Depression kids was humility. They realize they are but smaller pieces of a large puzzle; very little arrogance or cockiness remains in them.

2. **Be grateful.** They are appreciative of the people who played a part in their progress. They realize that while they worked hard, they did not achieve their goals alone.

3. **Be a good worker.** Work ethic is a staple for senior citizens. Even if they felt they weren't great models of an industrious spirit, they still knew it was the barometer for a quality employee.

4. **Be kind.** They learned to look out for one another during the dark days of the Depression and World War II. They're marked by the acts of service among neighbors in their earliest memories.

5. **Be resilient.** Enduring several societal setbacks while they grew up, these Depression kids had to learn to bounce back after hardship. Grit and resilience were normal and expected.

6. **Be resourceful.** Because most didn't enjoy lots of resources between 1929 and 1945, they had to learn to be resourceful.

They made much out of little and discovered how to make life work on less.

In 2013, Ardyth Stull wrote a graduate dissertation called "Stories of the Children of the Great Depression: What I Learned from My Parents." This thesis provides quantitative and qualitative research from interviews she did with Great Depression kids, suggesting what we can learn about the values adults embraced during the Great Depression that enabled them to provide for the physical and emotional needs of their families during economic hardship. She wrote,

What other qualities did this generation model for future generations?

> I was surprised to discover the fond memories and good experiences that were shared, despite the fact that all the participants' families had endured hardships. The Great Depression was difficult, but not devastating for most of them. I asked if they realized they were living during the Great Depression when they were children. Several spoke at once and said they did not, stating that "Everyone was the same. We didn't know any different."

One of the fascinating outcomes of poor economies is that they can cultivate both people who are risk-averse *and* those who are entrepreneurs. My dad was an entrepreneur, going into business for himself with his brother, Gene. They built a solid business in San Diego assembling security cameras for stores and other outlets to prevent shoplifting and vandalism. They met a need, and the business grew up the coast of California before they sold it and retired. Thanks to their resourcefulness and resilience, the Builder generation spawned millions of entrepreneurs in the workforce.

SIX QUESTIONS THE BUILDER GENERATION MUST ANSWER

For a Builder in the marketplace, the key will be *adapting*. As I've mentioned, team members come from different worlds, speaking different languages, embracing different customs, and often having different values. We must be ready to play on a multigenerational team.

We must lead better. We must adapt better. We must think better. We must communicate better. Our problem, however, is we are weary. And we're leading people who are scared and uncertain about the future—their health, their income, their families, their work, and whether they'll be able to reinvent themselves if needed.

Let me suggest some questions for Builders to answer as you attempt to lead better:

1. **When was the last time you did something for the first time?**
   The older I get, the more I must pose this question to myself. Am I still attempting new feats, trying new adaptations, and launching new hobbies, or have I gotten stuck in my routines?

2. **Do you appreciate new team members' differences as individuals?**
   Be honest with yourself. Do you care for team members as people and not just as commodities to help you reach your bottom line? Do you know and love them as humans and not just as workers?

3. **Do you normalize defects when you're tired?**
   When start-ups grow, they tend to solve problems rapidly with quick fixes that aren't best in the long run. It becomes an *efficiency defect* over time. Do you allow these to continue?

4. **Have you fallen in love with your products more than your purpose?**
   Drill companies must not fall in love with the drill bits they make. People buy bits to make a hole. The hole must be the focus, not the drill bit. Methods come and go. Mission remains.

5. **Are you open to new ideas when they're from less-experienced sources?**
   Four generations serve in the workforce today. Do you welcome ideas from younger team members or do you assume their inexperience eliminates them from contributing?

6. **Can you see disruption as an *introduction* instead of an *interruption*?**
   Can you reframe an intrusion in your day as a possible opportunity to rethink things? If you saw the interruption as an introduction, it could enable you to see possibilities.

Do you remember Hank, the man I introduced you to in the beginning of this chapter? Hank is a Builder generation member who has much to offer, not just in handiwork but in wisdom. I put him in touch with a nonprofit organization that could benefit from his talent and experience. I encouraged the president of this nonprofit to begin by getting acquainted with him, then interviewing him before the entire team, both paid staff and volunteers. Hank was a hit. His stories gave everyone fresh perspective. He not only began doing repairs and lawn work around the property but, regularly met with team members to offer wise counsel to the problems they encountered each week serving people in need.

Everyone won.

Similarly, I love how one retirement village brought a sense of purpose to dozens of Builder generation members and added value to the community at the same time. During the COVID-19 quarantine and pandemic, there was a great need for masks in a lower socioeconomic area of the city. The village joined hands with a local company and enlisted members—all eighty-five to ninety-five years old—to sew masks for this community. They produced over one thousand of them in a matter of two weeks to give to those in need. Once again, everyone won.

I believe, however, the Builders felt like they received more than they gave.

─────────── **Talk It Over** ───────────

(1) Are there members of the Builder generation you could welcome to play a role on the team or even be interviewed in front of your team?

(2) What are some virtues your team displays that reflect the Builder generation? Which of the Builder generation virtues could you use more of on your team?

(3) How could you position any Builder generation members to be successful?

(4) How can you capitalize on the virtues the Builder generation brings to the team?

(5) What changes should you make to help them connect better with other team members?

5

THE CONTRIBUTION OF THE BABY BOOMER GENERATION

I AM A MEMBER OF THE BABY BOOMER GENERATION. I WAS BORN IN 1959 and have vivid memories of the 1960s, including the music, icons, demonstrations, riots, and heroes. John F. Kennedy's assassination took place during my fourth birthday party, and I remember my parents stopping the celebration to watch the events unfold on our black-and-white television. I didn't understand it all, but I knew something tragic had just happened. As a preschooler, I just remember wanting to get back to the party—but it was not to be. It was the beginning of a new tone in our American culture.

I was eight when Dr. Martin Luther King Jr. was shot and killed, and I was nine when astronaut Neil Armstrong stepped onto the moon. Our family watched it all. I was among the first generation that grew up watching footage of major news events on TV as they occurred. I distinctly recall watching newsreels of the Vietnam War on the evening news with the host Walter Cronkite, and I remember watching the last soldiers return from that war in April 1975.

But it was the end of *another* war thirty years earlier that launched my generation.

As soldiers returned home from World War II, America saw a boom of babies we'd never seen before. Large and in charge, this new generation took risks and lived audaciously. They questioned everything, which led to change and even growth. It was needed, but it was different. There were demonstrations, riots, protests, and separation from tradition. America was turned upside down as this generation grew up in a faster-paced, modernized age.

The end of the war had a huge impact on the US birth rate, which skyrocketed in an astonishing and unexpected reversal of the prewar decline. A mixture of factors created this baby boom: American soldiers returning home were battle-fatigued and wanted to settle down into a family life with their sweethearts. Further, GI Bill benefits promised decent pay, access to good jobs, and affordable housing that made raising a family possible. More than fifteen years of economic uncertainty were transformed into a hopeful time in the United States, and everyone seemed determined to make the most of it.

While there was a spike in marriages before soldiers traveled off to war, the spike was much larger after the war as they returned home. An unprecedented 2.2 million couples married in 1946, a record that would stand until the 1970s. With this record number of unions came a record number of babies. The low birth rates during the Great Depression were due to economics; couples couldn't afford a family. High birth rates following World War II were due to a hopeful economy. Birth rates went from about 200,000 babies per month before the war to nearly 350,000 per month immediately following the war. Twenty percent more babies were born in 1946 than 1945. This boom continued for eighteen years. An average of 4.24 million babies were born per year between 1946 and 1964, which amounted to 76.4 million babies during the baby boom period. This constituted a whopping 40 percent of the US population, which at the time was about 192 million people.[23]

Consider for a moment the results of such a baby boom. Retailers and marketers instantly paid attention to the Boomers as they saw them as the largest group of consumers ever born. Toys, gadgets, clothes, TV shows, commercial ads, and music all targeted these young customers. This may explain the audacious spirit Boomers grew up with, not unlike the gigantic Millennial generation that arrived some thirty-five years later. The times generated economic prosperity, consumer confidence, civic empowerment, and future hopes and dreams.

Let's examine some of the reasons why Baby Boomers act the way they do.

REALITIES THAT SHAPED BABY BOOMERS

As a member of the Baby Boom generation, I was born into change. The Beatles weren't even popular yet. Only girls had long hair. Bell-bottoms and hot pants had not hit the shelves. Dwight Eisenhower was president, and Americans' greatest fear was of nuclear bombs dropped by the Soviets. Yet during the next ten to fifteen years, Boomers would leave their mark on the world. Many countries experienced a Baby Boom because the war that ended in 1946 was a *worldwide* war.

The factors that played a role in shaping us were many:

1. **Because it was a time of expansion, not depression, we grew up idealistic.**

   Our generation began as soldiers returned from World War II. The war had boosted the economy and now our nation turned its attention to building domestic products instead of tanks, bullets, and bombs. Fast-food restaurants began to franchise, shopping malls sprang up, and like never before, we became primarily *consumers* who wanted our own unique looks, clothes, shoes, haircuts, and lifestyles. We were far more idealistic than our parents.

2. **Because it was a hopeful time, we became audacious.**

   Between 1946 and 1963, Americans resided in a state of

"normalcy." We wanted life to get back to normal after a terrifying world war—and to buy a house with a picket fence, have several children, a dog, a TV, and a good income. Dr. Benjamin Spock told parents not to *stifle* kids' ideas but allow them to *express* their ideas. So we did. After 1963, the United States witnessed protests, demonstrations, petitions, and a call for peace, civil rights, and lots of big dreams.

3. **Because information became accessible, we questioned authority.**
   The information age launched as Boomers came of age. We began hearing about a strange machine called a "computer." Before this time, computers were titles for jobs people had. As information expanded, we got the scoop on the failures of our leaders, and their reputations became tarnished. As young adults, we began to doubt their decisions. Fewer wanted to join the establishment. One very popular bumper sticker told us to "Question Authority."

4. **Because we grew up with television, our expectations climbed.**
   Both news media and television expanded our expectations and increased our exposure. With TV shows came visual advertising. With advertising came a message we began to believe: *we deserved better*. Better cars, better soap, better homes, better clothes, and better vacations were available, and the Boomer generation bought into it—literally. Our expectations of comfort, customer service, and possessions were measurably higher than our parents'.

5. **Because our generation was so large, we learned to compete.**
   All through my career, I felt I was competing against 76 million peers for jobs, homes to buy, market share, ideas, and recognition. Baby Boomers were the most numerous generation so far, which was good news and bad news. The good news is that we had retailers customizing products for this large batch of consumers. The bad news is that we were

constantly battling for a place in the world. This fostered progress, but it also led to insecurity and greed along the way.

Wayne is a vivid case study illustrating these realities. He is sixty-eight years old and lives in New Jersey. He didn't save his income the way his parents did, so Wayne continues to work instead of retiring. He wonders if he'll have enough to live on when he does retire. He spends sideways energy comparing himself to his colleagues, seeing the lifestyles they enjoy, and knowing that ten thousand Baby Boomers retire every day in America. He also ponders what his legacy will be. Did he really accomplish anything significant in his career, or did he abandon his ideals in the hunt for the almighty dollar? Do his kids still respect him after he divorced their mother? He recently told me he regrets the way he parented his children. He feels he wasn't intentional enough and was part of a generation of moms and dads who gave kids participation trophies, bought them

> Can you think of other realities that shaped Baby Boomers along the way?

any portable devices they wanted instead of requiring them to earn it, and told them they were awesome just for putting their fork in the dishwasher. It seemed to be what all parents did. As a young man, Wayne's search for a life of significance was eclipsed by his search for success. Now he wants significance again, but he questions whether it is too late. He longs for meaning. Millions of Baby Boomers like Wayne are scrambling to find ways to finish well.

Unique Boomer Caveats

There are a handful of caveats that make the Baby Boomer position interesting. The early Baby Boomers became teens and college students in the 1960s. It was the dawn of the postmodern age, when life shifted from black-and-white, linear thinking to colorful, abstract thinking, and almost every traditional structure was questioned. Since the Boomers were a large generation, they looked around and felt empowered to ask such questions and to participate in demonstrations and protests since there were more Boomers than elders. For example, few people questioned America's participation in World War II, but millions protested our involvement in Vietnam. Few questioned racial equality in the 1930s, but millions did so in the 1960s. Any sexual revolution in the Builder generation would have involved a marginalized group of people. In the 1960s and 1970s, the topic was mainstream. Bras were burned. Flags were burned. Buildings were burned. As a nine-year-old kid, I wondered if the world was going to burn down.

As time marched onward, millions of young Baby Boomers matured and joined the establishment they had protested against. Boomer college students, for instance, likely protested air pollution (ecology was a big issue in the early 1970s) and later got a job working for a company that contributed to the pollution by pumping an endless cloud of smog into the air. I have friends who've acknowledged such moves. Ready or not, Boomers entered their careers.

With some exceptions, mentors were few because my generation rebelled against an older generation that could have mentored us. While it wasn't true for every member of the Boomer population, by and large, our generation was *anti-establishment*. It wasn't uncommon to hear about communes, where several young adults lived together, sharing everything from food to products to sexual partners. In one focus group, a former commune member summarized his experience this way: "I am glad I did it. And I will never do it again."

The disproportionate size of the Baby Boomer generation has not had universally positive effects. Like a "pig in a python," as many demographers have characterized the group, the Boomer generation stretched and transformed American society as its members moved through life.

BABY BOOMER CONTRIBUTIONS

Today the Baby Boomers in the United States still number over 70 million, as immigrants of approximately the same age have made up for American-born Boomers who emigrated or passed away. As they age, the ratio of retired Americans compared to working Americans will shift significantly, placing considerable strain on hospitals and Social Security and other government agencies designed to aid the elderly. According to Zachary Wagenmaker, "The Census Bureau estimates that by 2030 one in five Americans will be over the age of 65. Furthermore, as the US birth rate is currently at an all-time low of just 12.5 live births per thousand population, by 2056 Americans aged 65 or older will outnumber those under the age of 18. What effect this aging population will have on US society remains to be seen."[24] What we do know is that Boomers have been around long enough to have garnered lots of wisdom and insight, giving them much to contribute to a team.

As you manage or work alongside Baby Boomers, it might be helpful to remember the valuable gifts they possess that could benefit younger teammates:

- **Stories from their journey.** Because these seasoned veterans began working three to five decades ago, they have loads of stories to tell—stories that could inform current events in your workplace.
- **Experience on the job.** This may be obvious, but because of their age, Boomers have loads of life (social) and work experience. They likely have performed tasks similar to roles that are needed on your team.
- **Lessons from comparable times in their youth.** Along with their narratives, millions of Boomers have picked up life lessons or tips to work efficiently and produce results more rapidly. Find places for them to share these.
- **An awareness of the pitfalls to avoid.** A second cousin to the lessons is the intuition and job awareness that stems from working on teams for years. Listen when Boomers offer cautionary tales of what to avoid.
- **Life coaching.** Finally, the mentoring and coaching they can offer to younger team members could be priceless. Even a Baby Boomer who's not a great communicator still has "pearls" to offer.

Toward the end of this book, I'll explain how our brains shift from fluid intelligence, where we innovate and ideate, toward crystallized intelligence, where we summarize and clarify for others. Since this is the stage Baby Boomers are in, we benefit from allowing them to apply this strength.

Steps for Connecting with and Leading Baby Boomers

1. Recognize their experience and expectations.

2. Ask them to share their past roles. Show appreciation for what they offer.

3. Allow them to take charge of a significant responsibility, if they're able and willing.

4. Give them space and resources. Don't micromanage.

5. Call on them to give back and coach others.

6. Remind them of their younger years when they get impatient.

EASING CONFLICT BETWEEN BOOMERS AND YOUNGER GENERATIONS

I recently spoke to an audience of HR executives on the topic of Boomers' views of the entitlement they see in younger generations. One executive—a fellow Boomer—approached me afterward to discuss my remarks. While he was grateful for the session, he didn't appreciate me saying that we Boomers ourselves had a sense of entitlement in our early years. He felt we "wanted" more but didn't act like we "deserved" more. I smiled and replied, "I think both are true. The research shows we acted far more deserving than our memories want to admit."

Pew Research Center data reveals that Boomers, as young adults, behaved with a high sense of entitlement. "This famously huge cohort of Americans finds itself in a collective funk as it approaches old age."[25] This is primarily because our generation must often say to the young, "Do as I say, not as I did." Millions of Boomers indulged in illegal drugs, free sex, and pleasure spending as young people. We protested the establishment, then joined the very establishment we protested against. We didn't save our money as our grandparents' and parents' generations did. When millions of Boomers reached middle age, they experienced a "midlife crisis." Why? We hadn't achieved or received all we wanted.

> What are some other "gifts" Baby Boomers have to offer?

The General Global Survey reveals some interesting longitudinal research. Baby Boomers have enjoyed less happiness on average than have other generations. When Boomers entered politics (as adults), the national debt was in mere millions of dollars. It became trillions, over $20 trillion to be exact, and it was mostly Baby Boomers who were at the helm of this shift. It was a generation that did not want to be denied what they wanted. "Absent changes to current law, more than half of the federal budget will go to Social Security, Medicare, and the non-child portion of Medicaid by 2022, up from 11 percent in 1960 and 30 percent in 1990."[26]

When a meta-analysis is performed on the Boomer generation over the last seventy years, there are some sobering realities we must remember, especially when Boomers become judgmental or critical of youth today. Baby Boomer journalists themselves evaluated their generation, saying things like,

> "a grasshopper generation, eating through just about everything like hungry locusts."
>
> —Thomas Friedman, author
> and *New York Times* columnist

"the most self-centered, self-seeking, self-interested, self-absorbed, self-indulgent, self-aggrandizing in American history."
—Paul Begala, TV pundit,
speechwriter for Bill Clinton

"[Boomers] squandered the legacy handed to them by the generation from World War II."
—Ken Burns, documentary filmmaker

Part of our problem was that our generation was so large, everyone catered to us. Now, those who follow us aren't so happy to cater to us.

Let's examine the following diagram, which I call "Three Valleys and Two Hills." This diagram illustrates the populations of the Boomers, Busters, Millennials, and Generation Z. The two hills are the larger Boomer and Millennial generations, measuring 76 and 80 million people in size. The problem is—the generations *behind* those larger generations are much smaller and will not be able to cover the demands for Social Security by the preceding retiring generations.

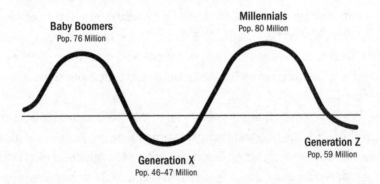

Baby Boomers
Pop. 76 Million

Millennials
Pop. 80 Million

Generation X
Pop. 46–47 Million

Generation Z
Pop. 59 Million

The Boomer generation represented a hill following the valley, as the economy felt promising. The Busters (Gen X) were another valley due to contraceptives and abortions. Millennials were another hill as American Boomers valued having children. Gen Z represents another valley as Busters, a smaller generation of parents, felt that the last twenty years represented a poor economic decision to have a big family. It's amazing how economies impact birth rates and workforces through families.

What Younger Team Members Wish the Older Generations Knew

In 2019, I hosted four focus groups of young professionals. The sixty participants were in their twenties, and they represented diversity in their ethnicities, genders, beliefs, and socioeconomic backgrounds. What they had in common was their perspective on the older generation leading them. The following are statements they made to me about managers in their workplace:

- "I wish they'd ask me what I thought about our new product line."
- "I hate the phrase 'pay your dues.'"
- "This company takes too long to make decisions and get things done."
- "These people don't really *get* social media."
- "They have no idea how stressed out I am."
- "I will stay as long as I think what I'm doing actually makes a difference."

Do you see any patterns in their perceptions? Collectively, these young professionals all feel their managers don't understand them or value their input. While the comments were offered with respect, the Millennial and Generation Z respondents felt a gap between them and their leaders. They perceived older people were "out of touch."

Misunderstanding is the clearest description I can give to this gap between young and old. In many ways, the evolution of TV illustrates what was happening in culture as early Boomers grew up. Televisions moved from small, black-and-white screens that broadcast predictable programs to larger screens broadcasting epic, edgy, and unconventional shows in full color. Remember, *Laugh-In, Bewitched, Till Death Do Us Part,* or *The Monkees*? Content took its first step out of the box.

Anyone fifty years old or older will remember the groundbreaking television sitcom *All in the Family*. The show aired from 1971 to 1979. It was a story of generations in one family. Archie Bunker (played by Carroll O'Connor) was the father figure who embraced traditional values. He was old-fashioned, a bit prejudiced, cantankerous, and used derogatory terms to describe anyone unlike him. Yet despite his bigotry, he was not motivated by malice. He just wished for times like they used to be—the good ol' days.

His daughter, Gloria (Sally Struthers), and her husband, Michael (Rob Reiner), or "Meathead," as Archie called him, represented the young Boomer generation. While good-hearted, Michael could be just as stubborn as his father-in-law. Archie was conservative; Gloria and Michael were liberal. Archie longed for the past; Gloria and Michael longed for the future. The comedy was almost always built around the differences between the young and old, even fifty years ago. Much of the humor surrounded Edith Bunker (Jean Stapleton), Archie's ditzy wife, who frequently played the role of peacemaker between her husband and kids.

Does this scenario sound strangely familiar to anyone today?

WHAT YOUNG TEAM MEMBERS NEED FROM BABY BOOMER SUPERVISORS

Because Baby Boomers have so much experiential wisdom to offer younger teammates, I want to challenge those Boomers to put that experience to work through mentoring. I've heard that the stages of life can be summarized with these simple descriptive words:

LIFE STAGE	DESCRIPTION
Childhood	It's about memories.
Teens	It's about mischief.
20s	It's about majors.
30s	It's about mastery.
40s	It's about multiplication.
50s and 60s	It's about mentoring.

I'm right there at the mentoring stage. Some of my most rewarding activities these days (now that I'm in my sixties) are spending time with younger leaders and investing in their lives—personally and professionally. I plan conversations and experiences with young professionals in their twenties and focus on empowering them to launch a meaningful career. (One is graduating from his university and anticipating a career post-pandemic.) I spend time with team members in their thirties, helping them zero in on their strengths, master them, and scale them. (One is planning to write his first book and is asking questions about how to do it efficiently.) I spend time with leaders in their forties enabling them to multiply what they've built so far in their careers. (One is working on his PhD and seeking to apply his academic research to his work.) Each relationship is satisfying because I can speak out of my own mistakes and successes while I was in their life station. If nothing else, I am able to say, "You have never been my age, but I have been your age. Let me offer you the gift of learning from my failures without having to commit them."

> How would your young professionals describe your relationship to them?

Baby Boomers can play their rightful role as mentors and empower young team members to assume the role suitable for them at their life stage in the marketplace. In fact, the question that consumes me these days is, "How can I prepare graduates and young professionals for a career regardless of when they enter the marketplace?" In other words, how can I build timeless skill sets that are relevant in 2020, 2030, or 2040? I believe this is possible.

What skills do I suggest we equip young people with as they graduate?

Help Them Focus on Learning Technical Skills and Soft Skills Simultaneously

In the past, we referred to academics in school as the three Rs: reading, writing, and arithmetic. Two more Rs have become just as important: *resourcefulness* and *resilience*. These are the soft skills required to succeed in the future. Resilience is in demand because jobs and even industries will be turning over rapidly in the future. Kids who are resilient and can adapt will be the ones to flourish. Resourcefulness is in demand because the way to succeed today is not to *memorize* (because information is at our fingertips) but to *research* and find new solutions. While technology is not going away, neither is the need for soft skills like these nor others like active listening, empathy, reading social cues, and clear communication.

Help Them Build Both Timeless Habits and Timely Problem-Solving Skills

I believe the graduates who get ahead are those who've pursued both *timeless* skills and *timely* skills. By this, I mean they develop skill sets that meet the need of the hour, such as coding, computer programming, or software development. At the same time, they don't neglect the timeless skills like relationship management, self-regulation, and social awareness. These are evergreen social and emotional skills.

I have said for years that the fastest way to gain influence on a team is twofold:

1. Solve problems
2. Serve people

When anyone can solve current problems their organization faces, he or she will always be in demand. In addition, if they're willing to serve those around them, without assuming the task is below them or beneath their pay grade, they will go far as well. The very acts of solving problems and serving people position a team member to be valuable.

Help Them Both to Blend In and Stand Out at the Same Time

As graduates enter the workplace, they'll soon realize it is important to both *blend in* and *stand out*. By blend in, I mean there is a benefit to discovering how things get done around an organization and demonstrating they can play team ball. They don't demand that everyone adjust to them but rather, vice versa. At the same time, they must find ways to stand out, to set themselves apart from others through their talent, initiative, creativity, and ambition. Without calling attention to themselves, they will find themselves in the spotlight by achieving goals, creating products, or surpassing expectations while they're still new and young. This will take walking the extra mile.

I recently asked three high school seniors to prepare and then offer a persuasive speech to an audience of school administrators. It was at that point I realized how self-aware they were; these students knew they were not "career-ready." Although they were honor roll students, they understood that academics were not enough to prepare them for what lay ahead. I was intrigued to find they chose to speak on the topic "I Wish My School Taught a Class in Life Skills."

Baby Boomers are readily accessible in our homes, communities, schools, and workplaces. And they have a lifetime of experience honing the very "life skills" younger generations yearn to learn. Exponential value can be found simply by bringing these two generations together.

For example, I want to close with a classic example of how a Builder generation and a Boomer generation team member can play their appropriate roles on a team. When the COVID-19 pandemic was in full swing in the summer of 2020, the entire staff at H&H sheltered in place and worried about the future. Most of them had never been through anything like 2020, with a pandemic, protests, political polarization, pay cuts, and panic attacks around the world. Susan, the CEO, asked Mel, age eighty-six, and Steve, age sixty-one, to host a roundtable discussion with her team. Susan interviewed them, asking about how Mel (who now did lawn care for the company) made it through the down economy of the Great Depression and World War II. She asked Steve (who now served as an executive vice president) what he remembers about the Hong Kong Flu (the last pandemic we endured in 1968) and the protests that happened during his childhood. These two colleagues were able to share some sage wisdom on staying calm, keeping a steady pace, and committing to doing the right things they knew to do even when the future was unknown. Hearing about past difficult times from people they knew gave context and perspective to everyone. It had a calming effect, especially among the Millennials and Gen Z staff.

The team benefited from generational diversity.

Talk It Over

(1) How can you capitalize on the value and skills a Baby Boomer brings to the team?

(2) What changes should you make to enable Boomers to connect better with other team members and adapt to the changes they bring?

(3) In what ways could bridges be built between Millennials and Baby Boomers?

6

THE CONTRIBUTION OF THE BABY BUSTERS (GENERATION X)

I AM A MIDDLE CHILD. I HAVE AN OLDER SISTER AND A YOUNGER sister. I don't despise my birth order; I am a well-adjusted adult who's enjoyed a meaningful life. My experience growing up, however, was one of feeling as if I were sandwiched between two special people. A psychology pioneer named Alfred Adler introduced the idea that birth order affects the development and potential of a child.[27]

My older sibling, Lisa, was the firstborn in the family; she was the "boss" of her brother and sister. In fact, she did all the talking for me my first two years. (I did not say much until I was two, but I've made up for it since then.) By age ten, Lisa was our babysitter; she was large and in charge. My younger sibling, Lynda, was the baby in the family. Our parents knew she was the final act of their offspring, and, being the last born, she got loads of attention and was nurtured in ways that Lisa and I both agree were ... well, special. Lynda continues to play a special role in our family.

The traits of a middle child are often stereotyped, but Adler identified them for a reason. Some classic characteristics of a middle child are that they can feel overshadowed; they often don't have a strong sense of belonging or don't feel as special; they are frequently more mobile; and they can feel they need to play the role of empathizer and peacemaker. Most of all, they can feel as if they are sandwiched between two special siblings.

In many ways, these "middle child" traits illustrate the generation we'll examine in this chapter. The Baby Busters, or Generation X, are like a "middle child" population sandwiched between two larger generations, the Boomers and the Millennials. Gen X (Busters) are positioned in the midst of these special, vocal, and visible populations that received much more press than they did. In many ways, it explains how and why Gen Xers have reacted to society the way they have over the years.

THE MIDDLE GENERATION

Born between 1965 and 1982, this generation was smaller than the Boomers and grew up with an unstable economy, assassinations, and skeptical parents watching news clips of the Vietnam War and the Watergate scandal on TV. Consequently, the Baby Busters became cynical themselves, introducing our culture to doubts, tough questions, and a need for authenticity. This generation's response to the Baby Boomers' audacity was to unplug. Packed tightly between outspoken Baby Boomers and Millennials, Gen Xers are the bridge between the past and the future. Perhaps this is the reason they call themselves the least distinct generation of the three.

Although "Baby Buster" was the first title given to their population, Generation X is the one that stuck. The "X" refers to an unknown variable or to a desire not to be defined. Over the years, they've been called various names: the New Lost Generation, Latchkey Kids, MTV Generation, and the 13th Generation (the 13th generation since American independence).

Pew Research Center (which is bipartisan) describes them as "America's neglected middle child." This overlooked generation ranges from almost forty years old to their mid-fifties. They are smack in the middle portion of life, which tends to be short on drama and scant on theme. Recalling the Three Valleys and Two Hills diagram on page 106, Gen X's population represents a valley between two big hills—the Boomers (76 million) and the Millennials (80 million). They are smaller because of the introduction of the birth control pill, which became popular as their generation launched. Abortion rights also played a role in the reduced size of their generation. Abortions peaked in America during 1980 to 1981, just as early Gen Xers were coming of age.[28] So they are a condensed demographic sandwiched between two expanded populations, playing the role of a middle child.

At this point, they express themselves in the middle of many issues:

- Socially, they lie in between the more conservative Boomers and the more liberal Millennials.
- Regarding technology use, they have higher adoption than Boomers and less adoption then Millennials.
- In terms of patriotism, they're precisely in the middle between Boomers and Millennials.
- Their number of Facebook friends lies between those of Baby Boomers and Millennials.
- They feel less unique and distinctive than the generations on either side of them.

Pew Research Center reminds us,

Gen Xers are bookended by two much larger generations—the Baby Boomers ahead and the Millennials behind—that are strikingly different from one another. And in most of the ways we take stock of generations—their racial and ethnic makeup; their political, social and religious values; their economic and educational circumstances;

their technology usage—Gen Xers are a low-slung, straight-line bridge between two noisy behemoths. Even their name is a retread. World War II photographer Robert Capa first coined the term Generation X in a photo essay about the young adults of the 1950s, but the label didn't stick the first time around. It was revived thirty years later by Canadian author Douglas Coupland, whose coming of age novel in 1991, Generation X: Tales for an Accelerated Culture, *was set in Southern California."[29]*

At that point, the generation's identity had become an enigma.

REALITIES THAT SHAPED GENERATION X

Because this generation began with the public introduction of the birth control pill, the "boom" became a "bust." Yet as the initial title given to them morphed into Generation X, it became clear the "X" merely meant they couldn't be nailed down to a clear persona. They were a mystery. They refused to be pigeonholed by a term. They were, in fact, an X generation.

Generation X is now in the peak of their careers. Most are in midlife or just beyond and often have been promoted into management positions. They are experienced, they are savvy to the workplace, and they are, by and large, authentic. In fact, as they grew up in a difficult period of the late 1960s and 1970s, they saw leaders still hiding behind facades and still pretentious. As a result, the Xers grew distrustful of that artificial style. It seemed fake.

Here are some realities that shaped this generation as they grew up:

1. **Because national leaders lied to the public, Xers grew up skeptical.**

   Imagine you're an early member of Generation X. By the time you were eight years old, you'd heard your parents discuss the tragedy of the Vietnam War, the assassinations of Martin Luther King Jr. and Bobby Kennedy, and the Watergate scandal in the White House. It was a dark time as America lost her innocence and leaders were caught lying in their reports. Even though Gen Xers were kids, as adults grew cynical, these kids became skeptical themselves.

2. **Because times were harder, Xers grew up guarded.**
For almost fifteen years, times were more challenging, with combative groups lobbying for and against societal issues, such as women's rights, abortion rights, equal labor rights, and civil rights, as well as anti-war, anti-censorship, and anti-poverty. Each was characterized by a rejection of conventional norms. The countercultural era rejected the societal standards of their parents, specifically regarding racial segregation, ecology, and pollution. As Gen X grew up, four famous political figures were assassinated in five years. Turmoil increased. Trust decreased.

3. **Because divorce rates had climbed, many Xers grew up self-sufficient.**
For the first time in American history, divorce rates not only climbed but even became normalized. Gen X was described by some social scientists as a *latchkey generation* where both Boomer parents worked or where one parent felt okay to leave a conventional marriage to "find themselves." In response, millions from Gen X were forced to be self-reliant and self-sufficient, figuring out how to get by alone after school.

4. **Because their generation was smaller, Xers lived in the shadow of the Boomers.**
Depending on what data you study, the population of the Baby Boomers was about 76 million; the population of the Baby Busters was somewhere between 47 and 48 million. As both generations aged, Xers could see they were growing up in the long shadow of the previous generation who seemed to get the jobs, promotions, and opportunities they wanted. For many Xers, this fostered a withdrawal from climbing the "corporate ladder."

5. **Because the economy was uncertain, Xers grew up pragmatic and jaded.**
As I've mentioned, all of this led Generation X to become
a raw, practical, and often jaded population. During their
childhoods, they realized life wasn't full of sunshine and
rainbows as they watched OPEC cause long lines at gas
stations and witnessed huge inflation rates, the Cold War,
double-digit mortgage interest rates, the AIDS epidemic,
and shortages of some staples. Many Xer comedians
grew dark and sarcastic in their stand-up routines. No
doubt, there are loads of Gen Xers today who have positive attitudes about life, family, and the future. As a whole,
however, Xers will contribute a "keep it real" mindset to the
conversation.

Pew Research Center reports, "For Xers, there's one silver lining
in all this. From everything we know about them, they're savvy, skeptical and self-reliant; they're not into preening or pampering, and
they just might not give much of a hoot what others think of them,
or whether others think of them at all."[30] In 1990, *TIME* magazine
published a cover story headlined "Twentysomething," examining
the post-Boomer generation and asking if they were "laid back, late
blooming or just lost."

We understand Gen X better as midlife adults when we consider
the fact that their generation came of age as larger numbers of women
were engaged in a career; fewer were stay-at-home moms. As divorce
rates climbed, a greater percentage of them (compared to the past)
grew up in single-parent homes and with minimal adult supervision,
hence the term *latchkey kids*.

Like younger generations Gen Y and Gen Z, Gen X contains
microgenerations within their membership. The older members look
and act a bit more like Baby Boomers, and their younger counterparts appear more like Generation Y (Millennials). Society continued
to shift as they grew up, and Gen X was influenced as much by the

culture as they were by their parents and family. Some movies that illustrated the psyche of Generation X were:

- *Kramer vs. Kramer* (1979 movie about the consequences of divorce)
- *Reality Bites* (1994 movie about the bitter truth of a disenchanted life)
- *Philadelphia* (1993 film about an attorney with AIDS who sues his firm when he's fired)

As these kids matured, rock music evolved as well. It became acid rock, psychedelic rock, grunge rock, and alternative rock. Lyrics became more jaded and sometimes even combative. In *Billboard*'s Top 100 songs, the word *love* decreased by half and the word *hate* first appeared in the 1990s. Subsets of pop music emerged as well, such as disco and early forms of rap. Music became more niched, a trend that continues to this day.

> From your observation, what other factors played into the development of Generation X?

One way to describe the era is to say the Boomer generation brought a new, childlike viewpoint to the world that questioned everything, just as kids do. By the time Gen X arrived, we'd evolved into an adolescent viewpoint; the innocence was gone and skepticism had set in.

It Wasn't All Bad

It's certainly true that Gen X saw a considerable amount of institutional incompetence: Watergate, Three Mile Island, Bhopal, the Iranian hostage crisis, the Iran-Contra affair, and the Clinton-Lewinsky debacle, just to name a few. But to be fair, a number of cool new realities surfaced while Generation X was still in school that were sources of hope and optimism to their population. While they were still young, the computer was introduced to the public; the Berlin Wall came down, marking the beginning of the end of the Cold

War; home video games went mainstream; and the space race led us to the moon and beyond, including the introduction of space shuttles in the 1980s. Consequently, seeing both the positives and negatives growing up, they entered adulthood with a broader perspective than their Boomer counterparts:

- Some call them cynical, but Gen X might say, "We're critical thinkers."
- Some call them renegades, but Gen X might say, "We're self-reliant."
- Some call them disloyal, but Gen X might say, "We're adaptable and fluid."

Heather (not her real name) is a stellar member of Generation X and a great case study of its characteristics. She is forty-eight years old, manages a productive team at work, and is also a single mom who finds a way to manage three kids at home. I consulted with Heather because she wanted to build a "trusting culture" on her team but found it difficult since she struggled with trust issues herself. She confided in me that she loved reading Brené Brown's books and watching her videos on vulnerability and trust, but she had a hard time translating it to her leadership.

Heather grew up as a latchkey kid, like many other members of Gen X. Her parents were divorced so she was forced to become independent, raised by a single parent who wasn't home when Heather returned from school each day. From this experience, she could now be described as self-sufficient, a hard worker, individualistic, genuine, and guarded in relationships but longing to be part of a team of people who are interdependent. Those who know Heather well would also describe her as a bit cynical, spotting what could go wrong with a new idea very quickly. She's the kind of person any team would want but is also the kind of person who may unwittingly prevent the trust that a team needs to work closely together.

While Gen Z and Millennials teamed up to poke Baby Boomers with the subtle "OK, Boomer" jab, Gen Zers also decided to take a few stabs at Gen X by calling them the "Karen generation." What exactly is a "Karen?" *BuzzFeed* explains: "Karen is the middle-aged, white mom who is always asking for the manager and wondering why kids are so obsessed with their identities."[31] I suppose clichés surface for a reason, right? All of this to say, Xers have a unique role to play on a team today.

WHAT GENERATION X HAS TO CONTRIBUTE

As you manage or work alongside Gen Xers, it might be helpful to remember these valuable benefits they bring to a team and their younger teammates:

- **Realism:** Because they grew up as a "keep it real" generation, they often keep a planning meeting from becoming too idealistic. They have no illusions that life is less complex than it seems.
- **Authenticity:** Millions from Gen X introduced an informal and genuine spirit to the marketplace as they entered the workforce. They have little time for platitudes or pretension on a team.
- **Balance:** Work-life balance was actually introduced as Xers, not Millennials, came of age. Seeing Baby Boomers "marry" their careers, Xers have desired balance between the tensions of home and work.

> What are some other benefits you see that Generation X brings to a team?

- **Resourcefulness:** Generation X learned to be resourceful as latchkey kids since adults were not around much of the time. They became talented at figuring out how to get a job done with few resources.
- **Pragmatic wisdom:** Gen X is fine not only expressing doubts but asking questions as well. They often take a contrarian point of view (as a whole), challenge the status quo, and offer wisdom on teams.

When we stop and consider these contributions, it is clear to see that Gen X plays an important role between pessimism and idealism. Almost every team needs this bridge today.

Steps for Connecting with and Leading Baby Busters

1. Listen and communicate understanding. Build a genuine relationship.

2. Allow them to function outside the conventional office.

3. Be brutally honest with them. They know life is tough. Don't pretend it isn't.

4. Give them places for authentic community.

5. Furnish a meaningful cause to embrace; let them lead.

6. When you give them boundaries, keep them minimal and explain them.

7. Influence through your relationship, not your position.

INTERFACING WITH MEMBERS OF GENERATION X

Shawn is our vice president of business development and a member of Gen X. He shoots straight, has a keen sense of humor and a strong wit, and has no room for pretense. At the same time, he is not arrogant; he doesn't have an inflated view of himself and has never gotten away from the lessons he learned early on to be resourceful, always on your toes, and to maintain a big-picture perspective. Due to how and when he grew up, Shawn is one of our best problem-solvers. In many ways, Shawn is that "middle child" who doesn't overplay who he is and whom everyone seems to like. He keeps it real.

I have always appreciated the people I know who, like Shawn, are part of this "middle" generation. I led an entire department of them from 1987 to 1994. They never fail to bring a sense of honesty and transparency to the conversation. They are now well into their careers, so they likely don't need anyone to cater to them, butter them up, or remind them that they are special and play an important role on the team. However, offering them the respect they deserve will send that message in a very genuine fashion.

What Do Young Team Members Need from Generation X?

My encouragement to Generation X team members is to step up and set the example for what you want to see in other team members. You have experience and are often managing a team at this point in your career. You are now the heart of the workforce. Taking your place means you not only offer direction and wisdom but provide a model to follow by the way you carry yourself. People need to *see* a sermon more than *hear* one these days. If Baby Boomers are in a prime life station to *mentor*, Generation X is in a prime spot to *model* the way.

For example, Gen X stands as a living example of why careful personal money management is so important. While Baby Boomers are likely wondering where their retirement savings have gone, due to the 2020 pandemic, Generation X is the generation that is in the greatest financial trouble, even compared to the Millennials, who accumulated the biggest tuition debt in American history. A recent study by LendingTree found that Gen Xers have the highest average debt burden of any generation as their average debt rose by about 10 percent ($11,898) between 2016 and 2019. Another note from that study is that Gen Xers have the most credit card debt of any generation while spending the most on nonessentials such as dining out and lottery tickets.[32]

This likely happened because marketing and advertising came of age as Gen Xers did. As young consumers, Xers believed they "deserved" great products and services and didn't have to wait for them. So they racked up debt—lots of it. This has set a poor example for future generations. It is easy, in this scenario, for Xers to feel like victims of the "system," but our world needs them to step up and lead the way in delayed gratification, ethics, commitment, and gratitude.

What else do the younger generations need from their middle-aged, Baby Buster friends and colleagues?

1. **Young team members need your stewardship.**

   Those who are younger desperately need Xers to see their talent, time, and treasure (finances) as stewardship. Everyone is stewarding a trust that has been given to them by former generations, either poorly or excellently. The mission of your company and your family should be viewed as a trust that you will one day pass on to younger people. Millions of Millennials and Gen Zers may have given up on modeling after Baby Boomers, but they're likely still watching Generation X, who is a step ahead of them. Set the pace.

2. **Young team members need your relationship.**

   Our surveys of members from both the Millennials and Generation Z revealed that these young people actually want a relationship with older generations; they just don't know how to ask for it. They aren't asking for a lecture, but they are asking to swap stories and to learn from those who believe in them and who can ask good questions to make them think better. This is your chance to "keep it real" and offer what you wish you received when you were younger.

3. **Young team members need your leadership.**

   Generation X has an opportunity to enable younger generations to learn to think for the *long term*, *big picture*, and *high road*. America saw three old, white males, all of them above the age of seventy, run for president in the 2020 election: Bernie Sanders, Donald Trump, and Joe Biden. While I am not disrespecting these men, how sad for us not to have a large quantity from Generation X able and willing to take this spot and lead. Remember, ten thousand Baby Boomers retire every day. This is the time for Generation X to step up and lead the way for younger generations.

Let me close with a little perspective on how Gen X can connect with younger teammates.

Because you grew up in tumultuous times during your childhood, you can relate to Generation Z, who is also growing up in some challenging times. Both of you suffered from sour economies and unethical politicians, and you have similarly savvy yet jaded perspectives. But because you were a young professional in the 1990s, when America experienced almost full employment across the nation and your generation moved up the corporate ladder briskly, you can relate to Millennials—whom we will discuss next. They grew up confident and feeling upwardly mobile as young people. I encourage you to speak from the portion of your life and career that enables you to identify with each generation you work with. Again, *read* them before you *lead* them.

For two years, Amanda served on our team as our human resources officer. She's a member of Generation X. I noticed she often played the part of a mediator between our young team members and Steve (our president) and myself (the founder and CEO). While Steve and I work to stay connected with the twentysomethings on the team, Amanda's "power gap" was smaller, and she felt more accessible to our staff. As a Gen Xer, she has experienced both what it feels like to be in the middle of a team and what it feels like to manage a team. It's been enriching to watch her help the old and young understand one another's perspectives. Obviously, it's about far more than merely being a part of Gen X. But her experience helped her identify with and relate to everyone. She was in a perfect spot.

If you are part of Generation X, you are at the peak of your career and productivity. You are in midlife or beyond and are seen as an experienced veteran of the workforce. People will look to you for cues on how to handle tough situations, how to read nuances in conversations with team members, how to put fires (conflict) out by tossing water on them rather than gasoline, and how to facilitate a meeting that is productive rather than just reactive. You are to lead like a flight attendant on a turbulent airline flight. Have you ever noticed while on an airplane that when the air gets a bit rough, people grab their armrest first, but if the turbulence continues, people tend to intuitively look at the flight attendant? That attendant will often determine whether passengers can experience peace or if they should feel panicked. If the flight attendant is still smiling, serving Diet Cokes, and joking with the other passengers, then all is well, even in tough rides.

So it is with you. You are the flight attendant. The rest of the passengers look to you.

Talk It Over

1. How can you capitalize on the value and skills a Gen Xer brings to the team?

2. What challenges have your team faced in which a Gen Xer could play the role of mediator and connect two perspectives on an issue?

3. How can you help Gen X leverage the tough times in which they grew up in order to benefit younger team members who experienced tough times as well?

7

THE CONTRIBUTION OF THE MILLENNIALS (GENERATION Y)

RACHEL GRADUATED FROM WHEATON COLLEGE WITH A DEGREE IN economics. She entered college with a positive attitude, healthy relationships with her parents and family, good grades, and a busy social life. In one sense, she was a classic Millennial. Unfortunately, Rachel finished college the same year the Great Recession hit and the housing market collapsed. She applied for job after job, but nothing in her field opened up. It felt as if she were competing for jobs against millions of her peers, and in a very real sense, she was. After a month of fruitless job inquires, Rachel moved back home and ended up taking a position as a barista at Starbucks. Seeing old friends and neighbors there, she felt embarrassed. She had left town with so much promise, so many hopes and dreams. When her $110,000 student loans came due, Rachel decided to go to graduate school. (She'd always heard that a master's degree is the new bachelor's degree.) It was her way to defer the loans until later. Rachel is still a positive person, but she is far more realistic than she was a decade ago. She now works as an accountant, which is not exactly what she'd planned to do—but it's helping her pay off her loans. Rachel would never say her *dreams* became *nightmares*, but she would say life has given her a big wake-up call.

Some form of Rachel's story has been told Millennials of times over.

The Millennials became the largest generation to date as their parents chose to prioritize families and children, with "Baby on Board" signs in the back of the minivan, diaper-changing tables in public restrooms, and trophies awarded to kids just for playing. These Millennials brought with them an energy, sociality, and love of family as they grew up. Born in the 1980s and 1990s, they were made to feel special. In many families, they were the top priority. They grew up assuming the economy would remain strong, opportunities would always be plentiful, and the future would be bright.

As they became adults, millions realized how difficult career-building really is. The economy tanked for a season as the first batch of Millennials came of age (2000–2001), then the Great Recession hit (2008–2009), and then the COVID-19 pandemic surprised us all in 2020. Many of those idealistic Millennials were forced to move back home with a huge college debt to pay off, and some found themselves at jobs that didn't require a college degree (such as serving as a barista at Starbucks) after graduation. Millennials (also called Generation

Millennials became the largest generation in the labor force in 2016

Labor force in millions

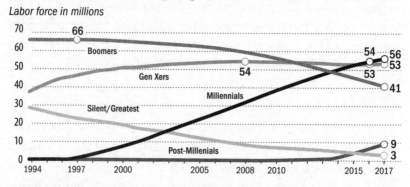

Note: Labor force includes those ages 16 and older who are working or looking for work. Annual averages shown.
Sources: Pew Research Center analysis of monthly 1994-2017 Current Population Survey (IPUMS).

Y, following X) were forced to adjust their expectations, and they are doing that even now. By 2016, they became the largest demographic working full time, and in a few years, ready or not, they'll be taking over.[33]

REALITIES THAT SHAPED THE MILLENNIALS

These young professionals now make up more than half of America's workforce, and Millennials and Generation Z will make up 70 percent of the workforce by 2025. We'd better get to know them.

They matured in a day of digital customization and see life as one large "cafeteria," where they pick and choose from a plethora of options and can personalize their purchases, their playlists, and their lifestyles. While many older generation leaders mourn their narcissistic tendencies, I should remind you that we're the ones who gave birth to them and raised them. If they were unready for the workforce, we must look in the mirror and ask, "What did *we* fail to do to get them ready?" In any case, here are some highlights that shaped them as they grew up:

1. **They grew up in a healthy economy and most entered adulthood feeling confident.**

   Past generations of parents worked to get their kids everything they *needed*. Millennials' parents worked to get them anything they *wanted*. While this sounds like hyperbole (and perhaps it is), it illustrates a shift in what we feel entitled to as emerging adults. Millennials entered their careers with confidence and high expectations that they needed to navigate with their employers. Their confidence energized their team, but it also needed guardrails.

2. **They grew up in a protective culture as parents became obsessed with their safety.**

   Dr. Peter Gray at Boston College warned us that parental protection of children would not only lower their grit and immune system but produce unready adults as they turned eighteen.[34] Moms and dads, however, made an unconscious shift in their own report card—believing that preventing children from pain was vital. Parents did not want their child to fail, to fall, to fret, to falter, or to fight (struggle) as they matured. It was not always a good trade-off.

3. **They grew up in an affirming culture as adults chose to build a high self-esteem.**

By and large, Millennials grew up with overfunctioning parents who served as their agents (negotiating with teachers for grades), trainers (coaching them in competition), and financiers (providing cash for them). Trophies and ribbons were awarded for participation. Everyone is a winner. Many were told they were amazing merely for making their bed. Far too often, adults prepared the path for the child and not the child for the path.

4. **They grew up in a collaborative and pressurized culture that cultivated stress.**

These young professionals experienced school and extra-curricular activities in communities. They participated in academic assignments on a team. They played soccer on a team. They regularly formed study groups and even began to date others in a social group of more than two. The good news is they're used to collaborating. The bad news is they felt high pressure to make the team, make the grade, make the cut, make the play. They feel stressed.

5. **They grew up with options, so many bring a "free agent" mindset to work.**

Indeed, they are a generation of "free agents." Loyalty in companies has declined the last forty years on both sides of the coin. Team members often observe that management treats them as commodities, so they act like free agents—always on the lookout for the best new offer. Their entire life furnished them digital and retail options, so life is like a buffet where you choose your items to suit your tastes. Opportunity trumps loyalty for Millennials.

A Generation of Firsts

Because technology was evolving so rapidly as they grew up, they inaugurated many realities as children and adolescents. They were the first generation to grow up with cell phones. They were the first to grow up with computers. They were the first to grow up with the Internet. In fact, they became a "generation of firsts," and it affected their teachers and employers. Millennials were the first generation that:

- didn't need adults to get information.
- could broadcast their every thought or emotion.
- enjoyed external stimuli at their fingertips 24/7.
- were in social contact at all times yet were often in isolation.
- would learn more from a portable device than a class.
- adults actually enabled many of their narcissistic tendencies.
- used a phone instead of a watch, camera, calendar, alarm clock, road map, or board game.

I wish you could meet Josh and Jessica. They're both Millennials about eight years into their career, and they are vivid case studies of what many from their generation experienced. They have been friends since middle school and now are thirty-one years old. It was an assumption in their families that they should attend a university in order to land a good job and enter a good career. As each graduated, the "freshman year of their career" (as we call it) was tough. Jessica found a job about four months into her search, but it was not in the industry she had studied in college. Josh didn't find a job for seven months and was forced to move home after graduation. Life did not look like what parents and teachers had predicted it would. Neither Jessica nor Josh plan to get married anytime soon. They feel behind in their careers and a little disappointed with the way life has turned out. Jessica feels pressure from her mom to get married and have children, but she doesn't feel ready. While Josh's

Have you spotted any other characteristics and causes shaping the Millennial generation?

dad tries to be encouraging to him, Josh feels like he's let his parents down. Both Josh and Jessica are in a "quarter-life crisis." Like millions of their peers, they now wonder what will happen to their dreams in this post-pandemic economy. Will they ever be able to pay off their college debt? Will they ever be able to afford a home?

These are all valid questions—and ones millions of young adults are asking themselves.

SUBSETS IN THE MILLENNIAL GENERATION

In 2010 I wrote a book called *Generation iY: Our Last Chance to Save Their Future.* It details a meta-analysis of these Millennials and reveals that this generation morphed as the 1980s progressed into the 1990s. In other words, the early Millennials have a set of characteristics that differs from the later members of their population. Because change happens so rapidly today, there are subsets even within a generation. Following is a quick comparison and contrast of the early Millennials (Generation Y) and the later Millennials (Generation iY). I call them "iY" because their population not only owned the first set of products from Apple (iPods, iPhones, iPads, iMacs, and so forth) but life became more about "i." Dr. Jean Twenge's book *Generation Me* details the narcissism that set in as these kids became young adults. Once again, I don't fault them for this shift. I think both they and their parents were ambushed by this new world.

Generation Y Morphs: The 1980s vs. the 1990s Kids	
Early Generation Y	**Generation iY**
Born in the 1980s	Born in the 1990s
Highly compassionate	Low empathy
Activists	"Slack-tivists"
Technology is a tool	Technology is an appendage
Civic-minded	Self-absorbed
Ambitious about the future	Ambiguous about the future
Accelerated growth	Postponed maturation

Once again, let me offer a disclaimer. Certainly not every member of those born in the 1980s is highly compassionate and civic-minded, nor is every member of those born in the 1990s low in empathy and self-absorbed. But something happened to this demographic, call it a perfect storm of elements, that nudged them as a whole toward an individualistic lifestyle that cared more about its own progress than the big picture. The sociology department at the University of Michigan noted that college students' empathy dropped 40 percent in the first decade of the twenty-first century at the same time the mobile phone became ubiquitous. Activism, which once manifested as young people serving, marching, or demonstrating for a cause, shifted to signing a petition on a website and getting a wristband. It's called "slack-tivism." It's akin to posting a black square on Instagram and claiming you protested for "Black Lives Matter." Posting is a lazy way to protest. Most notable among the shifts from Y to iY were the emotional maturity levels that diminished in Generation iY. It was as if their maturation was postponed by the childhood they had. I lost count of the university deans who, after interfacing with students, said to me, "Twenty-six is the new eighteen."

While both subsets are catching up in their career readiness, millions of Millennials discovered the gap between their confidence and their preparedness as they entered their careers. The adults who raised and led them as young people unwittingly cultivated a "me-first" culture as parents and educators focused on their status. It appears that as a whole, adults focused on helping Millennials feel they were special as kids. We wanted them to get into that prestigious college perhaps even more than they did. Gen Y became an extension of their parent's success as they grew up, and (as I mentioned) some had parents join them at their first job interview. Moms and dads might have avoided this clash had they followed the adage: "It is better to prepare the child for the path instead of the path for the child."

This cultivated a new kind of team member as they entered full-time jobs.

Through the Eyes of the iYs

If you were to ask me to describe the later Millennials and their view of an appealing workplace, I would describe that work environment in the following manner. The following items are the results of focus group feedback from young professionals who've been in the workplace five to ten years:

- **Openness and Contact:** They're not into hierarchies or ivory towers; they want access to their boss and a flat organizational chart.
- **Fun and Play:** They want to feel as if they're with friends at work, gamifying their tasks and enjoying their day.
- **Speed and Change:** They get bored quicky and like routines to change regularly to keep jobs interesting.
- **Balance and Flexibility:** They like to have their hours and locations in which they work to be adaptable as their needs surface.
- **Meaning and Mission:** They long to feel that what they do really matters, that their job makes a difference.
- **Growth and Learning:** They want to develop new skills and learn insights that help them progress in their career path.

Reviewing this list, I am reminded of the fact that younger generations tend to introduce new norms to the workplace. In the future, perhaps these descriptors will be the norm for all of us.

WHAT MILLENNIALS HAVE TO CONTRIBUTE

It's important to keep in mind that Millennials will likely play the most important roles transforming the workplace before their careers are over. Not only are they the largest population in the office today, but the changes they brought with them—a precursor to Gen Z changes—have already caused a shift in the way Americans approach work. The first batch of them is reaching midlife, and millions of others are still in the first half of their careers. As you manage or work alongside Generation Y, it will be helpful to remember the valuable benefits they bring to a team:

- **Confidence:** If any generation brought confidence to their jobs, it was the Millennials. Like the Boomers, they feel large and in charge; unlike the Boomers, they welcome organizational mentors.
- **Energy:** Millennials are often the team members who bring energy to meetings. This vitality can be motivating to colleagues and invite momentum into an ideation process.
- **Tech Sense:** Because their generation grew up with cell phones and computers, they intuitively understand technology and can find ways to leverage it for marketing and commerce.
- **Sociality:** Millennials grew up extremely social, even if their relational connections were on screens. They love working in groups and often relate to teammates as a community of friends.

: How are you accomplishing these with your young team members?

- **Creativity:** Even though they tested lower in creativity while in school than past generations, they often bring innovation to their jobs since they think differently than past generations.
- **Optimism:** Like Baby Boomers, they are idealistic about future prospects (as a whole) and are optimistic about reaching goals. It's possible that their positivity can rub off on others.
- **Love of Family:** Year in and year out, Millennials reported prioritizing family in nationwide surveys. They tend to relate to others in warm, relational ways and cherish the balance of work and home life.
- **Awareness of Their Influence:** They grew up watching social media posts go viral and seeing protests form movements that changed politics. This made them aware of their own influence as adults.

For thirty-five years, I have welcomed interns into the teams I've led. For half of that time, those interns were Millennials. I am an eyewitness to these traits. In fact, we chose the college students who joined our team because of these qualities. It was just what we needed. I sought shared values and vison but also diverse perspective and skills. We became better because of them. Two of those interns were my own children, who brought a different experience with them.

THE CHALLENGES MILLENNIALS ARE FACING

In the summer of 2022, my daughter, Bethany, turned thirty-four and my son, Jonathan, turned thirty. They are both Millennials who are several years into their careers, but both are still considered young professionals. In many ways, they are "classic" Millennials, especially Bethany. She is far more progressive in her political views and felt a great sense of agency even as a twentysomething. We've had many conversations over the years in which she helped me better understand her generation, and I helped her understand how her employer might perceive some of her comments on social media.

What are other benefits you've observed that Millennials bring to a team?

Both of my adult children provide vivid illustrations of the plight of young professionals today and may just help both you and me empathize with them as we lead them. Three scenarios surfaced over this past year that illuminate this plight.

I remember discussing home ownership with Bethany during 2020, right in the heat of the COVID-19 pandemic. She recognized we were experiencing the third economic downturn in the last two decades, and she remembers them all. In the midst of our conversation, she asked me, "Dad, will I ever be able to afford a home?"

I wish I could've responded with, "Of course you will!" But I couldn't. She graduated into a tough economy (not unlike the one I graduated into in 1982), but this time salaries were not keeping up with inflation, and tuition costs had skyrocketed. Her mother and I agreed to cover the costs of her undergraduate studies but not her master's degree. She is still paying off a large loan and has a legitimate question about home ownership and equity. I never mentioned that I bought my first house at twenty-five years old. It was a different day.

My son, Jonathan, graduated and got married a few years later to Ashleymae. They met at college in Los Angeles, where he majored in screenwriting. He wants to work as a writer in the entertainment industry. After living in Atlanta a few years, they moved back to LA—less than three months before the pandemic broke out. He's working full time, making ends meet but not getting ahead, and he is not working in the field he'd studied and planned to enter. I asked him recently, "Do you think you'll be able to enter the field you chose to study anytime soon?"

He smiled but couldn't say. He desperately wants to write scripts for film and television, but that world has been limited since the quarantine began in 2020. His networking hasn't produced any leads yet. He's not discouraged and has kept a good attitude as he executes his current job, but he clearly has had to serve in a field he did not plan to spend years working. It's often the story of the Millennial generation. Whether graduates entered an already-saturated industry or they bumped into a poor economy, many are doing "gigs" as they wait for a break. I don't remind him that I had three opportunities to work in my field of study upon graduation.

Finally, both of my kids have partners but they do not have kids. They both want to have children one day, but right now they're wondering whether it's even wise. My wife and I work hard to put no pressure on them to furnish us with grandchildren, but some time ago we discussed the question, "Is it even a good idea to bring a child into the world today?"

The world seems like such a crazy place to raise a child, and neither of these couples believes they have the income right now to provide for another mouth to feed. Like millions of Millennials, they've chosen careers over kids—at least for now. Not only are careers important to this generation, but for most couples, two incomes are necessary for the lifestyles they've chosen. In contrast, my wife and I were parenting both of our children by the time we'd reached their ages.

With all these challenges in mind, I encourage older generations that leading or collaborating with Millennials at work requires both empathy and wisdom. If you're managing young professionals on your team, following are some suggestions to do it wisely.

Steps to Connect with Them or Lead Them Well

1. Create incentive for them. (Clarify the "why" behind their tasks.)

2. Micromanage at first. (Offer consistent feedback.)

3. Let them share ideas. (They want to upload their ideas, not just hear yours.)

4. "Gamify" the tasks and goals. (Find ways to create competitions with peers.)

5. Launch a mutual mentor initiative. (Match them with older colleagues so both can add value.)

6. Communicate the importance of their work. (Connect the dots between their tasks and the goals.)

7. Tell them the truth. (Some may have never been criticized in a gracious manner.)

8. Celebrate any and all progress. (Enable them to see improvement in their work.)

9. Manage by objective. (Eventually, give them a goal and let them reach it their way.)

10. Mentor more than manage. (Relate to them as a coach more than a scrutinizing boss.)

INTERFACING WITH THE MILLENNIAL GENERATION

Recently a department head spoke to me about the number of young team members who expect immediate freedom on the terms and times of their labor. She said, "Millennials and Gen Z employees often expect to set their own hours, establish their own boundaries, and even dictate the tasks they'll take on."

Another vice president told me he had three employees approach him questioning their "career path." It's a term describing the course each person will take to be promoted and receive pay raises, ultimately resulting in the arrival of an ideal position in the organization. The VP frowned and said, "I would have never brought that up to a supervisor when I was young. I would have felt I was being selfish, focusing on my own growth rather than the company's." I had to agree with him. As my career began, I focused on executing my job with excellence, and I counted on my superiors to move me up.

Today, times have changed.

Terms of Engagement: Four Rules That Govern the Workplace

Whether you're a Millennial who is still learning the systems in your workplace or you're a Baby Boomer or Gen Xer, the following four rules may be fodder for good discussion. In our office at Growing Leaders, I find myself talking to young leaders about their potential career path and the steps they can take toward promotion, leadership, and deeper influence. About half of our team is under thirty-five years old. It dawned on me that I had not taken the time to explain to our team *how work works*. By this, I mean there's a natural order of laws that govern the way freedom, influence, and even pay raises tend to operate. While there are exceptions to these rules, the following are four that I embrace that usually make sense on the job.

1. Autonomy Increases with Productivity

In 2019 we had a growing number of team members who requested days each week to work from home. It's obviously quite normal in our culture today. Over the last decade, we've allowed several team members to do this. But I have always based my decision on a simple principle: *autonomy increases with productivity*. In other words, we all earn our right to work on our own terms. Those who demonstrate they are producers and need little or no supervision to meet and exceed expectations get to enjoy greater levels of freedom. Each director must evaluate the production and results of employees and make that judgment. Freedom isn't free; it's earned. As Dave Ramsey says, "Your raise is effective when you are."

2. Promotions Always Follow Testing

When team members inquire about promotions and pay raises, our COO and I are not put off by that conversation, but we always try to clarify: *testing always precedes promotion*. By this, we mean tenure alone doesn't earn the right to be promoted or given bonuses. Academic degrees alone don't automatically translate into pay raises either. By "tests" I mean rising to challenges and capitalizing on opportunities. Just like a product in a store is never used until it is tested, so it is with team members. The deeper the testing and the more team members display they can pass those tests with flying colors, the more likely they are to be invited into greater levels of responsibility and are rewarded with greater remuneration. Simply doing a job doesn't equal progress. Promotion follows performance at a higher level.

3. Rules Decrease as Results Increase

Sometimes it's hard for a young, inexperienced team member to see a supervisor experiencing high levels of independence and authority. Similar to "autonomy increases with productivity," this close cousin explains that the more results a person produces in their work, the fewer rules are needed to legislate their activity on the job. Working under Dr. John C. Maxwell for twenty years, I learned this rule quickly. John was crystal clear about the fact that results were his "love language." My work ethic and my track record of reaching outcomes were all he needed to allow me great independence, even in my twenties. He never asked me to clock in; he only asked me to put out or produce results. I was happy to do so. This is how work usually works.

4. Influence Rises by Providing the Scarcest Resource

This one occurs naturally, but few people notice it. Our influence (and ultimately our leadership role) rises when we provide a rare resource. Consider a simple example: if you're with a group of people in a car, traveling in an unfamiliar city, and only one person has a GPS, he or she is the one with the most influence. Similarly, if I bring a skill, talent, or ability that is scarce to my team, I tend to gain more influence. It's just how the marketplace works: supply and demand. If what you have is in short supply and great demand, you'll have influence. In fact, the scarcer your ability, the more remuneration and the more influence should come your way.

> Have you spotted any disparity between young staff members' expectations and yours?

Four Ideas Millennials Can Leverage for Change at Work

Mary-Hunter (Mae) McDonnell is a professor at the Wharton School of Management at the University of Pennsylvania. Dr. McDonnell suggests four ideas for younger team members who want to see change occur on their team but may not be sure of the best way to achieve it:

- **Stand *for* something, not merely *against* something.** This was the flaw of Occupy Wall Street years ago. Translate your grievance into a positive vision. Martin Luther King Jr. said, "I Have a Dream," not "I Have a Complaint."
- **Your request should be rooted in a broad identity.** In short, don't lobby for change for a small special-interest group but rather one that will make the whole organization better.

Keep in mind who your organization is and what it's always been about.

- **Look for allies in positions of power.** Change is always easier when you can find a person of influence who could accelerate your message to those at the top.
- **Start building a coalition on the team.** Slack, Notion, and other communication platforms make it easier today to gain traction with those who align with your ideas. Leverage those sources in a positive way and become so big they can't ignore you.

In my experience, most young employees desire to see change happen in the workplace. These steps enable a young team member to lead and influence even when they're not in charge.

LEADING MILLENNIALS

As I've mentioned, the transition from school to career was a big one. By and large, adults did not do a great job getting their Millennial kids career-ready. In addition, millions of them came of age just after the terrorist attacks on September 11, 2001. For many, the world went from awesome to awful. It was a dark rite of passage. As we lead them, we must remember the world that their leaders created while this generation was in childhood and adolescence often did not remotely resemble the one they've entered as professionals. Let me offer some counsel as you lead these young team members:

1. **Lead with empathy and understanding.** We'll get better results if we begin not with frustration but with empathy. Seek to understand before being understood. Our listening earns our right to be heard.

2. **Launch conversations called "The Elephant in the Room."** Some topics feel off-limits at a job. Find time to talk about these topics that no one talks about in public. They're "elephants in the room" that we would do well to address and explain.

3. **Create safe spaces for them to ask "dumb questions."** Often young staff don't ask questions because they're embarrassed that they don't know the answer and feel they should. Find spaces for them to ask questions anonymously.
4. **Provide training in areas in which they may lack experience.** Work with them to create a career growth plan. If they need training to do their job or get promoted, we should offer that as leaders. We can either get mad or get busy.
5. **Communicate that you see their strengths and value to the team.** As a young employee, they can feel unimportant and think you don't see their value. Be sure to relay you do see their talent and skills and point out the value they offer.

It's important we never forget the value those Millennials bring to a team.

Jared is a Millennial who always brings energy to a room. In fact, while some older team members believe he's a bit "too much for them to handle," you can always count on Jared's positive attitude, idealistic approach, and belief that the team can pull off the goals they've set. Once he learned the products and services his company offered, he was selling like crazy. I consulted with this team a few years back and heard from colleagues that Jared was a bit too creative in his techniques and wouldn't stick to the plan—but few could argue with his success. He is valuable to their mission. He still has the energy, creativity, and optimism that older team members who've become jaded over the years desperately need.

My advice to their CEO? Keep Jared around and let him play this role.

——————————— **Talk It Over** ———————————

(1) How can you capitalize on the value and skills a Millennial brings to the team?

(2) Data reveals that the largest chasm on work teams today is between Baby Boomers and Millennials. Do you see this? What can you do to bridge this chasm?

(3) Generation Y is now the largest part of the workforce and will soon become the largest population of customers in US history. How can you prepare them to lead on your team?

8

THE CONTRIBUTION OF THE CORONIALS (GENERATION Z)

Ethan and Emma are both members of Generation Z and classic illustrations of what's trending in this demographic.

Ethan's primary group of friends meets mostly online, playing video games such as Fortnite and Minecraft. He's already created an app at the age of twenty-one and plans to work for himself once he begins his career. While a junior in high school, Ethan came out as bisexual because he wasn't sure whom he might want to hook up with; each gender seemed like a potential option. He is forgoing attending any four-year liberal arts college and is instead taking some Massive Open Online Courses (MOOC), getting an internship with Google, participating in two master classes, and connecting with some business mentors his parents put him in touch with.

Emma decided to attend a university, but she always felt a little out of place. She wasn't a traditional student and is a self-described "socialite." Her digital "coming out" happened when she was in the sixth grade when her mom bought her a smartphone. Neither Emma nor her mother had any idea how that device would become all-consuming; it ambushed her entire adolescence. She has suffered from both panic attacks and bouts with depression and endures the weekly low-grade anxiety of comparison traps as well as online bullying. Sometimes Emma is the tormenter; sometimes she is the tormented, even at twenty years old.

Both Emma and Ethan experience FOMO (Fear of Missing Out) and FOMU (Fear of Messing Up). They each entered their careers recovering from compromising videos posted by peers; Emma's boyfriend (at the time) shared a bedroom video she had meant for his eyes only. Ethan was filmed on an iPhone at a party, and the video is still out in cyberspace and has sabotaged two job interviews. Fortunately, he plans to work for himself in the end. Each of them spend about eight hours a day on their portable devices. Mental health issues are front and center in their minds. They're both afraid that this reality may trip them up in their careers. Both want to succeed in their jobs but will likely meet mentors and supervisors who are unlike them and may require some time to get accustomed to their ways.

Ultimately, both Ethan and Emma describe their lives as absolutely overwhelming.

NEW KIDS ON THE BLOCK

Generation Z is now the talk of the town as they represent the newest and youngest employees on the job. They are the team members who've grown up in the twenty-first century. They don't remember Bill Clinton as president or the Monica Lewinsky scandal; they don't even remember the Columbine High School massacre or, for that matter, the September 11, 2001, terrorist attacks. But they did grow up in the aftermath of both.

Parents of Gen Zers were scared for their safety and health and did not realize how the "smart" technology of their childhood would affect them. For instance, if a Gen Zer has a phone, they likely consume adult information (such as news reports of a bombing or mass shootings) at twelve years old. They take in so much content that most are overwhelmed. Consider this: while Millennials grew up with cell phones, Generation Z grew up with smartphones. Millennials grew up connecting with friends through a text message; Generation Z grew up connecting with friends on social media. Most from Generation Z have been on a smart tablet or portable device since they were in preschool. Some call them "Coronials" because their childhood and adolescence was interrupted by the coronavirus pandemic of 2020. As they enter their careers, they will exhibit some new characteristics. The newest generation in the workforce today has been called many names:

- Screenagers
- Coronials
- Mosaics
- iGen
- Centennials
- The Touchscreen Generation
- Generation Zoom
- Zoomers
- Generation Z

Generation Z grew up in an age where technology was virtual and smart. Interacting with it as early as two years old, they're the most overwhelmed and anxious yet most savvy and entrepreneurial generation of hackers to date. As I said, historian Neil Howe calls them the Homelanders because their generation started about the same time as the Department of Homeland Security. Terrorism has been a normal part of the conversation. In fact, President George W. Bush described the post-9/11 era as a "new normal." American society began to use that term again in 2020 as the pandemic changed the way we did life. So Generation Z has been conditioned to expect the rules and the terms of engagement to change.

REALITIES THAT SHAPED GENERATION Z

The first twenty years of the twenty-first century were so different than the previous twenty years. While smart technology was enticing and novel, there was a downside. The last two decades have provided us darker times in general. Step into Gen Z's shoes for a moment and ponder these dark realities:

1. **They wrestle with mental health issues more than ever.**
   As Gen Z began, cognitive behavioral scientist Dr. Robert Leahy said that the average US teen experiences the same level of anxiety as a psychiatric patient did in the 1950s.[35]

2. **They are aware of national and global tragedies younger than ever.**
   When I was a teen, my biggest problem was, "Where is my baseball mitt?" Today kids are exposed to news of bombings, tragedies, trauma, and terrorist attacks as young as fifth grade.

3. **They witnessed more mass shootings in 2019 than we had days in the year.**
   There were 419 mass shootings in the United States in 2019, an average of more than one a day. High school students recently told me, "When we hear any loud noise at school, we all duck."

4. **They feel undue academic and social pressure to perform/ compete.**
   Gen Z is growing up in an extremely competitive time. Everything is organized and they feel pressure to excel in school, sports, and anything else they do. Few items are just for fun.

5. **They feel they're constantly captured (on video) and critiqued (when posted).**
   If I had dropped my tray in the lunchroom at school, the table near me would have laughed, clapped, and then moved on. Today this mishap is videoed and posted on a half-dozen social media platforms. It doesn't go away.

6. **They witness polarized adult generations who often behave poorly.**

   Let's face it. When we challenge young people to act maturely, many could say they've not seen any adults do that yet. "Snowplow adults" overfunction, intruding on teachers and managers.

7. **They are now part of the "pandemic population" in an economic crisis.**

   The COVID-19 pandemic caused the third economic downturn since the twenty-first century started. Many Gen Zers feel "postponed and penalized." They feel uncertain and hesitant.

Certainly, these young employees don't all feel like life is "dark." But we would do well to recognize the strange period of history in which they grew up. According to a 2022 Barna Research study, over half of Generation Z (56 percent) say they tend to expect the worst to happen. Ponder that reality. Just like the September 11 terrorist attack was the Millennial coming of age tragedy, the COVID-19 pandemic marks Gen Z's coming of age.

We'll examine several of the positive qualities Gen Z brings with them into their careers in a moment. First, though, allow me to illustrate how they are not merely continuations of the Millennial generation. The Deloitte Global Millennial Survey 2020 reveals that close to half (48 percent) of Generation Z and 44 percent of Millennial respondents in the primary survey said they're stressed all or most of the time.[36] Half of respondents said they believe it's too late to repair the damage caused by climate change. The good news, though, is that a Pulse Survey reveals the pandemic has brought about an even stronger sense of individual responsibility. Nearly three-fourths said the pandemic made them more sympathetic toward others' needs and that they intend to take action to have a positive impact on their communities. Here are shifts they bring:

The Shifts Generation Z Makes Away from Millennials

- Confidence is morphing into caution. (They refuse to repeat Millennial errors.)
- Spending money is morphing into saving money. (Think anti-debt.)
- Attacking an education is morphing into hacking one. (Think DIY after high school.)
- Idealism is morphing into pragmatism. (Think safety and security first.)
- Consuming media is morphing into creating media. (Think upload and create.)
- Viral posts are morphing into vanishing posts. (Think Snapchat.)
- Feeling special is morphing into feeling savvy. (Think "woke.")
- Entitlement is morphing into empowerment. (Think smartphone.)
- Text messages are morphing into iconic messages. (Think emojis and GIFs.)
- Anticipation is morphing into anxiety. (Think panic attacks and depression.)

The CDC reported in fall 2020 that one in four young adults (ages 18–24) contemplated suicide in the previous month. Not one in one hundred or one in fifty. *One in four.* It was mostly due to the pandemic and their fears that the world would be less than it was prior to 2020.

This is part of what makes Generation Z a game changer.

IMMIGRANTS AND NATIVES: WHO'S IN FOREIGN TERRITORY?

As Gen Z members enter their careers in the coming years, you will likely notice new habits and attitudes; they will be different to say the least. The world is changing rapidly (socially, ethnically, technologically, and in terms of rules of engagement), and the youngest population is usually the type who adapt the soonest. In fact, some of these new rules will be ones they create and introduce to the working world.

As the future unfolds, those who are thirty-five and older will feel increasingly like they are interfacing with foreigners as they interact with Gen Zers. The language, customs, and values a young team member embraces are likely to be so strange to you that you'll have to work to find commonalities. Keep in mind, however, that in the Land of Tomorrow, *you* are the foreigner. They are the natives; we are the immigrants. High anxiety, volatile economies, heightened terrorism, and artificial intelligence (AI) are all elements they've grown up with and that have been normalized. I often feel like a missionary in a foreign land attempting to reach them and teach them. Simultaneously, I recognize they have so much to teach me.

> Have you spotted any other distinct characteristics among Generation Z?

Following are some key descriptions the Generation Z population possess. To make it easy to remember, the terms spell the word FOREIGN. We are in "foreign" territory:

F – Fluid

Even more than the Millennials, this population is always changing, even in their sense of self. At younger ages, Gen Z is experimenting with their identities, their gender preferences, and the terms they feel most comfortable using to describe themselves. A 2016 study by trend forecasting agency J. Walter Thompson Innovation Group found that only 48 percent of thirteen- to twenty-year-olds identify as "exclusively heterosexual." The LGBTQ+ community expands, even if it includes those merely experimenting with new gender identities or tastes. These decisions are frequently fluid, too, so they may be different in six months. Colleagues must get used to adapting to their dynamic sense of self and leading with empathy and understanding.

O – Overwhelmed

This research became public as early as a decade ago. University students said the top word they use to describe themselves is *overwhelmed*. More than half are so overwhelmed it is difficult to function, and nearly one in ten contemplated suicide the year prior.[37] Mental health issues have moved from the margins to front and center. At least part of the source of their anxiety, depression, and panic attacks is the ridiculous volume of information coming at them (or anyone) from social media—almost ten thousand messages a day. Just 45 percent of Gen Zers report that their mental health is very good or excellent, according to the American Psychological Association. Further, the stigma of seeing a counselor is dropping. Mental health care will need to be part of what workplaces offer going forward.

R – Reinvention

While earlier generations may be satisfied with incremental tweaks and facelifts, Gen Z desires fundamental changes. Forget the facelift; they want an overhaul. We're fine with an evolution of change; they want a revolution. In fact, make that reinvention. They often desire to completely switch up tastes, approaches, and even causes for which they will be activists. Alternative music, clothes, tattoos, and lifestyles are no longer on the fringes. The past two generations have had music artists that are alternative, such as Marilyn Manson and Nirvana. Today Billie Eilish is considered an alternative artist, except that her music downloads are "pop" or popular. She has hundreds of millions of fans. Alternative is now common. Get ready for *different* to be *normal* ... or to explain why your company's values require them to remove a piercing and cover a tattoo.

E – Entrepreneurial

One national survey reports that 72 percent of Generation Z high school students plan to be an entrepreneur.[38] Millions see themselves being their own boss, including creating a product or service, launching a new organization or even industry, and then releasing an app to distribute it. A disproportionate number of teens and young adults have already launched their own start-ups. It makes sense—this is a generation that grew up with a smart device in their hands where they could search and find answers on their own instead of waiting for an adult to provide the information. In fact, Gen Z doesn't need their elders for *information* but, for *interpretation*. We must help them make sense of all they know, to provide context to all the content they've digested. This entrepreneurial spirit is something we should leverage on our teams.

I – Independent

While Millennials grew up playing soccer on teams, working on school projects in groups, and embracing all things "community," Generation Z grows up in a world where they learn to be alone on a portable device, where indoor games have increased more than outdoors games, and where they play on a screen alone while sedentary. They are used to being "social" while in isolation. They do more things alone than Millennials or Generation X, which may illustrate why so many claim they struggle with loneliness. The pandemic has only deepened this pattern as kids were forced to learn, play, and work virtually on a screen. In short, whereas Millennials are true team players, Gen Z are independent, competitive, and more individualistic in their habits. Fifty-six percent say they prefer to customize their career paths rather than have a company do it for them.[39]

G – Geek

The term *geek* meant something different in the past. It was a stereotype. Today nearly all Gen Z members could be considered *geeks* merely because they are so at home in the digital world. They haven't merely mastered technology; they've mastered *smart* technology. By 2020, over 90 percent of toddlers were on tablets or other portable devices, and by age two 75 percent owned their own devices, according to the American Academy of Pediatrics. This reality has cultivated a "hacker" mindset in almost everything they put their minds to; they are savvy and they possess a DIY disposition. They are intuitive when it comes to smart tech, and the sooner organizations capitalize on this strength, the better.

N – Networked

While this term has been around for three decades, Gen Z members have given it new meaning. Smart technology has enabled these digital natives to be connected 24/7. Yet while these social creatures are on multiple platforms for the time equivalent of a full-time job, they are also more private, having learned from the digital mistakes of the Millennials. Their connectivity has fostered a greater sense of tolerance for all lifestyles than older generations. As I noted earlier, they are far more social and consider themselves a global generation—global citizens—that is apt to know peers in other countries. Employers should utilize this strength as they consider future customers and employees. Their relationships are more than transactional. They are personal. Gen Z wants *real* friends, not *deal* friends.

Let me say it again—in the Land of Tomorrow, Gen Z are the natives, and we are the immigrants. The emerging generation is usually seen as strange at first, and eventually everyone sees they bring those oddities into the future and often become the norm. These descriptions above are actually characteristics of the future for *everyone*. Our culture is migrating toward these realities, like it or not. This is all the more reason we must lead well.

THE RULES MAY BE CHANGING

While Generation Z are niched in a thousand different subgroups, Austin may be a vivid case study for us on this new generation. He was born in 2001 and identifies with Billie Eilish, the top Grammy Award–winner in 2020, whose songs are often about things that are dark and depressing. Austin is a nice guy who has different groups of friends on TikTok, Snapchat, and Instagram. If he were honest with you—like he was with me—he would admit to having major questions about his gender identity. Like many Gen Zers, he doesn't identify as binary. He's pretty sure he's not heterosexual.

As a college student, he was overwhelmed by school, life, and an uncertain future. He takes meds for an anxiety disorder and would say anxiety has been normalized among his friends. Having older siblings, Austin feels he's growing up in the shadow of the Millennial generation who are a step ahead in age and experience. He knows he'll be competing with them for jobs when he graduates, just as Generation X grew up in the shadow of the Boomers and felt they competed with them. He was diagnosed with ADHD in elementary school, and the meds for that have helped him become more focused. All the same, he still feels penalized by the whole pandemic.

More than anything, he is sure that no adult is going to swoop in and "save the day" for him once he begins his career. Austin said to me, "Why should I think that? Nobody knew what they were doing when the pandemic hit us all in 2020. I am going to hack my way through my career and figure it out myself." He is part of a different generation than any in America's past:

1. They're the most diverse population at work: 48 percent are not white.
2. They own a smartphone (96 percent) and multitask on five screens a day.
3. They're smart consumers: 35 percent plan to save for retirement in their twenties.
4. Salary is a top motivator (70 percent) and health insurance is a must (70 percent).
5. Almost 60 percent say they would work weekends for higher pay.

6. Unlike Millennials, only 38 percent consider work/life balance important.
7. Over 90 percent prefer to have human interaction at work instead of just screens.
8. Forty percent want daily interaction with their boss, and they feel something's wrong without it.
9. Sixty percent want multiple check-ins with a team supervisor daily.[40]

Get ready for a new normal when this young generation is all in the marketplace. They are genuinely different and not afraid to let you know.

WHAT GEN Z WANTS AT WORK

In preparation for this book, I looked at the quantitative data on Generation Z (some social scientists believe the generation began as early as 1995; some say 1997 or 1999). When I couple this data with my qualitative research done in focus groups with Gen Z, I created this list of desires they have for a work environment. This represents merely a wish list on their part, knowing that the economy may make a perfect work environment unattainable:

- **Accessibility and Connection:** They want supervisors to be reachable and available to them for questions or concerns.
- **Autonomy and Independence:** They're hackers and learned to figure life out on their own; they want this reality at work as well.
- **Appreciation and Respect:** They expect to be respected the same way the boss is; the organizational chart should be flat.
- **Adaptability and Change:** They prefer lots of change at work and desire it to happen fairly rapidly. This prevents boredom.
- **Acceptance and Inclusion:** They prioritize diversity, equity, and inclusion on a team, in language, and in company values.
- **Acknowledgment and Recognition:** They may not admit it, but surveys show they—like most humans—want to be rewarded.

If you read this "wish list" and concluded it's unrealistic, let me remind you that Gen Z will be the key to the future for your team if you successfully connect with them. Most Millennials in their thirties remember when they were the dictators of what was in vogue, including craft beer, Adele, rompers, rose gold, "Netflix and chill," and squad goals. Now millions of them get the foreboding sense from Generation Z that their AARP card is already in the mail.

> Have you noticed any other desires of Generation Z in your workplace?

As "generational shifts tend to go, there is a new crop of employees determining the norms and styles of the workplace," as journalist Emma Goldberg writes. We must acknowledge that what is "cool" and what products are trending evaporate more quickly than ever. I distinctly remember reaching midlife and writing an article where I admitted I'd given up on being "cool." I was no longer an "emerging leader"; I had emerged. The card I had to play was to be a listening leader of the emerging generations. The most pitiful thing I could do was to continue trying to be "dope" when no one was looking for those cues from anyone in my generation.

My kids needed a parent, not a pal; my team members needed a leader, not a wannabe hipster who was still trying to be their BFF. I wasn't giving up on relevance—in fact, quite the opposite. I was being more relevant by being my authentic self. Twentysomethings roll their eyes at the habits of their elders, and that will continue into the foreseeable future. There is a new boldness, however, in Gen Z today. Whereas the Millennials who graduated into the 2008 financial recession were happy to get any job in their desired industry, Gen Z have quit jobs during the economic downturn of 2020–2021 and sought out "pandemic-proof jobs." They felt the agency to do so. It's the gig economy. A fall 2021 survey of Gen Z job candidates from the recruitment software company RippleMatch found that more than two-thirds wanted jobs that will indefinitely stay remote.[41]

Gabe Kennedy, the thirty-year-old founder of the herbal supplement brand Plant People, says, "Older generations were much more used to punching the clock. It was, 'I climb the ladder and get my pension and gold watch.' Then for millennials it was, 'There's still an office but I can play Ping-Pong and drink nitro coffee.' For the next generation it's, 'Holy cow I can make a living by posting on social media when I want and how I want.'"

Believe it or not, we must meet Gen Z where they are.

WHAT GENERATION Z HAS TO CONTRIBUTE

As you manage or work alongside Generation Z, it will be helpful to remember the valuable benefits they bring to a team. They add value in unique ways to their older teammates.

- **Hacker Mindset:** Millions of Gen Zers are not going to college but are hacking their postsecondary experiences. As adults, they're becoming resourceful and self-sufficient cultivating useful skills for a job.
- **Entrepreneurial:** Many imagine they will create an app, invent a digital product, or become YouTube or TikTok famous and are finding ways to launch projects. This spirit could be useful on your team.
- **Cause-Oriented:** If you make them aware of a societal or cultural need, they can be passionate about working tirelessly to solve a problem or serve people. They love to support a mission that matters.
- **Social Media-Cunning:** They were familiar with social media apps in middle school. They could be useful finding ways to monetize it for an organization, by telling a company's story, and giving shout-outs to customers.
- **DIY Disposition:** They've had a portable device in their hands all their lives and love figuring out how to do a project by looking it up online. Their do-it-yourself disposition is greater than any since the Builders.

- **Fresh Perspective:** Because this generation grew up in a subculture of their peers on social media, they'll bring a new paradigm and outlook to every system you have or problem you need solving.
- **Savvy:** They've been overexposed to information and consequently feel savvy about the world and about culture. While this may be a wrong assumption, they may know more than you expect.

> What other contributions have you noticed Generation Z can make?

The more I'm around this generation, the more excited I get about how empowered they feel. No doubt they'll need experienced guides who can help them navigate the workplace. But I believe they bring just the spark that most teams need.

Steps for Connecting with and Leading Generation Z

1. Listen to them and affirm their dreams and goals.

2. Provide them with a sense of purpose as they perform (sometimes) menial tasks.

3. Give them short-term commitments they can keep and put wins under their belts.

4. Help them to focus on one meaningful objective and pull it off.

5. Encourage them to simplify their lives and remove some self-imposed pressure.

6. Discuss personal values with them and help them to become value-driven.

7. Build a relationship with them before expecting trust.

8. Express both high expectations and high belief in them. Both are essential to be complete.

9. Give them short-term projects to help them see they're contributing to the overall mission.

10. Include them in brainstorming meetings and ask for their input and "hacker" insights.

11. As they demonstrate responsibility and results, allow them to work from anywhere.

12. Let them "own" a project along with the responsibility and authority that come with it.

A FINAL WORD ON GEN Z

Many from Generation Z are a bit skeptical about leaders because they've seen too many of them fail morally, relationally, financially, emotionally, or vocationally. They've seen the "dirt" on social media or in digital articles on *BuzzFeed* about how unethical leaders act, and they can enter a workplace suspicious of what's really going on behind the curtain. My advice to employers is this: don't assume they trust you just because you have a title and position. Even though you are paying them a salary, imagine they are a volunteer and work to earn their trust. I have had to do this with several of my team members from Generation Z. It isn't because they believe I am a bad person; it's because I need to overcome a past stereotype in their mind. I had one young employee recently tell me, "When I meet a new leader, they start with the grade of F and have to earn an A." I smiled and replied, "Wow. I am just the opposite. When I meet someone new, they begin with an A and have to earn an F."

Even if they don't know how to ask for it, Generation Z long for relationships with their leaders but may not know how to approach that desire. We must build bridges of relationships that can bear the weight of honest self-disclosure. Trust and transparency are earned and come over time, not overnight. Once I have built these with a young employee, I have noticed they will go to great lengths to serve the mission—far beyond the job description requirements.

Now, let me share one more sobering reality.

Remember, the American population is made up of two mountains and two valleys (see the diagram on page 106). The Baby Boomers are about 76 million strong. They're a mountain. The Baby Busters (Xers) are about 49 million strong. They're a valley. Millennials are about 80 million strong. Another mountain. Gen Z is about 59 million strong. Another valley. This creates a supply and demand dilemma for leaders.

As I've mentioned, ten thousand Baby Boomers retire on average, every day. Even if everyone in Generation X were a brilliant leader, there would not be enough of them to fill the vacancies left by the Boomers. Managers and leaders will need to be selected from among the Millennials and Generation Z. Ready or not, they will be called up to lead because of the need.

We must get them ready to lead.

Hannah was just eighteen years old when she joined her company as an intern. At first, nearly everyone at her organization saw her as they did most interns—as a way to get tasks done that no one else wants to do for a small price. That is, until they saw what Hannah could do. The company gave her a cornucopia of tasks, from operations, to sales, to editing, to marketing. When she was assigned to handle social media posts to market to their tribe, things took off. Likes and shares increased, customer engagement increased, and the company's followers increased as well. Her supervisor asked Hannah if she'd ever handled marketing tasks like these, and Hannah had to admit she hadn't. But as a member of Generation Z, she intuitively understood how to enlist people's participation on social media. She'd grown up with it. The good news is that her team recognized her value and invited her to join their staff full time upon graduation. When I spoke to the company president, she told me, "We all know

Hannah needs some training; she's raw as a teammate. But she has the abilities to not only serve our mission but to lead our marketing efforts in time. We are so glad we found her."

Truth be told, many want to lead . . . as long as it's not about privilege. They desire to be on a *leadership journey* so long as it's not a *power trip*, like so many of the Baby Boomer stereotypes they've witnessed in politics and business. Worldwide, Generation Z has a keener interest in leadership than the previous three generations according to a survey by Universum. After the March for Our Lives in March 2018, two Gen Z high school students were asked by a journalist how they could be so mature at such a young age. One of the students responded, "Because so many adults are acting like kids, I felt it was time the kids acted like adults."

I spoke recently to a college student who was volunteering with us at Growing Leaders. He was hungry to grow and ready to serve people and solve problems. I was stunned when I asked if he was volunteering to get extra credit for his transcript. He smiled and said, "No, those hours were invested months ago. I actually started my own nonprofit organization this year and am simply here to learn how to lead it better."

This is the bright side of Generation Z. And they're wondering if we'll help them lead.

———— Talk It Over ————

(1) How can you capitalize on the value and skills a Coronial (Gen Zer) brings to the team?

(2) What changes should you make to connect better with Gen Z team members? How could you connect a Boomer generation member or a Gen X member to a Gen Zer who would identify with the challenges of a tough economy?

(3) As you reflect on the challenges this newest team member brings into their career, how can you equip them to perform at their highest level?

PART
THREE

BRIDGE
THE GAP

9

LIFE IS ABOUT MANAGING PREFERENCES, TENSIONS, AND EXPECTATIONS

A FRIEND RECENTLY RECOUNTED THIS STORY: "TWO SUMMERS AGO, when my daughter was nineteen, I was giving her a ride to work one morning. She was running late so I stopped what I was doing in order to take her as quickly as possible.

"At that moment, I was paying bills. I do some bills online, but I still like to mail checks for some of them. I had time to seal the outgoing mail but not to put the stamps and return addresses on them. So I brought them with us on the ride, figuring I'd have my daughter finish them during the trip. I handed her the envelopes, stamps, and stickers with our return address on them and asked her to finish getting them ready so I could mail them.

"The next thing I know, she's on her phone, searching for a YouTube video on how to mail a letter. She had *no idea* where the stamp went because she'd never actually mailed a physical letter and, apparently, she had paid zero attention to where the stamps go on the envelopes we send and receive at the house every day.

"I wasn't sure if I should feel disappointed or outdated. In retrospect, I can see how a kid born in 1999 could make it into adulthood without ever learning where to put a stamp on a letter. Unless I showed her, why would I expect her to know that?"

This dad had an epiphany many of us need to have.

One mistake I've made is expecting young team members to have had the same experiences I had at their age. We may fail to recognize our youngest team members had a very different reality than leaders may have had. Further, because younger generations have had unique experiences, they often bring unique expectations with them to a team. It's a tension we must manage. In fact, navigating this tension is essential for leaders.

PREFERENCES, EXPECTATIONS, AND REQUIREMENTS = TENSIONS

- Different experiences lead to unique expectations.
- Unique expectations lead to ongoing tensions.
- Tensions are something to manage, not solve.

Every challenge we encounter is either a *problem to solve* or a *tension to manage*. We must remember that tension is a normal part of leading a team of people. We will never rid ourselves of certain tensions. They are to be managed and not expected to disappear. However, different people from different generations who join our team come with problems that need to be solved or, better yet, prevented.

What makes this tricky for leaders on our team is that sometimes a young Millennial brings a lofty expectation that isn't realistic. They expect something impossible because of an idealistic perspective based on sheer inexperience. One human resources executive told me two young team members wrote a letter demanding the company provide them with opportunities for discussion on each decision the organization makes. They'd seen a smaller, privately owned company do this, but this company was publicly traded and much larger. The pace of improvement and "speed to market" on new products would have slowed down to a snail's pace. Minimally, it would have been a board decision, and there was probably no one on the board who would vote to approve the motion. It was simply a naive expectation on the part of two "rookies."

Conversely, there are times when those rookies can expect something that could shake an organization out of its lethargy, such as requests for better practices in equity and inclusion. This happened on our team, and it led to a positive step forward. I am grateful for those young outliers on the team who pushed for improvement. It has been said, "On the front end, change often appears to be improbable. On the back end, it appears to be inevitable."

The fact is, each person, depending on who they are and what generation they're from, brings with them varying *preferences* (personal opinions), varying *expectations* (personal assumptions), and varying *requirements* (personal demands), which can produce tensions on a team. Effective leaders identify these differences and spot which ones exist in team members. Is a suggestion made by a Gen Xer merely a preference, or is it a requirement for them to stay on the team? Is it an expectation that can be handled even if their supervisor doesn't meet it but helps them adjust it instead? And are the differences team members experience tensions that can be managed so the team can stay on course with their mission?

Our goal should be to distinguish between problems and tensions and lead efficiently.

Navigating the Differences

Let's examine these three tensions and illustrate how team members can navigate differences between them. Wise managers aid in this process and enable teammates to collaborate instead of collide. This is an art more than a science and requires social and emotional intelligence.

Many leaders failed to navigate these preferences, expectations, and requirements in 2021. Millions of employees left their jobs for something else. A feature article in *Inc.* magazine called it "the Great Resignation." In April, May, and June of 2021, some 11.5 million team members quit their jobs. Later that year, more than four million left in a single month. Many called it the "Pink Slip Revenge." So many companies had to lay off workers during the pandemic in 2020, and a year later workers were demanding more pay or better conditions if they were going to stay. Employees were asked to work double shifts because fewer staff felt comfortable coming back to work. It wasn't all about the pandemic, however. Texas A&M professor Anthony Klotz predicted this great resignation in 2019 after seeing the sense of agency many employees felt and the work dissatisfaction they expressed on surveys.

When researchers dug into this, some discovered a generational problem. In an Addison Group study of one thousand workers representing multiple generations, 90 percent reported satisfaction with the diversity of age ranges in their workplace. However, the study also found that 35 percent felt their company's culture and processes favored one generation over others. Forty-five percent of respondents felt their employers were biased toward Millennials.[42] Generational conflict arises whenever the interests or ideals of one generation collide openly with those of another.

I believe we can begin to build a bridge between our differences by understanding preferences, expectations, and demands that lead to tensions on our team.

Managing Preferences

Preferences are the softest of the three and should be the easiest to manage, but sometimes team members from different generations can confuse them with expectations or demands. Boomers, for example, may prefer that a task be performed in the manner they used in the past, but Millennials may want to approach the task in a new way. If either person makes a preference a requirement, trouble brews unnecessarily. Conversely, a young team member may expect everyone to be open to their new methods for approaching a task and fail to appreciate the effective system that's already in place. Perhaps that young teammate is a creative and despises confining systems and processes, but every veteran knows they actually enable efficiency.

What's the advice I try to follow with preferences?

Avoid winning a Pyrrhic victory. Thousands of years ago, Greeks were fighting the Battle of Asculum against the Romans. It was forty thousand Greeks versus forty thousand Romans. King Pyrrhus of Greece finally brought in elephants and broke through the Roman barrier to win the battle. Sadly, it was at the expense of thousands of men, horses, and weapons. As he surveyed the battlefield afterward, King Pyrrhus was congratulated on his victory by one of his captains. His response? "One more such victory, and I shall be lost." He meant, of course, that his win cost him more than he gained. This happens all the time on teams and in families. We win the battle but lose the war. We win an argument but lose a relationship. We must ask ourselves,

- *What is it I want to gain from this conflict?*
- *Why do I want to win? What are my motives?*
- *What will it cost me and what am I willing to sacrifice?*

Leaders must model and teach team members how to choose wisely the hills they will die on. Teach everyone how to distinguish between a preference and a requirement by pitting the bigger-picture goal and the relationships with teammates against the conflict at hand.

Managing Expectations

As I've said, people joining a team from different generations will likely bring different expectations. Kids entering the workforce today have had a life almost wholly unto themselves, interfacing on social media with peers more than mentors. Leaders must discover these expectations and manage them for the team to collaborate on a goal.

Let's examine some foundations for managing expectations:

1. **Satisfying people is pretty much about managing expectations.**
   When Abby joins a team at age twenty-two and expects autonomy and agency from teammates although she's never worked on a professional team, she may unwittingly feel confined or distrusted. She needs someone to explain that collaboration requires mutual accountability up front.

2. **People cannot be disillusioned unless they are first "illusioned."**
   When our communication and expectations are clear, we lower the probability of a team member being disillusioned. They despair if they carry with them an expectation that is unrealistic. With those illusions comes the likelihood of disillusionment.

3. **Conflict is created by the distance between expectations and reality.**
   If I tell my wife I'll be home at 7:00 p.m. for dinner and then come home at 7:10 p.m., it's no big deal. If I return home at 9:30 p.m., we're going to have a discussion. It isn't because she can't live without me for two and a half more hours; it's because an expectation was created.

4. **Conflict expands as that distance widens.**
   When expectations are both unmet and unspoken, conflict begins to percolate inside people. The longer it marinates, the greater the chance of internal and external conflict causing problems on a team. The key is to talk about them and see what can be done.

Stacy serves as a human resource executive at her company; she is fifty-two years old with thirty years of career experience. Marianne works under her in human resources and is thirty-one years old. She has about seven years of career experience. Gabby is a recent college graduate who's just been hired at the company and obviously has less experience than Stacy or Marianne. I recently discovered that

Marianne serves as an unofficial "translator" between Stacy and Gabby. She's young enough to interpret for Stacy what Gabby is feeling or thinking, or even her meaning, when she makes a remark. Yet Marianne is old enough to explain it in terms Stacy recognizes and catches their meaning. Once again, it's like two different cultures that require a translator. This may be an ongoing need for years to come, but my goal is to eliminate the need for such translators.

Managing Demands

When a team member brings demands with them, far too often it can lead to an impasse. Team members must learn to distinguish between something they demand of their boss or workplace and something they prefer. This is difficult for certain temperaments. A person may offer an opinion, and at first, it's only a preference. As differences emerge, their ego gets involved. They dig their heels in and later treat a preference as a demand. To use a phrase we've all heard, "They die on hills that aren't worth dying on."

When this happens repeatedly, there may be little alternative than to let this person go. When demands interrupt the flow toward achieving the mission, something's gone awry. "Me" becomes more important than "we." This is why leaders must create environments to discuss such topics privately, to discover whether an issue is a preference or a genuine demand. If it is a demand, the choices are few: you can either meet that demand or communicate that you cannot and then allow the team member to adjust or to leave. In our current world of polarized populations, people can escalate into adversarial positions unnecessarily. We will discuss this more later.

Managing Tensions

I've learned that while I strive for *perfection* on my team, I must settle for *excellence*. People working together bring friction. It's part of the human experience. There will always be a bit of tension between the sales department and operations or between production and fulfillment. Once we realize it's an ongoing tension to manage, we're liberated from feeling like lousy leaders and teams. And we can manage tensions. For years our team has discussed the tension between *cultivating meaningful relationships* with our clients and *scaling our work.* Our younger team members were focused on the relationships and began to believe we couldn't scale and still experience customer intimacy. Our older team members were consumed with scaling in order to reach our numbers, even if it meant handling client relationships differently. Our vice president of business development is fifty years old and knew how to achieve both. Why? He had done it before with a previous company. We are now scaling our work, but it remains a tension on our team that we can all appreciate. We try to manage both sides with the help of one another.

Have you seen evidence of differing preferences, expectations, and demands on your team?

If we don't manage tensions, teams can reach an impasse. Take, for instance, this cautionary tale written by Arlene Hirsch for the Society for Human Resource Management:

> When Brian Formato began working as an HR manager for Golden Books, the editorial staffers of the now-defunct publisher of children's books were mostly in their late 50s or early 60s and had been with the company for 25 years or longer.
>
> After the company was purchased, it added more than 200 new jobs in one year, with most new hires being recent college grads. The new generation of employees brought fresh ideas but were also far more focused on immediate gratification than long-term success, Formato said. As a result, many veteran employees took early retirement because they couldn't stand by and watch the company they had devoted their careers to change so drastically overnight.
>
> "What was left was a group of high-energy amateurs that lacked the industry knowledge, as well as the discipline, to negotiate attractive

deals with the writers," Formato said. Revenues soon fell. "After more than 50 years in business, the company was forced into bankruptcy."[43]

My conclusion? Leaders must ensure tensions don't lead to such impasses and loss.

THE CHALLENGES TO COLLABORATION AMONG GENERATIONS

Let me say again: generational differences are not the only reason for varying expectations. A person who is twenty-four years old may share a similar expectation with someone who is fifty-four years old if they share a similar temperament or tastes. The challenges, in fact, are many.

Following is a list of basic challenges facing today's teams. I suggest you examine the list and discuss it as a team. This list is not exhaustive, but I hope it will spark other examples of the challenges you face in your organization.

1. Diverse generations that embrace diverse mindsets
2. Mental health issues: anxiety, depression, stress levels
3. A "free agent" mindset in today's employees
4. Smart technology that diminishes our social skills
5. Various personalities, strengths, and styles
6. Technology that leaves our emotional intelligence low

> What other elements lead to conflicting expectations and capacities to cope with differences?

One nonprofit organization illustrates this quandary. During the pandemic, every team member worked from home for months, meaning they no longer enjoyed spontaneous meetings in the hallway or in the kitchen on a break. If someone wanted to talk, they had to set up a Zoom call, but often the issues didn't seem important enough to actually plan a meeting. So information was shared less frequently, creating vacuums in the minds of those who didn't know the details of what was going on with certain projects. It created speculation and distrust.

The teammates from Generation Z were particularly impacted. Since they were new and had less experience, they usually were not in the leadership team meetings where decisions were made. Since they weren't present and didn't get a report from the meeting quickly, they began suspecting something was being hidden from them. Perhaps they were going to get furloughed. Since they felt ill-informed, their internal narratives began straying far from reality.

Clear, consistent, and accurate communication is paramount. I learned this the hard way.

Leaders must operate like dentists.

I love teaching timeless leadership principles through the power of images, which is the language of the twenty-first century. We call them *Habitudes®—Images That Form Leadership Habits and Attitudes.* One of my favorite images is called "Dentists and Cavities." Have you noticed when you visit your dentist and have a cavity, that dentist will often say, "Could you stay a bit longer so I can fill that cavity now, or if not, can you return as soon as possible to get it filled?"

Do you know why dentists say this?

Because they know if *they* don't fill the cavity, bacteria will fill it. In fact, the longer they wait to fill that crevice with the right stuff, the more the wrong stuff gets in. That is precisely what happens with people. In times of change and disruption, people have mental "cavities." There are parts of the narrative they're unsure about. If leaders don't step in with an accurate narrative, all kinds of inaccurate stories begin flowing through their minds and eventually through the team. Leaders must play the role of dentists, especially on a multigenerational team. Your style and lack of communication can create cavities—which lead to gossip and speculation—and can be avoided.

I have noticed this dilemma is widened when multiple generations are on hand.

Common Preferences and Expectations of Different Generations

At the risk of stereotyping, I'd like to suggest how different generations may perceive your leadership differently. The way you communicate, motivate, evaluate, and orchestrate change can be received well or poorly based on the receiver. For example, university admission counselors told me a decade ago that they'd found the need to change the way they communicated with freshmen candidates. Those high school seniors were rarely on email and preferred text messages. Eight years later, those same admissions counselors commonly use social media apps they know those candidates are on. Phone calls are used only in case of emergencies.

My point is not to say older leaders must surrender to the up-and-coming style of young team members. It is, however, to suggest we begin where they are and offer them the reasons why we want them to use Slack or email or some other vehicle of communication. In other words, start where they are and build a bridge to where they need to go.

Read Them before You Lead Them

Each generation brings both value and vices. Each generation also faces issues based on who they are and the life station in which they live. Looking at data from 2020, there is a high probability that leaders are facing the following realities:

- **Millennials and Generation Z bring with them higher levels of diversity.** They are ethnically more diverse than past American generations. More than half are minorities.[44] It should be easier to create a diverse pipeline of diverse candidates.
- **Millennials and Generation Z bring with them higher levels of anxiety.** Forty-four percent of Millennials and 48 percent of Gen Z report they're stressed all or most of the time.[45] This

anxiety can and will impact their work, and we must learn to navigate it.

- **Millennials and Generation Z express higher expectations of equity and inclusion than older generations.**[46] Most of them will even select a job based on the organization's stance on equity and inclusivity.
- **Millennials and Generation Z bring higher levels of formal education to work than past generations did.**[47] Nearly 40 percent have a college degree compared to 25 percent of Boomers. This creates a greater expectation of weighing in with their ideas on decisions.
- **Millennials and Generation Z now make up two-thirds of the workforce.**[48] As Boomers and Xers retire, this number will only grow larger. We'd better learn how to connect with them.

I have appreciated using Patrick Lencioni's personal histories activity to help team members from different generations build trust and find common ground.[49] Each person on a team prepares a slide with photos and answers these three questions:

1. Where did you grow up?
2. How many siblings do you have, and where do you fall in that order?
3. Describe a unique or interesting challenge or experience that shaped who you are.

We have found this activity brings team members closer together. They find common interests, experiences, and places in their story, and they get to know the whole person. There is something about getting personal that reminds us we are all humans first, not workers.

Comparing and Contrasting

It is wise to always consider the person in front of you when you attempt to communicate, motivate, evaluate, or stimulate change. The ideas below may even explain why different people respond to your leadership differently. My goal, once again, is not to place people and generations into specific categories; it is only to foster empathy and understanding that someone from another generation may value something different than you. The best step to take is to converse with them to find out what they value. Conversations beat categories every day.

Let's look at some common differences:

1. **Self-Awareness**

   Each generation may see themselves differently in relation to the team:

   - **Baby Boomers:** I am who I am; I'm set in stone; it's hard to see myself differently.
   - **Generation X:** I have too much to lose to acknowledge my weaknesses.
   - **Millennials:** I've been conditioned to focus on myself and to build my brand.
   - **Generation Z:** I've learned to filter photos and choose my persona.

2. **Communication with People**

   Each generation may prefer different communication styles:

   - **Baby Boomers:** Give me the bottom line.
   - **Generation X:** Keep it real.
   - **Millennials:** Make it interactive.
   - **Generation Z:** Keep it short.

3. **Motivating People**

   Each generation may be incentivized differently:

   - **Baby Boomers:** Corner office; position; bonus.
   - **Generation X:** Freedom to work on my own terms.
   - **Millennials:** Meaningful work that makes a difference.
   - **Generation Z:** Let me do it on a screen, my way.

4. **Feedback and Evaluation**

   Each generation may respond best to their preference in feedback:

   - **Baby Boomers:** Annually and with full documentation.

- **Generation X:** Steady and honest; please share all the pros and cons.
- **Millennials:** Immediately and frequently. Be nice.
- **Generation Z:** Short and on a screen. Then, in person.

5. **Philanthropy**

Each generation seems to be motivated slightly differently as donors:

- **Builder Generation:** Gives to *programs*. They often give out of loyalty to tradition.
- **Baby Boomers:** Give to *productivity*. They usually give to what generates results.
- **Generation X:** Gives to *people*. They frequently develop loyalty to specific individuals.
- **Millennials:** Give to a *passion*. They give to causes they believe in and care for.
- **Generation Z:** It's too early to tell. (Teens often donate their *parents'* money.)

6. **Dealing with Change**

Each generation may handle change differently:

- **Baby Boomers:** It worked fine the way we've done it in the past.
- **Generation X:** I love change ... when it's my idea.
- **Millennials:** I want change every few months.
- **Generation Z:** My attention span is eight seconds.

A CASE STUDY: WISE STEPS FOR LEADERS TO TAKE

As Generation Z moves from school to career, many enter their first job with not only different expectations than those of their employers but speedier ones. They want to move up the organizational chart faster than their manager believes they're ready for that move. "More than 75% of Gen Z members believe they should be promoted in their first year on the job, according to a recent survey of 1,000 participants ages 18 to 23 by *InsideOut Development*, a workplace-coaching company. Employers see similar patterns among younger millennials in their late 20s and early 30s," reports the *Wall Street Journal*.[50]

But this makes sense if we weigh their previous reality:

- Most young adults have not worked a job in high school so they have no work experience to help them understand precedents for promotions at a job.
- Since they may have no work experience (they have only school experience), they're used to "moving up" every year; junior year is followed by senior year.
- Most of their life has been a succession of regular promotions. Think video game levels, club or school athletics, and extracurricular activities.

This pattern has employers scrambling to manage young team members' expectations. It is imperative we remember a principle I shared previously: *conflict occurs when there is a distance between expectations and reality.* The conflict expands as this distance widens.

The *Wall Street Journal* states that managers don't want to put off a young employee by "driving them out the door" because they can't seem to agree on what's realistic. Some of the latest data I've drawn from focus groups is that Generation Z team members are requesting four-day work weeks instead of five. It isn't necessarily that they want to work less, but they want to condense their work time and expand their play time. What's more, many Gen Z team members are asking for pay at the end of the day instead of a paycheck every two weeks. The reason? Many young professionals are living hand to mouth and need the money now to pay their bills. And they're not ashamed to talk about it—their low income, mental health, stress levels, and so on.

> What have you observed as differences in age groups in these categories?

One vivid example is how comfortable Gen Z feels about bringing their personal life and emotions to work. Emily Fletcher is a Gen X executive at Ziva Meditation who noticed her youngest team members were comfortable stretching the bounds of what is considered professional conversation. *The New York Times* reports,

> *This became apparent when the staff participated in an exercise she calls the "Suffie Awards": sitting around a campfire and sharing personal sources of suffering from last year, trying to one-up one another as corny award show music played in the background. It was the Gen Zers, Ms. Fletcher said, getting the most vulnerable by speaking about partners cheating on them or the loneliness of a solo quarantine.*
>
> *"They celebrate human emotion, instead of having an outdated framework of what corporate should be," Ms. Fletcher said. Her company culture has relaxed even more since the departure of her oldest employee, who was 48. "Now everyone feels safe to be a little more weird."*
>
> *As the millennials have made clear through their own workplace ascent, one generation's weird can quickly become the new normal.*[51]

So what can we do?

If you have young team members who want instant change on the team or who desire to be promoted quickly, you have to talk about it. You can't allow an "elephant in the room." Here are some steps we're currently taking at Growing Leaders that might spark some ideas:

1. **Talk about the subject; don't avoid it.** I have found the issue doesn't go away by ignoring it. Be up-front and transparent. Talk about specific reasons for slowing their pace if you believe you must do so.

2. **Carve out a step-by-step growth plan for team members.** This year, we're creating this growth plan for our leaders, and subsequently their teammates. People feel and perform better as they see a clear path toward promotion.

3. **Incentivize growth.** We are now offering bonuses (even when we can't do automatic raises in compensation) to those who achieve goals. A goal and a reward should always go together, whether it's financial or emotional rewards.

4. **New titles and authority.** When we can, we provide new titles and new levels of authority to challenge our team members with new mountains to climb. Even if they're small achievements, they can be important.

5. **Celebrate milestones.** This fiscal year, we've celebrated work anniversaries, noting the team members who've been with us two to five years on the job. We also give shout-outs to team members who help us reach collective goals.

6. **Talk about crockpots and microwaves.** This imagery is one of our *Habitudes®* in our book for new professionals. Most people's careers should be viewed as a meal prepared in a crockpot—not nuked in a microwave within minutes. The slow cooker meal tastes better.

Building Hungry Employees

The other side of this coin is that managers must cultivate team members who are humble and hungry to earn their right to move forward, no matter their age. The answer is not to simply give more money or positions because someone asks for them. *The Wall Street Journal* continues:

> *Young employees who push too hard risk derailing their careers by projecting a sense of entitlement. Alex Klein, a vice president and recruiter at VaynerMedia, a large global agency based in New York, says new recruits are constantly questioning him about promotion opportunities. Many also ask to be considered for a raise earlier than the agency's customary timetable. "Those are great questions to ask. I want to hire people who want to grow," Mr. Klein says. "But you also need to leave the employer with the impression that you want to earn it."[52]*

Both leaders and team members must remain hungry and ready for growth.

———————————— **Talk It Over** ————————————

(1) How can you better manage unmet or unspoken expectations on your team?

(2) What communication changes should you make as you manage multigenerational expectations?

(3) What's been your current approach to navigating varying preferences, expectations, and tensions on your team? Are there any insights you could employ from this chapter?

10

HOW TO BE FLEXIBLE
WITHOUT GIVING IN

OUR TEAM EXPERIENCED SIGNIFICANT TURNOVER AND MEASURABLE change in our strategy in 2019. A mutual decision led to the departure of a senior executive, the second-most influential person in our organization. We restructured our team and reconfigured our organizational flow chart from boxes to circles—which meant we began a shift away from a top-down model. Our organization was moving forward in our life cycle—and we were feeling the growing pains. That year, we hired both new C-suite executives and new staff members. (Almost a third of our team was new.) We introduced a new strategy, a new CRM, and some new technology to achieve our key objectives. Needless to say, this represented a lot of new realities for everyone to grow accustomed to each day. Yet there was one more reality I didn't consider that made life more complex: by that time, we had four different generations collaborating on our mission.

As I've suggested, this can be good news or bad news, depending on how well we lead these multigenerational teams. It is clear to me that the challenges I faced were not due to poor performers but rather to the friction that stems from varying styles and approaches:

- We had Generation Z team members who felt empowered to weigh in on issues in which they had no experience or background. We faced ideological differences.
- We had Millennial team members who appeared fragile and could be easily triggered, feeling that much of my feedback included microaggressions. We faced trust issues.
- We had Gen X team members who brought twenty years of successful experience with them but came from very different organizations. We faced culture issues.
- We had Baby Boomers (I'm one of them) who were used to doing things a certain way and wondered about the apparent disrespect from teammates. We faced alignment issues.

When I reflect for a moment, however, it begins to make sense.

Of course Generation Z feels empowered to weigh in on everything—they were raised with a smartphone, obtaining instant input from Google, Wikipedia, Siri, and Alexa.

Of course Millennials may feel criticism is harsh and full of microaggressions. Many were raised with participation trophies and told they were special for making their beds.

Of course Generation X brings their own ideas to the team. They have loads of experience they bring with them and feel they've earned their right to manage the strategy.

Of course Baby Boomers feel people should get on board with the program and stop being disrespectful. They have few years left in their career and want to work efficiently.

What's ironic is that everyone claims they desire a "culture of feedback," but what many of them really mean is that they want a culture in which they can *give* feedback rather than receive it. I find myself wondering why people don't align with the mission while many of my wonderful teammates wonder why I don't listen more. I guess we're human after all.

Over the last year, I did a lot of reflecting. I asked soul-searching questions such as, *Do I still want to be here and lead this team? Do I still love these team members? Do I still believe this team can fulfill our mission?* In the process, I had an epiphany. In 2021, I wrote a letter to our board of directors in which I attempted to address some of the misgivings we had on our team. I shared that many of the conflicts we'd experienced could be defined as DNA issues. Staff had different views on who we were as an organization (our identity) and what fulfilling our mission should look like (our vision). In the end, our leadership team had to wrestle with two big issues.

Should We Adapt or Adopt?

Some of our board reminded me of my own writings: we need to adapt to today's culture and the new kind of young person we see on campus or on a team. I agree. But I believe there is a difference between *adapting* to the needs of culture and *adopting* what's occurring in culture. I once had a university professor tell me, "Hasn't every generation of adults complained about kids? They did when we were young and look at us—we turned out OK!"

I replied, "You're right. Every generation since Socrates has mourned disrespectful youth. But I don't agree with your conclusion—that we turned out OK. Today half of marriages end in divorce; the average American spends 103 percent of their income, has a $90,000 debt, and is 23 pounds overweight; our federal government can't seem to balance a budget. I believe we've simply lowered our expectations and adopted what's occurring in culture." We must decide where the line exists between adapting and adopting. Organizations need a plumb line or a compass to let them know when they're off course. We decided to recruit countercultural team members and board members and to clarify our big goals along the way. My job is to maintain our standards.

Should We Be Flexible or Forceful?

I began to wonder if I needed to be more flexible, to be more open to change. I certainly can use that advice, especially at my age.

We need to change when necessary. As I reviewed our "fuss and discuss" conversations in our leadership team meetings, however, I noted that when I appear to be inflexible, it's usually not about an inability to change—it's been about our identity and DNA. Recently I shared these core issues with our leadership team, and many said they were not aware of some of them. Somehow, as our vice president left and I was on the road, I neglected to consistently relay these "core" principles we live by and lead by. As we added new people, I was appropriately allowing others to do the hiring and managing. At times this led to misalignment. So to be clear, I relayed my stance to our team: *we must be forceful on what our core principles are but flexible on everything else.* If we fail at distinguishing between core issues and current issues, our team can become confused.

Once an organization determines what the issues really are, tough decisions may need to be made. Along the way, I believe leaders and team members must work to win over those who want to stay yet still struggle with the decisions. In other words, quitting should be the last resort; fighting for and winning over team members should be our first resort—especially when the dissenting team members are from a generation dissimilar from yours.

WINNING THEM OVER

Let's talk about how to win them over. How do you lean in and trust someone who is not like you? Often a supervisor can encounter a team member with a different ideology, and they reach an impasse. They may not know how to handle the friction or the conflict. There's a way to win over teammates at the heart level while not compromising your values. This is a must for leaders.

Five Essentials to Win Them Over

In light of these realities, I have come to believe I must live by five essential guidelines.

1. Trust Must Be Earned

For years, I approached new acquaintances as well as people I knew well with a predisposition of trust. Trust was assumed on my part. In our current society, I no longer have that luxury. I now assume I will need to earn their trust through my personal credibility, not through a title. As I began my career, trust between leaders and teammates was more common. People didn't seem to begin working on a team from a place of suspicion. But that was then and that was me. I reflect past times. Culture is different today. I now enter a relationship prepared to earn their trust with my trustworthiness and integrity.

2. Relationships Must Be Established

The younger the generation, the more important relationship-building becomes. Generation Z is swimming in information but longing for relationships with leaders and teammates. They've experienced plenty of programs, products, promotions, and pop-ups. What they want is something personal. The latest surveys reveal they prefer face-to-face interaction at work, even though they're more at home on a portable device. Going deep in a relationship is a solid way to deepen trust. Brené Brown says it the opposite way: "It is hard to hate people up close."[53] I believe leaders must build bridges of relationship that can bear the weight of truth. Even hard truth and honest disclosure.

3. Incentive Must Be Cultivated

The average young adult (age 16–24) consumes approximately ten thousand messages a day when you consider social media, TV, emails, DMs, radio, billboards, playlists, and so on.[54] The best way to engage a team is to incentivize them. While money is important to them, it's not the only way to build incentives. Share the "why" on the project they're working on, then let them get creative on how they pull it off. Talk about the benefits of finishing a project and reaching a goal. Illustrate how people are helped when they use your product or service by telling stories of your raving fans. Since we are competing against so many other messages and distractions, incentive is key.

4. Ownership Must Be Given

Far too often, leaders, coaches, educators, and parents have been *prescriptive* in our leadership style rather than *descriptive*. We've given a team a job and prescribed exactly how they should pull it off — sometimes complete with steps to be taken. This removes a sense of ownership, when it's our task and our steps, not theirs. What if you described the goal your team needs to reach and let them own how they reach it? Their methods may not be as efficient, but they'll be practicing metacognition and experience greater commitment in the end. Remember: people support what they help create. They are more determined when they have an internal locus of control.

5. Hope Must Be Offered

Especially after the COVID-19 pandemic, the workforce needs leaders who can provide a clear path forward and a deep sense of hope. I am not talking about being superficially positive with a "go get 'em" pep talk. People can see right through that. Your team, especially young team members and certain temperaments, need someone they respect to articulate this thought: "We will not only get through this, but we will be stronger for it." This may not always include a specific plan in the moment. While you need a plan, this hope I speak of is spoken to the heart of your teammates. This enables staff people to operate out of their frontal cortex (reasonable hope) instead of their amygdala (unreasonable fear).

Do They Even Like Me?

Let's double-click on an issue I introduced earlier. Very often, the biggest conflict can surface between the most different generations—the oldest and youngest. According to research from Morning Consult, younger adults from Generation Z are losing trust in all major institutions in the United States.[55] Fewer than one in ten members of Generation Z reports they trust the media, Hollywood, or Wall Street much. Less than one-fifth say they trust the public education system or the US government. These numbers skyrocketed under the intense scrutiny of leaders during the pandemic and the racial unrest in 2020.

> Which of these five practices do you do well? Are there any lacking?

So who does Generation Z look to for guidance? According to a Barna Group study, the answer is clear. Generation Z in large measure is looking to older generations:

> Barna has long studied the impact of intergenerational relationships, and their significance in the life of Gen Z aligns with previous findings. More than two thirds of U.S. adults report having intergenerational friendships—and these are most prevalent among the youngest adults. On top of that, the Morning Consult data show that Gen Z trusts older generations more than any other social institution.[56]

Step into their shoes for a moment. While a twenty-two-year-old may appear confident on social media, that young professional is likely overwhelmed. They finally finished the only world they've ever known—the classroom—and have entered a new world they'll be in for the next several decades: full-time work. Further, there are so many conflicting messages coming at them each day, they are looking to someone they know who is more experienced to guide them. Did you catch that?

- Someone they know. (They have a relationship with regularly.)
- Someone with experience. (They can benefit from that person's insights.)

This is good news, indeed, and it's news you and I must take advantage of on our teams.

They may not trust institutions, but they just might trust you. This is why cultivating relationships is crucial among younger and older generations.

Almost twenty years ago, I started a nonprofit organization called Growing Leaders. I had worked under Dr. John C. Maxwell for two decades and felt compelled to launch a mission that was all about equipping youth for leadership just as he had done for corporate leaders. I chose to focus on social and emotional learning, character development, leadership habits and attitudes, and equipping kids to be career-ready when they graduate. All of that was clear to me. What wasn't as clear was website development, electronic ads, and marketing our mission in the world of the Internet. It was 2002, and I was not tech-savvy. The dot-com bubble had just burst, and I didn't want to make the same mistakes that had bankrupted so many.

So I called Jeff. Jeff was in his twenties. I was in my forties.

I explained to Jeff what I wanted to do and humbly asked him for help. He obliged, and we went to work launching several web-based elements. Months later I found myself in a conversation with Jeff, who needed help from me. He was struggling in his relationship with his partner, Avery, and with his controlling parents. While I didn't claim to be a therapist, I offered him some sound counsel that helped him. Jeff acknowledged something to me later that illustrates the very point I am making here. Jeff said to me,

> I appreciate the help you gave me with Avery and my mom and dad. When you first called me to help you with your start-up, I didn't know you well and didn't even know if I liked you. But you asked me for help, and that meant a lot to me. In fact, it made me start to trust you and feel safe enough to ask you for help when I needed it. I guess we both won.

I believe Jeff was right. It was a double win. It required transparency on both our parts as well as the courage to be vulnerable about our weaknesses and strengths. When people do this, it doesn't matter much what generation they're from.

WHAT IF YOU REACH AN IMPASSE?

Maggie, a general manager of a restaurant, experienced the turmoil that can come when two generations see an issue fundamentally differently. Maggie was fifty-nine years old and had been working in the franchise for over thirty years so the job was second nature. She knew every product, price, and policy the brand was known for, and she embodied that brand as well as any leader could. Her life aligned with her high standards for team members.

One of those policies for all team members was no tattoos.

You can imagine the conflict that surfaced when she noticed a large, bold tattoo on the arm of one of her best team members. Antonio was twenty-five. At the end of his shift, Maggie called Antonio to her office behind the stockroom to talk about it. She tiptoed into the conversation by reminding Antonio how valuable he was to the team and how much she liked him as an employee. She could tell Antonio was becoming suspicious of her reason for the meeting.

"What's wrong?" he inquired, knowing something was up.

"Antonio," she replied. "You know our restaurant policy on tattoos. Why did you get one anyway?"

"I had this when you hired me a year ago," he retorted, beginning to get defensive.

"Well, I obviously didn't see it in the interview, nor have I been on the same shift with you enough to notice it until now. I don't understand why you weren't honest with me about it."

"Hey, you just said I'm a good worker. The tattoo is my personal business. What difference does it make if I can do my job?" Antonio was now braced for battle. His whole countenance changed.

"It makes all the difference in the world. If I let you stay here and people see the tattoo, they'll know I made an exception for you and may expect one too. Not only that, but I'm sure this will get back to corporate headquarters, and my leadership will be questioned," she explained. "Minimally, it will look like I'm playing favorites because I've had other team members ask if I'd let them stay on staff if they got one—and I said *no*."

"This is bulls***!" Antonio's voice cracked and was shaky. His lips were quivering. It was as though Maggie was invalidating part of his identity.

No matter what Maggie said to explain her predicament, it did no good. Antonio had never served in a leadership position nor been accountable for anything but his own life. The two saw the issue differently and were stuck. Antonio quickly stormed out of her office. In the days that followed, the debate got messy. Maggie's value system was colliding with Antonio's. If the two of them could list their core beliefs, it might look like this:

MAGGIE	ANTONIO
1. Integrity and honesty mean everything.	1. Individuality and self-expression are everything.
2. Follow the core values of the corporation.	2. Follow your heart and be yourself.
3. Trust is earned by being forthright.	3. You should trust me without question.
4. Our appearance should be professional.	4. Our appearance is part of our unique identities.
5. We all sacrifice for the sake of the team.	5. The team should accept me for who I am.

If you're like me, you can see the benefits of both perspectives. Unfortunately, the discussion had drifted from the crux of the issues above. What these two had in common was ignored and their differences were highlighted. The next thing Maggie knew, Antonio had made this about race (he was Latino), gender prejudice, and socioeconomic differences. In this case, those were not the issues; they were smokescreens for the real issue.

While the two had much in common (their work ethics, their commitment to serve customers, and their abilities to do their jobs with excellence), they had a major difference: their ideologies. Maggie is a Baby Boomer whose personal philosophy is about being a team player, about making sacrifices for the sake of the whole, and about team camaraderie being more important than individual rights. She could not comprehend Antonio's selfish attitudes and deceptive spirit about the tattoo. Why couldn't he just have been honest in the interview? And at this point, why couldn't he either get it removed (it happens all the time; it's an entire industry now) or quit? On the other hand, Antonio could not comprehend why Maggie was inflexible. If she really did value him as a team member, why did she have to make such a big deal about a stupid tattoo? Wasn't her relationship with him more important than an antiquated rule?

Without stereotyping the two generations, this is a vivid illustration of a debate that happens every week in our country—and it's not just about tattoos, piercings, or hair color. Those who are over fifty years old understand the value of personal expression but often feel they've gotten past the immature, superficial demand to look however they want to look. (Certainly not all the time, but this is more commonly true about Generation X and Baby Boomers.) I've heard many folks over fifty years old whisper the words, "I wish those kids could just get over it."

The bottom line? Maggie and Antonio had reached an impasse. Both had dug their heels in, and neither seemed willing to budge. Either Maggie would need to give in or Antonio would have to leave. Technically, she was right: there was a policy in place and she was merely enforcing it. Yet Antonio was such a promising team member, and it would be a loss if he quit. As you can imagine, the staff were beginning to take sides on the issue. Team morale was at stake.

Would you like to know what happened?

In the end, Maggie put on a "clinic" in great management and made it a lesson for her team. She ultimately met with Antonio, and she extended a handshake. He reluctantly shook her hand. Once they sat down, Maggie outlined her game plan and allowed Antonio to accept or reject it:

- Tattoos were against franchise policy, but Maggie had failed to ask about Antonio's.

- Antonio had known about the policy but had hidden the truth about his tattoo.
- They both committed to total transparency, and she would allow him to stay on staff.
- Antonio would have to wear clothes that totally covered the tattoo when working a shift.
- The entire staff met to discuss this resolution, and both Maggie and Antonio apologized.
- Finally, Maggie made this a teachable moment in trust and transparency for everyone.

Whether you agree with her or not, Maggie actually deepened the respect her team had for her. Because she put a person before a policy and still found a way to demonstrate integrity, she won over everyone on her team. She met with two corporate executives, communicated her decision, and got their buy-in. She committed to always inquire about any tattoos and share the company policy during employee interviews. She also began to encourage corporate headquarters to rethink its policy and to consider updating it without compromising its core principles.

In the end, Maggie won the hearts of her team without losing her values.

Winning Their Hearts without Losing Your Values

If you haven't had an experience like Maggie's, my guess is you will in the future. How do you think you would handle it? Have you figured out a way to be flexible without giving in?

As you consider leading others and managing relationships, let me offer six shifts that will position you to win the heart of a person with whom you're at odds while not discarding your own values. I have found this list applies both to work and at home.

1. Don't Think *Control*, Think *Connection*

Because we're human, we have a tendency to try to control people when things go awry. We do it with our children; we do it with our teams at work. Unfortunately, you and I both know control is a myth. We can't control a teenager's attitude, nor can we control the attitude of a colleague. *Instead, we should pursue connection with them.* Forget the issue for a moment and spend time trying to understand them, and vice versa. When we make a personal connection, we are more likely to be able to smooth over friction and reach a solution, even if it's a compromise. A team is more than a collection of people—it is a connection of people that leaders must initiate. Always work toward heart transformation, not behavior modification.

2. Don't Think *Tell*, Think *Ask*

The best managers lead with questions, not imperatives. Most people are intelligent enough to figure out how to resolve a dilemma if the right questions are asked. When leaders lead with questions, a team owns the solution because they worked for it. Instead of getting people to "rent" your vision or your ideas, you get them to "own" the ideas because they helped develop them. Some of the greatest leaders in history are known for offering direction by the questions they asked. Why not join their ranks? This is especially true when you've reached an impasse with someone. They may be resistant to an idea coming from your mouth, but they may come up with the same idea and embrace it because it came from their own.

3. Don't Think *Rules*, Think *Equations*

Life is all about equations, and when everyone understands them, rules are less necessary. An equation basically goes like this: "If you do *this*, that is the *consequence*; if you do *that*, this is the *benefit*." When your team operates on equations, it can remove some hard confrontations along the way. If I fail to make a mortgage payment three months in a row, my bank doesn't yell at me. I simply get a notice and may lose my house. It's an equation. If a police officer pulls me over for speeding, I can expect a citation. My wife and I raised our children on equations and got them ready for life. I believe teams can run more smoothly if everyone understands the equations that govern everything. Some are natural (e.g., we must sell products to get our paycheck). Choose yours.

4. Don't Think *Prescriptive*, Think *Descriptive*

Sometimes conflict arises because teams are conditioned to look outward for an answer—to look for policies or bosses to solve problems. It's because leaders manage in a *prescriptive* way; we prescribe every step they should take to solve a problem. What if you led in a *descriptive* way? What if you described a goal a team member should reach and then expected them to initiate the list of steps toward reaching it? The best leaders place a sense of ownership in the hands of the team; they create an environment where team members are responsible for cultivating the culture at work, for solving problems, and for sustaining morale among teammates. This requires us to lead differently—we must create a place where they solve problems and serve people.

5. Don't Think *Impose*, Think *Expose*

This requires leaders to move from an "old school" mindset to a "new school" mindset. When a problem arises, most leaders are tempted to simply impose an action plan or a policy on the team. We act like enforcers. Let me suggest a more convincing way to foster change. Instead of arguing your point, can you illustrate it by exposing team members to a situation that makes the point? I have found that when I think differently than one of my team members does, I should first listen to see if they bring some insight to the issue that I don't have. But if I'm sure it's a matter of their inexperience, I should ask myself, *How did I come to my conclusion?* Then I try to expose them to a similar set of realities or situations so they can come to their own conclusions.

6. Don't Think *Manage*, Think *Mentor*

The term *manage* is used in various ways almost everywhere. Teachers use the term *classroom management*. Sports franchises use the terms *general managers* and *managers*. Employers and retailers do as well.

Sadly, I think it's painted a picture in our minds that's not as conducive to relationship and growth. What if you began to see yourself as a mentor? When your team sees you as a mentor as much as a manager, you become a "welcome intruder" in their lives—someone they know has their best interests in mind. Because it has a positive connotation to it, they'll receive your "coaching up" and insights as helpful rather than interruptive. I know very few people who want to be managed. I know a bunch who long to be mentored.

The bottom line about these shifts?

I am not suggesting this list guarantees everyone will get along and proceed in harmony. Some people and personalities actually look for trouble; conflict seems to find them around every corner. Practicing this list, however, creates the best environment for various generations to avoid reaching an impasse. When you get stuck, it becomes a tollbooth, not a roadblock.

I was born in a small town outside Indianapolis. As a kid, I remember seeing a covered bridge along an old country road nearby. The bridge was narrow so there was room for only one vehicle to pass through at a time. When you approached the bridge, you noticed a yield sign, reminding you to watch for people coming the opposite direction. Interestingly, as you approached the bridge from the other side, the same yield sign was posted. The town was communicating to all drivers—look out for others and yield to them.

That's not bad advice for a team made of diverse generations, don't you think?

—————————— **Talk It Over** ——————————

(**1**) Have you experienced a scenario like Maggie and Antonio's? How did you handle it?

(**2**) How do you earn the trust of others? What's your "go-to" method?

(**3**) How committed are you to winning over your team members who differ from you?

11

MANAGING DIFFERENT PERSPECTIVES ON DIVERSITY, EQUITY, AND INCLUSION

IN THE SUMMER OF 2020, MOST OF US WERE SHOCKED WHILE watching the video of George Floyd being murdered at the hands of Officer Derek Chauvin. This incident, along with the deaths of other Black individuals over the past month, set off a series of protests in major cities across America. In fact, marches occurred from the East Coast to the West Coast and in other countries as well. Signs with the mantra "Black Lives Matter" could be found everywhere. Millions were frustrated by the racial inequality that still existed more than fifty years after the civil rights marches of the 1960s. This time, however, a much larger percentage of the population was involved.

What I wasn't prepared for was the number of families that were split over the issue.

By the end of June, I had interacted with sixteen parents of adult children (their kids were ages 18–32) who said their own sons or daughters wouldn't talk to them. Families that had enjoyed rich relationships over the years were suddenly torn apart because the kids felt that Mom and Dad were not engaged enough in the protests. One young lady grew angry because her mom did not post a BLM square on Instagram. (She felt this was the legitimate report card to declare where someone stands.) For a while, she refused to talk to her mom or bring her baby (the grandson) to see his grandmother. Clearly, our nation both *came together* and *became divided* on this issue of racial equality, as people chose their response to the topic. While it was not a purely generational issue, I observed a pattern in how older and younger populations responded to the marches, violence, and protests.

Everyone I spoke to, from all generations, agreed that racism is wrong and equal rights should be enjoyed by every American. The team that I work with each day believes in social justice, and many of us have found ways to demonstrate that belief. The differences I heard in larger society, however, could be summarized this way:

- Millennials and Generation Z were frustrated that older generations allowed racist behavior in institutions and were not acting quickly enough on behalf of the marginalized. This led to ideas such as "defund the police" and "affirmative action" initiatives at work.
- Generation X and Baby Boomers were frustrated that younger generations seemed blind to the hidden agenda of the larger BLM organization and didn't want to return to ethnic quotas at work. This led to debates over equal opportunities versus equal outcomes.

Once again, I am not claiming an entire issue can be divided along generational lines, only that there is a disproportionate number of younger generations pushing on one side and a similar percentage of older generations pushing back on the other. It reminds me of that humorous quote attributed to Anselme Polycarpe Batbie in an 1875

French book of biographical portraits by Jules Claretie. It's been para-phrased over the years. Here is one summary:

> If you're not a liberal before you're age forty, you have no heart.
> If you're not a conservative after age forty, you have no brain.

Sadly, the debate in the workplace often drifted toward extremes. Some people felt that folks on the other side are merely capitalists. And those folks felt that people on the other side were merely social-ists. Most of the time, these conclusions were too simplistic. But, alas, we felt a divide in our nation. Social media lit up over ethnic issues, and millions on every side of this issue declared they were "outraged" on platforms such as Facebook, Twitter, and Instagram.

The data reveals that there is, indeed, a difference in how Millennials view policies related to race compared to previous gener-ations. In fact, both Millennials and Generation Z were much quicker to join in the Black Lives Matter marches in 2020 and see systemic racism as a larger problem than do those from Generation X or the Baby Boomers. Nick Davis published data regarding younger popu-lations' attitudes and viewpoint toward racism. For example, Davis writes,

> This polling suggests that Millennials are much more likely to support ending cash bail—a policy that has clear racial implications—than Boomers . . . racial and educational differences on attitudes toward cash bail are modest, at best. Instead, there are clear generational differences among respondents, with Millennials most open to removing a policy that jails more persons without a conviction than other countries' entire incarcerated populations. While this is but one policy, it is not something to gloss over.[57]

So what are the implications of these differences on a multi-generational team?

DIFFERENCES BETWEEN OLDER
AND YOUNGER EMPLOYEES

A look at older and younger generations reveals a significant and measurable difference that may explain some of the challenges employers face in their workplace. Older generations tend to lean toward professional conduct, while younger generations, because of the times in which they were raised, tend to lean toward personal conduct. Older ones tend to compartmentalize their lives, especially at work, while younger team members "bring their whole self" to work. Of course, being professional and being personal are not mutually exclusive. The way these approaches cascade into workplace conduct, however, is noticeable. Below is a summary of what I've observed when interviewing people over forty years old and those under forty:

Over Forty Years Old	Under Forty Years Old
* Conduct should be professional.	* Conduct should be personal.
* Leave your personal problems at the door.	* Bring your whole self to work.
* Keep your emotions in check.	* Emotions play a huge role in my expression.
* Keep politics and work separate.	* Political issues can't be divorced from work.
* The workplace is run by a benevolent dictator.	* The workplace is a democracy for all to weigh in.

If you think the last phrase in the two columns is an exaggeration, let me remind you of some headlines from 2021. Hundreds of Google employees protested work projects for the Pentagon. Whole Foods employees sued their employer for not being allowed to wear their Black Lives Matter masks at work. Hundreds of Amazon employees chose to risk their jobs by violating company policy. Wayfair employees walked out to protest sales made to migrant detention camps. I am not suggesting there have never been workplace protests or litigation, simply that social media has multiplied the volume of people who believe that work is a place in which to take a stand for causes they embrace. An increasing number of employees expect to weigh in and voice their opinions about inclusivity and social justice. Employee activism is on the rise.

What's more, the court of public opinion is one that more employers fear today. They are afraid of a social media–driven boycott against their products or a narrative that gives them a bad reputation. Clearly, the issue of diversity, equity, and inclusion are paramount for younger generations (and for many Gen Xers and Baby Boomers), and the difference is simple. You are in one of these two categories:

- Woke (meaning you've been awakened to the current issues in culture)
- Zeezed (meaning you're asleep, catching some Zs when it comes to current issues)

Organizational psychologist Adam Grant believes we are experiencing the "democratization of the workplace."[58] Employees, especially young employees, feel empowered to redirect how the organization functions, especially if they feel it isn't aligned with their point of view on social justice or isn't taking a stand on current social issues. Many feel like capitalism needs to evolve. After collating comments older and younger generations made in a focus group, here are my conclusions on today's narrative on diversity, equity, and inclusion in the workplace:

Healthy and Realistic	Misleading and Unrealistic
1. Everyone's voice should be heard.	1. Everyone should have an equal voice.
2. Teams should provide a place to let people weigh in and share ideas.	2. Teams should allow everyone to weigh in on each decision of the organization.
3. We all deserve equal opportunities.	3. We all deserve equal outcomes.
4. Inclusion means all are safe to share.	4. Inclusion means all get to make choices.

Consider the first item. While I believe everyone on a team should feel like their voice is heard, I do not know one organization that can honestly say everyone has an equal voice. If the CEO and an intern both speak up on an issue, both should be heard, but those voices are not equal. The wisdom and experience of the CEO has earned deeper influence, as unfair as that may sound. In 2012, I hosted a focus group of young professionals (all Millennials), and they agreed they all hated the phrase "Pay your dues." Yet it is still true. Perks and influence are still earned, regardless of how much we feel that sounds patriarchal.

The fact is, organizations need to be both *empowering* and *efficient*. By this, I mean they need to welcome ideas from everyone (even the inexperienced) on a team. At our organization, we've tried to live by the axiom "The best idea wins." This makes people feel empowered. At the same time, organizations must be efficient, operating at a good pace and practicing excellent "speed to market," which may prevent everyone from getting to speak into every issue. Effective workplaces are usually not democracies. Everyone doesn't get a vote on the functions that enable the company to succeed: sales, marketing, operations, renewals, and so on. When we asked each of our team members to furnish us with their own definitions for "inclusion," one suggested it means "people get choices, not demands." While I think everyone desires choices and freedoms, sometimes team leaders need to give directions. Imperatives do not equal bad leadership. Sometimes, we all need clear imperatives.

At the same time, leaders must be aware of what's becoming normalized. The data shows that young team members believe the issue of inclusion and diversity are front and center.

So how do we strike a balance?

FOUR BIG QUESTIONS

I believe employers and organizational leaders must respond to four questions. We can do so by choice or by force. If we fail to choose to do so, we will be forced to do so.

Is Diversity Merely a Preference or a Mandate?

First, workplace diversity expectations among younger team members are clearly different than older ones. *Washington Post* journalist Jennifer Miller summarizes it this way: "For younger job seekers, diversity and inclusion in the workplace aren't a preference. They're a requirement."[59] Younger generations tend to think that racial justice matters extend to how companies practice diversity and inclusion in matters within their own control and culture. Their views of systemic racism extend to how the company works and actually makes decisions on diversity and how power is shared. Once again, young and old tend to view this issue differently.

"This is a generational shift in the belief that these values are really important and foundational to their experiences as workers," says Alvin B. Tillery Jr., director of the Center for Diversity and Democracy at Northwestern University. "You can say there's no systemic racism, but Millennials and Gen Z don't believe that. If you're under 35, you expect these conversations, and if you don't offer them, you'll have trouble recruiting."

Don't believe it? Jennifer Miller says, "According to a September survey from Glassdoor, 76 percent of employees and job seekers said a diverse workforce was important when evaluating companies and job offers. Nearly half of Black and Hispanic employees and job seekers said they had quit a job after witnessing or experiencing discrimination at work. And 37 percent of employees and job seekers said they wouldn't apply to a company that had negative satisfaction ratings among people of color."[60] I see this across the board as my organization recruits and interviews job candidates. The issue has become front and center, and employers will need to commit, one way or the other.

According to Kevin Gray at the National Association of Colleges and Employers, "Since 2008, the National Association of Colleges and Employers (NACE) has asked new graduates to rank the importance of a diverse workforce. That first year, diversity ranked 12th out of 15 options. By the spring of 2020, it had risen to seventh out of

19 options; over 79 percent of respondents called it 'very important.' Edwin Koc, director of research at NACE, said employers are starting to recognize this shift."[61]

Is Diversity Merely about Justice or Success?

Second, there's a connection between Millennial views of diversity and their views of innovation. Millennials see inclusion itself as an innovation or a feature of a culture that fosters innovation. A young team member may claim diversity makes a team better. It is not merely about injustice or opportunity; it is about success. This might seem counterintuitive to someone from an older generation who perhaps has experienced moments of inclusion that were the first "barrier breakers," and thus the conversations were harder and caused conflict—therefore actually seeming to slow the team down and stifle the speed of innovation that might take place. There is often a transition period in a team that starts to diversify—and in that transition, it can seem like things are actually less efficient and innovative. Millennials are deeply past this transition and expect it to already have taken place—and a potential value conflict exists in organizations that are not truly embracing this transition. Consider what Katherine Martinelli writes:

> The 2018 Deloitte Millennial Survey suggests that this generation, which is expected to make up 75 percent of the workforce by 2025, takes a far more nuanced view of diversity. To them, it's less about gaining equal opportunity and more about holding to the conviction that working and collaborating with people from varied backgrounds will make a company smarter, richer, more creative and more successful. In fact, according to this same survey: 74 percent of millennials believe that their organization is more innovative when it has a culture of inclusion. This statistic sends a clear message: businesses taking active steps to build and maintain a genuinely diverse culture will reap the benefits. Results from the same Deloitte survey also reveal that 83

percent of millennials feel empowered and engaged in the workplace when they believe their company fosters an authentically inclusive culture.[62]

There is a growing body of research, all from various studies performed in the twenty-first century, that reminds us of this truth: teams possessing diverse perspectives tend to be more creative, more adaptive, and more productive. It eventually affects the bottom line. In short, companies reach their goals more effectively if they practice diversity and inclusion.

Is Diversity a Priority Just for Work or for the World?

Third, team members can sniff out disingenuous people, especially when they are bosses. They can tell if a leader is only meeting a "quota" for the workplace but doesn't really embrace the idea of diverse thought. This is where there are differences between Baby Boomers / Generation X and Millennials / Generation Z. According to Cara Wong, associate professor of political science at the University of Illinois-Urbana-Champaign:

A majority of young adults (ages 18–35) believe that increasing racial and ethnic diversity is good for our society and that racial discrimination is the main reason African Americans cannot get ahead; only a minority of older Americans agree. The vast majority of young people think that immigrants today benefit the country, and they oppose building a wall along the Mexican border; these are positions taken by only about half of those born before 1965. Young Americans today also are much more likely to attend college than older cohorts, and education consistently has been related to greater tolerance and support for racial equality. As a result, Generation Z is part of the multicultural vanguard: young people, compared with older Americans, are more supportive of descriptive representation and the teaching of ethnic history, and they are less likely to have ethnocultural or assimilationist notions of what it means to be a "true American." Gen Zers are not colorblind, but they shrink social distances between racial and ethnic groups in their physical, digital, and imagined communities.[63]

Racial residential segregation is still prevalent in many areas, which is inextricably tied to continuing racial segregation in schools. Nevertheless, members of Generation Z are much more likely than the Boomers, for example, to have and approve of friends and partners of different races. Increasing diversity accounts for a large part of this change, but people's beliefs are also shifting, particularly among the young. More than three-quarters of white Gen Zers would approve of a family member marrying someone of a different race or ethnicity; only about a third of white senior citizens are equally supportive. This reliance on psychology more than "biology" affects who Generation Z sees as belonging and for whom they feel a duty to care.

Is Diversity Merely about Demographics or Perspective?

Fourth, there is evidence that Millennials might see diversity of viewpoint and relational dynamics in a company as more reflective of true diversity than mere demographics, which can be more easily quantified. It's possible a Millennial would interpret a company that "has good diverse pictures of their leadership to show" to not actually be diverse, for instance, if more marginal voices and their opinions are not met with welcome arms. I have seen how this can cause conflict across the generations (and races), especially if the opinions are coming from a young white professional who was raised in an affluent background.

Chris Craddock, writing for *The Millennial Perspective*, notes,

Put the two perspectives side by side, and the differences are clear. The perspective of the older generation of business leaders is that diversity is based on demographics. The perspective of millennials (and Gen Z) is that diversity and inclusion refers to a diversity of ideas, thoughts, perspectives, and insights.

"Inclusion" for Baby Boomers meant things like hiring a certain percentage of African-Americans or creating work teams that reflected workforce or customer demographics. Inclusion for Millennials means giving all people opportunities to share their perspectives, network, and contribute innovative and creative ideas. Baby Boomers like statistics and goals, measuring factors like the number of women in leadership positions or the percentage of people hired or promoted who are minorities, disabled, veterans, and so on. Millennials are more interested in subjective factors like the level of employee engagement, the percent of the workforce that believes there is a positive workplace culture, or whether there is a sense of belonging. For Millennials, subjective factors are as important, if not more so, as hard statistics. [64]

This issue became personal to me between 2019 and 2021.

Our Story of Diversity and Inclusion

Our organization had been slowly evolving into a more diverse team over the years. Up until 2017, diversity had not surfaced as a crucial problem to solve, at least not among team members at the time. Over the next few years, however, I began to learn that some employees were finding other places to work because they didn't feel "included" and felt our team was not "diverse enough." Up until then, we had enjoyed an incredible culture of energy, vision, alignment, and a genuine love of collaboration as a team. But then things grew different. The change didn't happen overnight. By 2019 we'd lost some people of color on our team, and by 2021 we'd lost some board members who were also people of color, all women.

We were moving in the wrong direction.

When the topic of diversity, equity, and inclusion became front and center across the world in 2020, we recognized it needed to become one of our strategic initiatives. I began to meet with diverse board members in informal and ongoing conversations about the issue. From that discussion, we formed an agile team to create an action plan to recruit, hire, and retain diverse team members and board members and even partners (customers) worldwide. When this agile team did not produce results fast enough, we lost a few more teammates and board members. I then initiated round two of an agile team to pursue the same goal. We needed an action plan.

The chief hurdle we had to jump, however, caught me by surprise.

The issue was not just about race. It was current team members, mostly Caucasian, who felt we were not practicing inclusivity, at least not genuinely enough. As I surveyed the situation, I recognized this was also a generational issue. Some of our young team members felt they didn't really have a "seat at the table." To put it bluntly, I had no idea that some of our Millennials and Generation Z team members felt we were unwittingly practicing "segregation." The old people had the power, and the young people implemented what they said to do. No one put it that forthrightly, but that's what they felt was happening. No matter how brilliantly I argued it wasn't true, it was their reality. In our case (as in many organizations), it was older males who led the organization. We aren't bad people, just older people.

The key will be to capitalize on what everyone brings to the table.

Generation Z, as the multicultural "vanguard," may just be the "safeguard" for America's future. They will ensure that inclusion happens, that everyone experiences diversity and equity. What older generations will need to add is the *practical business sense*. Ideas are great until they cannot be monetized and people therefore don't get their paychecks. My former board chairman, Morgan Hill, likes to put it this way: "Everyone is spiritual . . . until the paychecks bounce."

Which brings us to the issue of trusting authority.

GENERATIONS AND THEIR
PERSPECTIVES ON AUTHORITY

My friend Rob Hoskins always sheds light on cultural issues for me. He and I were discussing authority and the modern cultural view of trusting those in power. In the summer of 2020, trust in police officers dipped measurably across the country, to the point that some communities considered legislation to "defund the police." The deaths of Black men and women set off a vocal crowd who distrusted authorities. For millions, trust seemed to shift to the Black Lives Matter movement. However, a year later, Americans' trust in the BLM organization declined measurably, according to a *USA Today* / Ipsos poll.[65]

The nation is clearly divided, and millions are not sure who to trust.

There has been an evolution of thought over the last century as it relates to loyalty. Society's view on authority and governance has shifted. Trust can no longer be assumed by leaders. Team members often enter an organization already questioning the motives, ethics, and perhaps even equity of pay on the team. If an older, senior-level executive thinks a younger team member is loyal to the same priorities, they may have another thing coming. Leaders must understand their people rather than make assumptions. Frequently a teammate will reflect a loyalty to the priorities of their generational cohort. Let's take a look at this in summary.

Seniors and Builders: Committed to the Institution

Those born between 1900 and 1945 usually retain a sense of loyalty to the institution to which they belong. It was normal for a person to stay at one company for decades, then finally retire and get a gold watch for all those years of service. If you were a person of faith, you belonged to the same church denomination, even if you moved to another city. You were loyal to brands and organizations (Rotary, Kiwanis, Lions Club, and so on) and often stayed for life. In many cases, older generations remain committed to the institution long after the original leader has gone.

Baby Boomers and Gen X: Committed to the Individual

If you were born from the late 1940s all the way to the early 1980s, your generation witnessed a shift away from loyalty to an institution, because too many leaders failed morally or financially. The emerging generations at the time found it safter to become committed to certain people they trusted over larger corporations or organizations. People who came of age during those years saw failed leadership in Vietnam, the Watergate scandal, the OPEC oil crisis, and the Iran hostage rescue. American institutions actually earned a poor reputation in those days.

Millennials and Gen Z: Committed to Ideation

The years between 1985 and 2020 saw so much failed leadership, and witnessed the stories of those failed leaders in the media, that the emerging generations at that time shifted their loyalties to ideas. They didn't put their trust as quickly in leaders because they observed too many of them failing at the commitments they had made. Due to corporate leaders' embezzlement and extramarital affairs or televangelists' sexual scandals and financial debacles, the two youngest generations prefer to follow ideals rather than attach themselves to a single leader.

Today they long for community but may not know how to experience it.

TEN IDEAS TO UNITE GENERATIONS ON DIVERSITY AND INCLUSION

Trust in institutions—corporate, government, education, even religious ones—has dropped measurably. Younger generations are trying to create accountability structures that are not corporate in nature. What does decentralized mission look like? How could it work? What earns currency in that community? These are crucial questions to answer.

Let me offer some ideas to begin to bring generations together on this issue.

1. Create an anonymous outlet for suggestions and ideas that expand diversity. Team members shouldn't have to write their names on the ideas they submit.

2. Leave some space at the leadership table for entry-level team members from time to time. If an idea affects them, they should be included in the discussion.

3. Host an "Elephant in the Room" day once a quarter and make this an issue. Allow team members to voice their thoughts, and then ask them to argue for other viewpoints.

4. Plan a day where the youngest team members run the show. Allow them to implement "diversity and inclusion" as they'd like to see it happen daily.

5. Follow the mantra "The best idea wins, regardless of where it came from." Even if an intern articulates the idea rather than a leader, honor the person and the idea.

6. As you plan for change and improvement, begin by allowing leaders and staff to write down their definitions of *inclusion*, and then discuss them.

7. Plan clear communication cascade times, where managers who are "in the know" cascade information to team members. This way, everyone is "in the know."

8. Plan biannual HR-hosted meetings for discussions on inclusion and diversity. Minimally, this enables everyone to have a platform to share their voice.

9. Host "get acquainted" interviews for team members during which a leader conducts an interview with an employee so that everyone can get acquainted with them.

10. As you implement a pipeline for inclusion and diversity, prioritize quality, not quota. In short, just adding more color without the essential talent won't help.

As practical as these steps are, you must recognize you'll not please everyone, regardless of how you attempt to do so. People from different age groups, races, genders, and perspectives will all bring their own experience (and dare I say, baggage), and perhaps some have never served in a leadership role. If you're like me, you'll find that everyone has an opinion on your leadership, many have a criticism of it, and some will even voice that criticism. One key is for leaders to remain in a posture of listening and learning without surrendering to all the armchair quarterbacks along the way.

Teaching and Learning

The best solution as far as I'm concerned is for each of us to remain in the posture of both a *teacher* and a *learner* at all times. We should speak as if we believe we are right but listen as if we believe we are wrong. Only then does the "armchair quarterback" come across as less dogmatic and recognizes there's likely a reason they're in an easy chair and not on the football field. This posture believes we can learn from anyone, both older and younger.

Tai Simpson is a Native American from the Nez Perce Tribe of Idaho. She gave a TEDx talk in 2019 about the intergenerational wisdom woven into indigenous stories. She claims each generation must learn from the others, from the elders to the babies. In her story, she remembers walking into her aunt's home as a teen and proudly announcing she had gotten straight As on her report card, she'd mastered a difficult song on her cello, and was very popular with the boys on campus. She was on top of the world. Sensing her pride was prodding her from interdependence to self-righteous arrogance, her aunt felt it would be wise to offer her perspective that day.

Tai's aunt asked her to look at her young niece outside, who was using a small spoon to clean out a fish she'd just caught in the river nearby. "Do you see what your niece is doing?" she asked. Tai said she wasn't sure, but said it looked like she was digging with a spoon. "Why don't you go out and teach her how to clean a fish." Tai hesitated because she'd never once cleaned a fish. After a moment, Tai replied, "I don't know how to do that. I've never done it."

Her aunt smiled and said, "Then maybe you could go out and learn."

It was her aunt's friendly way to remind Tai that she still had room to grow, that she didn't know everything, and that even a younger child could teach her something. Tai could either watch her young niece and be an armchair quarterback or she could keep learning. This is the spirit in which we must approach each generation when it comes to issues like diversity, equity, and inclusion. Our polarized culture today can lead to polarized workplaces that don't listen or learn anymore. Groups suffer from confirmation bias. Leaders must model the way in building a community that listens before it speaks, that is a learner as well as a teacher.

Truth be told, leaders really are quarterbacks. They spur teammates on, call the plays, and hand the ball off so the team can score. Armchair quarterbacks are often pretenders or posers as they sit on their sofas. I'm not saying they're useless . . . they can always go grab another bag of chips.

Let's reach our goals by being flexible and convictional.

——— Talk It Over ———

(1) Have you observed any generational differences in how your teammates view diversity?

(2) Would all team members agree that your team culture is inclusive and equitable?

(3) How do conversations take place on this issue on your team? Is it off-limits? Is it an "elephant in the room"? Or do people converse freely and learn from each other? How could you improve?

(4) How could different generations on your team enable one another to see something that was previously hidden because of the other generations' age and experience?

12

WHAT MAKES THIS SO HARD?

I HAD AN AMUSING EXPERIENCE WITH A SMALL COMPANY I CONSULTED with in 2019. I was scheduled to meet with a three-person department that happened to be made up of people from three generations: a Boomer, an Xer, and a Millennial. I called ahead to let them know I'd be a couple of minutes late due to a previous engagement but to go ahead and begin discussing the two questions I had provided to them earlier. They agreed.

When I arrived, I walked straight to the office of the manager, who was the Baby Boomer and host of the meeting. Upon my arrival, I witnessed a clear picture of what's happening today when teams meet. Each was on their personal device, and their choice matched their age:

- The Baby Boomer was on a desktop computer sitting on his desk.
- The Gen Xer was on a laptop and seated on the sofa.
- The Millennial was on an iPhone, seated on the floor.

It was not only a snapshot of three generations; it was also an illustration of what happens too many times when teams are not intentional. These three teammates were not discussing the questions face-to-face, even though they were in the same room. They were staring at screens and messaging each other. It happens at work and at home. I realize we talk about this so much that it's almost cliché, but clichés exist for a reason.

Is there a pattern here? What does the data show?

THE SOCIAL HABITS OF OUR TWENTY-FIRST CENTURY CULTURE

The socialization of the human population has morphed since the dawn of the smartphone. Much of today's smart technology, for instance, has made life easier and more efficient for us but has also diminished the soft skills needed in adulthood and in our careers. As I reflect on the forty years I've been an educator and leader, I believe we got ambushed. Few of us, if any, could see what skills would atrophy with the advent of portable devices. In one sense, today's population is advanced compared to past generations; in another sense, they are behind.

For example, educational psychologists measure maturation in children by using four categories: cognitive, biological, social, and emotional. Our culture seems to have cultivated these realities:

- **Cognitive Growth:** Advanced. (People know more and at younger ages.)
- **Biological Growth:** Advanced. (People are physically maturing faster.)
- **Social Growth:** Behind. (People are less able to navigate relationships.)
- **Emotional Growth:** Behind. (People experience more fragile emotions.)

Just read today's newspaper and you will see this illustrated. People express outrage on social media over the smallest issues.

"Cancel culture" has reached an entirely new level, where minorities are calling out other minorities for not using specific language. People will sooner call the police instead of their neighbor to work out a conflict. Some parents can't seem to muster civility at their kid's Little League baseball games. Critical thinking is down, but critical comments are up. People are impulsive and *react* more than they *reflect* on a tweet, Facebook message, or Instagram post.

We often failed to recognize what a portable device was doing to our social and emotional experience. Psychologists now talk about "phone addiction." The challenge has been summarized this way:

> *When our phones had leashes, we were free.*
> *Now our phones are free, and we have leashes.*

The Inverse Relationship between Technology and Soft Skills

What does this have to do with navigating generational diversity?

Everything.

If our differences didn't present a big enough challenge, we've now been conditioned to avoid hard conversations and difficult conflict. Connecting with people who are different represents too much work. The data shows that as new realities are introduced to our culture, many have had an adverse effect on our abilities to negotiate our differences. The following statements are not necessarily *causality* statements. They do represent, however, a *correlation* between one reality and another. The following statements illustrate negative correlations based on studies overlaid with each other:

- As technology increases, empathy decreases.
- As information expands, attentions spans diminish.
- As options broaden, long-term commitment shrinks.
- As life speeds up, patience and personal discipline drop.
- As external stimulation goes up, internal motivation goes down.

- As consequences for failure diminish, so does the value of success.
- As virtual connections climb, emotional intelligence declines.
- As free content swells, so does our sense of entitlement.

It's intriguing to me that when one reality changes in our culture, there are usually unintended benefits and consequences.

OUR SCENE TODAY

Our cultural SCENE is different today. We live in a world of speed, convenience, entertainment, nurture, and entitlement (SCENE). It's affected nearly everyone. This explains why the generational challenge has become more difficult and also suggests how we can overcome it.

When life gets more convenient, even small drudgeries feel bothersome. We get annoyed and impatient easier. We retaliate faster and more impetuously. We complain faster. In fact, we want to fill out comment cards at restaurants, retail outlets, or hotels if we feel the customer service was poor. I am not suggesting this is wrong, but imagine what growing up in this world of assumptions and expectations has done to Millennials and Generation Z.

Have you noticed any inverse relationships like the ones I listed?

A meta-analysis on the data shows people are more prone to quit something that's hard than to persevere and resolve the difficulty. For example, we'd all agree that relationships can be hard, even in our own homes. Disagreements, conflict, and spats often nudge people to walk away or avoid. It's too hard to stay connected. Compared to life fifty years ago:

- fewer people belong to civic clubs and churches.
- fewer people are marrying.
- more people are dining alone.
- more people are traveling alone.
- more people are living alone.

I don't think it's because we don't desire community and belonging; I think it's because the skill sets needed for such community are rare and challenging. Think about it—today it is rare to find a couple who's been married forty or fifty years. It's rare to find people who've remained in a workplace for more than twenty or thirty years. I am not suggesting it's wrong, just that it's rare. Kids look around and see adults walking away rather than working it out.

Years ago, I created two columns to illustrate the challenge our culture has given to kids growing up in the twenty-first century. While they may enjoy modern luxuries that make life physically easier, the unintended consequences are emotional hardship. Their emotional muscles seem to have atrophied. Check out the columns below. In short, this makes it clear how a high-tech lifestyle actually fosters entitlement and impulsivity for all of us:

Our SCENE Today

Our World Is Full of:	Consequently, Kids Can Assume:
S – Speed	Slow is bad.
C – Convenience	Hard is bad.
E – Entertainment	Boring is bad.
N – Nurture	Risk is bad.
E – Entitlement	Labor is bad.

I think we all love the modern-day speed and conveniences we experience, but Gen Z is growing up in a world that is faster and more efficient than ever, which may foster a wrong assumption in them. For instance, as I suggest, our world today is full of entertainment. It now travels with us everywhere on our phones. We can watch streaming video, programs, news feeds, sports—you name it. There's nothing wrong with that, but we've now become used to the stimuli it offers us. We hate to be bored; it has led many to believe that "boring is bad." But that's not true. While I remember hating boredom when I was a kid, today we recognize something we did not understand in my teen years. Neuroscientists today tell us that our brains actually *need* boredom. It is in times of boredom—when we have margin in our day and quiet time to think—that we develop creativity and empathy.[66]

So today, we sit more. We consume more. We watch more. We virtually connect more. But we experience higher levels of anxiety and fragility among today's emerging generation.

So how do we lead them?

The fastest way to raise anyone's level of grit, engagement, and performance is to express belief and hope. If you're a leader or manager, you must treat them as you see their potential, not as you view their past. Herein lies our struggle. In 2018, our organization, Growing Leaders, partnered with Harris Poll Interactive and surveyed over two thousand American adults. We asked them a series of questions regarding their view of the "emerging generation of young people." How do they treat them? How do they see them and what do they predict about their future? I commissioned this study because all of this comes out in our leadership. After speaking to employers, coaches, educators, and parents, I had a suspicion we were hindering the growth of Generation Z. The numbers confirm my hunch:

- 66 percent of today's adults report a negative rather than a positive emotion when they think about Generation Z. Two in three people expressed this.
- 64 percent of today's adults believe that Gen Z will not be ready for adulthood when they reach it. Nearly two in three expressed this.

I recently met with Brianna, a young professional who is six years into her career. She had just left her job in search of something better. When I asked her why she'd resigned, her response was telling:

I could tell my supervisor didn't believe in my potential or my future at the company. He didn't say this out loud, but all of his actions revealed he didn't trust me with the projects he'd given me. I tried to imagine working at this place five years from now, but I couldn't do it. Plus, this job isn't "pandemic proof." I gotta find a job where I am in charge of something, like Uber Eats or DoorDash; my last boss wasn't about to let me take charge of anything.

Interestingly, I encountered Shane, Brianna's former supervisor, five weeks later. In the course of our conversation, I mentioned that Brianna didn't feel like her boss believed in her, trusted her, or expected much of her. Shane's reply to this comment was equally revealing. He said bluntly,

I didn't believe in her. I don't think she was ready to take on the workload we needed to get done, and I was afraid it would cost us dearly. It was a blessing in disguise that she left.

How do you suppose it feels to be led by someone who is afraid for you, who feels concerned and doesn't think you'll be ready for the challenges that lie ahead? The answer is obvious: not good at all. Regardless of whether we say all the right words and feign all the right actions, they are savvy and can see right through our motives and fears.

Perhaps you were led by a worried parent, coach, or boss when you were younger. Did it show? Did they overfunction, bailing you out of tough situations or negotiating a conflict for you? While it might have felt good in the moment, the message it sends is: "You need me. You can't figure this out on your own. I will rescue you." It surfaces in our verbal, nonverbal, and paraverbal communication and leaves both parties vacant of the skills they'll need to develop.

So what's a step we can take to improve?

THE KEY IS PRACTICING SOCIAL
AND EMOTIONAL LEARNING

The solution to these challenges is to muster the courage to have tough conversations. One huge reason different generations fail to connect is that we've spent too much time on screens and too little time with one another developing our social and emotional intelligence—navigating complex relationships by managing emotions and interactions. Do any of the following sound familiar?

- Employees who decide to quit their job but don't have the courage to talk face-to-face with their supervisor. So they send a text and go home, never to return again.
- Parents of young team members who call their son or daughter's manager to tell them they feel their adult child deserves a raise. They, in fact, play the role of an agent for their child.
- Team members who are unable to have difficult conversations with one another or their boss. So they just avoid them altogether, calling in sick or using extended vacation days and paid time off.
- Supervisors who don't know how to encourage team members in a way that genuinely affirms them. So they just slap them on the back or grunt some generic "Attaboy," and walk out.

As I shared in a previous chapter, I served on an agile team to expand how our organization practiced diversity, equity, and inclusion. The team was made up of board members, team members, staff leaders, and a couple of outside experts. In one conversation, our cochair shared how our leadership team had been working on this issue and had begun to enter some authentic and vulnerable conversations about it. When our board chairman asked Monica (a young team member) if she was witnessing any of these improvements, she paused. Then Monica replied, "Do I have permission to speak freely?"

I jumped in and said, "Of course."

Monica proceeded to say she had not seen any positive changes. She said she was confused as to why we had reviewed our core values in our team time and why we were doing a weekly study on a new leadership book I'd written. Her tone changed and began to display hidden negative emotions. In fact, Monica's emotion outweighed the issue at hand. We were all quite surprised that she was confused; I thought it was clear to everyone exactly why we'd taken those steps, and I didn't understand her negative emotions.

I felt compelled to respond.

I unmuted my mic on the Zoom call and chimed in. "I think I can explain those issues and lessen your confusion, Monica," I replied. In the following moments, I reminded her what we had done and explained why we'd taken those steps; I walked her through why we'd made those decisions and explained I didn't know why she was confused. My language was masterful—but as I spoke, I watched her withdraw and eventually turn off her camera and microphone. She typed into the chat column, "I am still here, but I think I'll just listen and not speak the rest of the meeting."

I had shut her down.

It was the last thing I had wanted to do, but I'd been so impatient at her reaction that I'd taken over and dominated the conversation. I had unwittingly pushed her away. Even though everything I'd said was accurate, my words were anything but inclusive. She'd been silenced.

This is a clear case study in social and emotional intelligence—or my lack of it, at least in that setting. We don't develop social and emotional intelligence from reading a manual or from some YouTube video. It is the result of learning to read the air. It required me to foresee the outcomes of my words. The situation required social and emotional skills. On your team, it will likely be the same. The stakes are high, and many situations call for soft skills as well as hard skills.

Are you ready?

Social and Emotional Learning combines both the management of oneself and the management of one's relationships. It is the foundation on which any thriving civilization is built. If we fail at building these social and emotional skill sets, an intelligent graduate who made straight As may sabotage their future career or marriage because they lack fundamental life skills. There is nothing more common than a smart young person who does "dumb" things because they failed in their social and emotional growth. Their IQ may have been high, but their EQ was low. The good news is, a number of educators who've collaborated on the subject have concluded that EQ is a greater predictor of success in life than IQ.

Coming to Terms

Social and Emotional Learning combines *social intelligence* and *emotional intelligence*. Let's begin by defining those terms. (The following is not the only definition, but it is a good beginning to help us wrap our arms around the issue.) Science journalist and author Daniel Goleman popularized the topic in 1995 with his bestselling book, *Emotional Intelligence*, which remained on the *New York Times* Best Seller list for a year and a half. Goleman cofounded the Collaborative for Academic, Social, and Emotional Learning (CASEL) at Yale University's Child Studies Center, which then moved to the University of Illinois at Chicago. Following is a summary of his working definitions:

> SEL is how people learn to understand and manage emotions, set goals, show empathy for others, establish positive relationships, and make responsible decisions.

- **Social Intelligence:** The capacity to effectively negotiate complex social relationships and environments.
- **Emotional Intelligence:** The management of one's emotions, enabling you to interact wisely due to self-leadership.

The Collaborative for Academic, Social, and Emotional Learning is a clearinghouse for research on this subject. They define Social and Emotional Learning like this:

Social and Emotional Learning can be broken down into five core competencies:

1. **Self-Awareness:** Know your strengths and limitations, with a well-grounded sense of confidence, optimism, and a "growth mindset."

2. **Self-Management:** Effectively manage stress, control impulses, and motivate yourself to set and achieve goals.
3. **Social-Awareness:** Understand the perspectives of others and empathize with them, including those from diverse backgrounds and cultures.
4. **Relationship Skills:**
Communicate clearly, listen well, cooperate with others, resist inappropriate social pressure, negotiate conflict constructively, and seek and offer help when needed.

> Have you noticed the need for any of these five competencies in your workplace?

5. **Responsible Decision-Making:**
Make constructive choices on personal behavior and social interactions based on ethical standards, safety, and social norms.

Can you imagine a multigenerational team where everyone practices these competencies? Those who do end up going further, faster.

Does Social and Emotional Learning Really Make a Difference?

What would it look like for a classroom, a sports team, or a work environment where everyone practiced these skills and competencies? SEL is what genuinely enables people to move from a "group" to a "team." It enables people to actually collaborate on a goal. Over the years, employers and educators have used various terms to describe these essential competencies:

- Life skills
- Soft skills
- Transition skills
- Employability skills
- Career-ready skills
- Executive functioning

While these terms differ in their exact meanings, they are all close cousins. They represent the proficiencies that enable students to translate all their academic learning into real life. They make academics practical and usable.

I recently read about a student living in Belgium who graduated with an engineering degree from Eindhoven University of Technology—at the ripe age of nine. This child prodigy is named Laurent Simons, and he earned his electrical engineering degree in December 2019. His plans for the future? He intends to embark on a PhD program in electrical engineering while also studying for a medical degree. The faculty and staff call him "simply extraordinary."

Laurent was given test after test as teachers tried to work out the extent of his talents. "They told us he is like a sponge," said Alexander Simons, his father. He has no trouble consuming information. Both of Laurent's parents, Lydia and Alexander, are doctors, so the boy comes by intelligence honestly. Some have called him a "walking brain."

What I appreciate most about the story is that his parents are intelligent, but they also value emotional intelligence. They work to make space for Laurent to do ordinary things that boys his age do, from playing with his dog to enjoying his smartphone to traveling and meeting new people. The staff and faculty describe him as a deeply sympathetic student. His parents want him to develop holistically, not just cognitively.

"We need to find a balance between being a child and [using] his talents."

Due to his high IQ and EQ, Laurent has already declared a goal. He wants to help people. He plans on pursuing a career developing artificial organs for those in need.

I believe Laurent's story is a great example of parents and educators fanning into flame both the cognitive growth and the social and emotional growth of a student. In order to flourish, people need both. Certainly, it's easy to assume this young man could focus purely on academics and experience a happy life and grand career. I supposed that's true, depending on our definition of *happy*. Most students don't have the luxury of becoming a "walking brain" who has never experienced emotional intelligence.

Recently, I listened to an unusual number of employers mourn the recent graduates they had hired who were unready for a full-time job. Many had graduated with high GPAs but performed better in a classroom than a workroom. One employer shared that a recent graduate told him in her job interview that she would "have his job in eighteen months." She had no self-awareness that this would come across as arrogant. He dismissed her. Another employer told me he just wished his young team members would show up on time for work each day. They were conspicuously late every day. Another reported he'd just been "ghosted" by an employee who'd been on the job for three weeks. The young man stopped coming to work, without notice, and was never heard from again.

These stories demonstrate social and emotional skills these recent graduates failed to possess.

The fact is, work teams, marriages, families, and all sustainable relationships require them. If we don't address the need, it will only get worse. Face-to-face interactions are a growing challenge for Generation Z (who is often more comfortable on a screen than face-to-face) because interacting in person requires work. This is anecdotal, but I believe success in school is about 75 percent IQ and 25 percent EQ. Success in a career is likely just the opposite: 25 percent IQ and 75 percent EQ.

DOING LIFE ON A SCREEN

More and more teens are living much of their life online. They even date online. In fact, some will date for months and never meet the other individual in person. Generation Z has grown up online and is redefining dating. The new normal is people meeting on an app or online video game and beginning to see all they have in common. It's not hard with smart technology. Their interaction may evolve to meeting on Zoom, Google Meet, Skype, or Facetime, but it's virtual.

"Liking someone's Instagram is the modern-day equivalent of smiling at them across a crowded room. Every online service eventually becomes a chatroom—be it TikTok, Fortnite or any of the other countless distractions that allow people to connect," writes Christopher Mims for the *Wall Street Journal*.[67] "They might sound unusual: online relationships that bloom, reach a fever pitch of teenage intensity and—possibly—even wither before the two parties ever meet. But they're becoming more common than ever. Ask any teenager—if they haven't been in a relationship like this themselves, they can probably name friends who have."

Nadia and Daniel are two high school seniors I know who "dated" for a year and spent all of an hour and a half together. Then they broke up. One advantage is if you've only connected online, it's easier to break up. In fact, you can "ghost" your partner and just fail to show up any more for interaction.

Is This a Problem?

So what's the big problem with this? Many people are saying today,

> We just need to get used to this. It's a younger generation's way to relate to each other. Older folks should stop demanding they learn old-fashioned etiquette or common courtesies. They've got their own way of interacting.

I am sure there is a kernel of truth in this notion. We older folks do need to adapt.

Cultural patterns today reflect this preference for screens over face-to-face interactions. In fact, a growing segment of our population is living alone, dining alone, traveling alone, and dating alone (on a screen with someone else). It's easier to start or end relationships on a screen. It's certainly one way to deal with two demographic trends: earlier puberty and later marriage. Young adults can just connect online, and nobody gets pregnant. Stephanie Coontz, director of research and public education at the Council on Contemporary

Families, says, "So you have a period of life of 15 to 20 years where people have to manage their sexual, romantic and intimate needs in ways that are more flexible than they used to be, and young people are experimenting with how to handle that."[68]

In interviews I hosted with high school and college students, they communicated that they still want relational skills in the person they are dating. In the vast majority of these interviews, they place it as one of five top qualities they desire in a friend or partner. Most of the time, receiving empathy from someone else topped the list.

Yet so far, it appears it is very difficult to build empathy on a screen. It happens much more naturally face-to-face with people. I mentioned that the sociology department at the University of Michigan provides data on college students. During the first decade of the twenty-first century, as the cell phone became ubiquitous and the smartphone was introduced into mainstream life, empathy dropped 40 percent.[69] That's a tangible decrease. At the same time, impulsivity continued to rise. That's not a good combination. Further, the *Washington Post* reminds us our careers will usually require interpersonal skills:[70]

> The problem is, we all still desire people skills that are difficult to develop online.

1. At some point in our careers, we will need to rely on our relationships with others. Who is going to go out of their way for someone who's never taken an interest in them?
2. Collaboration wins the day in getting things done. If you are blind to the needs and the point of view of other teammates, you too will fail. We're all in this together.
3. You may not always be right! Someone else may actually have a good idea or reason to do things a certain way. If your mind is a lockout, you'll never grow.

The fact of the matter is, people who are different from us either compel us to learn or compel us to run. We will either put in the work to connect with a colleague, a friend, or a partner, or we will consider it to be too much work and walk away.

My wife, Pam, and I celebrated forty years of marriage in June 2021. I have recognized over that time that my marriage to Pam has forced me to combat my selfish desires, my narrow perspective, and my insistence that I am always right. Marriage is often the best example of welcoming diversity. She and I are different people who believe we are better together. I am an improved human being because of her. I've developed social and emotional skills because we are different. I've learned to welcome that.

Have you seen any benefits from Social and Emotional Learning?

THE FOUR BIGGEST HURDLES WE MUST JUMP TO BRIDGE THE GENERATION GAP

While visiting Singapore in 2016, I spoke both to faculty and students at Temasek Polytechnic, a post-secondary education institution there. While both audiences were very intelligent, I was most impressed by their pursuit of emotional intelligence. During my time on campus, however, I did see a "generation gap." One student described to me the "gap" she experienced in this way: "I have more in common with college students in your country (the US) than I do with my own parents here in Singapore." Her statement illustrates how Generation Z has so much common ground on the Internet that it often trumps the cultural commonalities shared with an older generation in their own country.

Did I mention we've got a gap on our hands?

Just as smart technology can play an adversarial role, disabling our connection with other generations, so can at least four other human factors. They are hurdles we must jump, each one positioned somewhere in the gap between generations. Only as we make the effort to leap over these barriers do we have any hope of closing the chasm between us.

Four Hurdles We Must Jump

1. Stereotypes

Over the last several years, the generation gap has shown up in the workplace in the form of age discrimination lawsuits filed by both young and old. Boomers and Xers believe their company is not promoting them because they're too old; Millennials and Gen Zers assume they didn't get promoted because they're too young. These are not merely small business challenges either; several Fortune 500 companies including Google, IBM, Marriott, WeWork, and Citibank are facing these age discrimination lawsuits. If nothing else, it's a picture of how so many feel they're being stereotyped. They believe bosses take "mental shortcuts" instead of working to understand who they are and what they bring to the table. Nobody likes to be stereotyped—including you and me. We must stop taking "shortcuts" and do the work to genuinely recognize who our people are and let them know.

2. Ego

As I've noted, people usually brace themselves when they encounter someone from a vastly different generation. Why? They can represent challenges to our own positions and opinions. Remember the *MarketWatch* survey, where more than half of respondents said they are unlikely to get along with colleagues from a different generation? Kelly Services posted a report revealing that 74 percent of hiring managers say the most significant trend shaping the recruitment world today is the rise of a multigenerational workforce. This is only a problem when we let our egos blind us and diminish our chance to benefit from one another. We must check our egos and logos at the door and prepare to learn. Developing a "growth mindset" that believes we can still develop at any age is our saving grace.

3. Laziness

I know an extended family who lives together, including grandparents, an uncle and aunt, three cousins, and the nuclear family who owns the home. After hanging out with them, I could hardly believe how people can spend so much time together and misunderstand one another so deeply. I'm sure they love one another, but I am also sure they don't like one another. The grandparents complained about how little respect the young people showed them, and the youngest family members complained how "out of touch" the older ones were. Each generation seemed to enjoy complaining about the others. I thought of psychologist Brené Brown's statement: "It's hard to hate people up close." Yet believe it or not, some do manage. How? They are socially lazy. They refuse to do the work to step into the shoes of others who seem so different. Laziness is our enemy. Labor is our ally.

4. **Disrespect**

Perhaps the saddest part of the multigenerational team is that we conclude the goal is to merely *tolerate one another.* Older team members sigh and say, "We gotta put up with those slacker Millennials." Generation Z posts on social media, "#OKKaren," as if to say: "I don't care why you're for asking for the restaurant manager, I think you're controlling." We fail to be respectful. Even if our stereotypes occur for a reason, disrespect is never the answer. If we care about solutions, we must begin with respect for one another. We've got to break out of our niche, the comfort zones where it's easier to inter-face with those who look like we do, talk like we do, act like we do, and vote like we do. We must do the work to seek out those from other generations and discover their "niche." This means we begin with belief.

Our Task: Ditch the Niche

My decision to "ditch the niche" was a game changer for me. It doesn't mean I never struggle with stereotyping or laziness anymore. It does, however, equip me to overcome my *implicit bias* toward my way of thinking. When we "ditch the niche" we choose to interact with people we'd normally avoid; we take the road less traveled and talk to new people from different generations as opposed to familiar people from our generation.

A decade ago, I became consumed with trying to solve an organizational health issue. I was part of the problem. My ego blinded me to how I was neglecting younger teammates. I hid behind excuses such as: *I'm busy with travel; I've got to generate more revenue; I don't have time for interruptions.* One day, a young employee poked her head in the door and asked if I had a few minutes. I'm embarrassed to say, this

:   Which hurdles remain
:   in front of you waiting
:   for you to jump?

young lady was someone I avoided because it took so much work to connect with her. I was tempted to say no. That day, however, I did the right thing and agreed to meet. My conversation with her—which was my reluctant version of ditching the niche—turned out to be transformative. In our discussion, she casually revealed the very solution to our organizational culture problem. And it came from a most unlikely source. My job was to listen, silence my implicit bias and break out of my own niche.

STRIKING A BALANCE BETWEEN SENSITIVITY AND PREPARATION

Did you hear how Columbia University handled its graduation ceremonies in 2021? No, I'm not referring to COVID-19 policies such as mask wearing or social distancing. I'm talking about the administration's decision to host six separate graduation ceremonies based on the graduates' income level, race, ethnicity, and gender preference. This had nothing to do with the pandemic as each ceremony was virtual. The issue was the school's attempt to be personally relevant to Native, Asian, Latinx, and Black students who graduated at the end of April. There was another ceremony, an "FLI Graduation" held for "first generation and/or low income community." The school also hosted a "Lavender" graduation for the LGBTQIA+ community.

It's all about tailoring the event for the kind of people with whom grads identify.

I Applaud the Sensitivity

The advantages to these ceremonies are clear. Each student graduating will be with "their people." Those first-generation students will be celebrated alongside others who also come from families with no previous college graduates. The words coming from the platform, including the student speeches and the guest speakers, will all be customized for them. Wow. Talk about sensitivity. Who can ask for more than that?

The statement Columbia University made was timely. Society is finally acknowledging minority groups publicly in these ceremonies and allowing them to feel like white students have felt since the beginning of modern public education. The protests and courtroom verdicts of 2020 and 2021 have led to decisions like this one. I applaud this.

I See Some Potential Consequences

My concern is just as real. In full view of cultural sensitivity, is this one more misstep we're taking in our failure to prepare students for their careers? The workforce they'll soon join will likely be eclectic and look little like a classroom or their graduation ceremony. People will come from different income levels, different races, different generations, and different genders. Jonathan Haidt and Greg Lukianoff released a book a few years ago called *The Coddling of the American Mind*. Much of the book is about the mistakes universities make in their well-intentioned efforts to create safe places for students and shield them from microaggressions. The gap between the campus and the cubicle is huge. Students graduate as "kids," not adults.

Further, where will tailored ceremonies end? I've already heard some minority groups say that even the action steps schools have taken are not specific or inclusive enough. Are we setting schools and students up for frustration because of the impossibility of making sure every special interest group (race, gender, or socioeconomic background) is given the proper attribution? This may feel silly, but I think it's a valid question.

In short, are we playing the short game and not the long game? Are we sacrificing future career readiness for current comfort? Making life feel homogenous seldom prepares students for life after graduation. Employers have consistently told me that colleges are not preparing graduates for the workforce. Young professionals have come across as fragile, unable to negotiate differences or conflict, and ill-equipped to collaborate with older generations. Is it because college felt like a silo with thousands of people living together, all between the ages of eighteen to twenty-four?

Finding Balance

Herein lies the struggle for schools today. How can we strike a balance between:

- You feel safe and can find others you identify with on the team.
- You feel stretched as you get ready for an unpredictable world.

I find myself in a quandary. I want to lead our young team members at Growing Leaders with incredible sensitivity. I want them to feel their leaders understand them and empathize with them. At the same time, because I believe in their abilities and skills, I don't want to communicate that I feel they're not strong enough because I keep removing stressors from their lives. My solution must balance both: I am sensitive to their unique needs *and* I believe they are capable of taking on tough challenges.

I know one of these recent Columbia University graduates, and I enjoyed his response to the various graduation ceremonies. He requested to participate in a ceremony that was different than the one he'd been assigned. When asked why, he said he wanted to be with people unlike him, to feel what it was like to be a minority.

His request was not granted, but I loved his spirit. He was saying, "Make it harder for me so I'll be more ready for different encounters in the future."

--- **Talk It Over** ---

(**1**) What has made building social and emotional skills challenging for you?

(**2**) Are you in any relationships that you feel require too much work to sustain? What have you concluded you should do?

(**3**) What social and emotional competencies do you feel you must work on the most?

13

SIX IMAGES TO LAUNCH
ESSENTIAL CONVERSATIONS

I HOPE BY NOW YOU'VE CONCLUDED WITH ME THAT INTERGENERA-tional connections might just help us all. Everyone wins when a seasoned veteran, who's worked for decades, can benefit a young rookie who's highly educated in a classroom but has precious little experience at a job. Further, I believe everyone wins when those same seasoned veterans pause and listen to input from the two youngest generations who now serve in the marketplace and might bring a completely different approach to a goal because they offer fresh perspectives.

Our problem is simple and clear: we don't do this naturally.

In March 2021, I hosted five focus groups that included Baby Boomers and Gen Xers. Every person in the study was over forty years old. The sixty-two participants were all professionals who worked in both blue-collar and white-collar jobs. Half were managers and half would consider themselves employees or labor. I included a mix of genders and races but just two generations, both older. My goal was to gain clear visibility on people in the final twenty-five years of their careers and what their perspectives were.

Three observations I made are likely predictable:

- There was a different perspective on reality between labor and management.
- There was a different perspective on reality between women and men.
- There was a different perspective on reality between minority races and whites.

What the majority agreed on, however, was their perspective on young people. More than three in four (77 percent) agreed that they did not understand young team members' behavior or values, and eight in ten (81 percent) believed young team members had poor work ethics. There was an enormous congruency and unity among races and genders on their outlook toward youth. In some cases, this was the one item they had in common.

The clearest downside was how this affected their own behavior.

I discovered not only that these negative attitudes surfaced as they worked (and were clear to those young team members) but that the attitudes among the veterans hindered them from initiating conversations with young team members. Each experienced a *culture of avoidance* at work. The Boomers and Xers were more apt to talk to one another during discretionary periods (lunch, water cooler conversations, break times), and Millennials and Generation Z were more apt to congregate together during their discretionary times. Why is this true? Quite frankly, it is easier and more natural to spend time with similar people. It is more work to spend time with someone who seems very different. Both the young and old can feel intimidated by each other. A 2021 Barna Research Group survey of Generation Z uncovered that while most Gen Z members feel supported by older generations, nearly two-thirds (64 percent) seek advice from their peers, not their elders. As I've noted, author Mark Bauerlein, an Emory University professor, concluded that young adults—thanks to their portable devices—have never spent so much time with one another than they do today.

So how do we spark great conversations among generations?

A PICTURE IS WORTH A THOUSAND WORDS

In 2002 I was forming the mission and core values of the organization I would launch the next year: Growing Leaders. I had a theory that the emerging generation (which at the time was the Millennials) needed mentors as they entered adulthood. Already, however, I had spotted a divide between the old and the young.

I began creating a tool that would ignite mentoring conversations between generations. It contained thirteen images, each of which illustrates a timeless life skill or leadership principle. (I mentioned some of these earlier.) I designed it to foster a dialogue, not a monologue, from a facilitator. I not only believe that pictures are worth a thousand words, but I also believe that *pictures beat lectures every time*.

The next year, I finished the first book (course) and had no idea how it would take off in schools, businesses, athletic teams, and youth organizations. In retrospect, I believe their popularity and memorability is because, for most of us, our brains think in pictures. Discovering and learning is much more engaging when it includes both hemispheres of our brain. So everyone can get involved in the learning process, young or old, and begin interacting over the metaphor and what it means to them. Over the years, I've concluded that there is no life *change* without life *exchange*.

That's what I'd like to spark with you.

SIX IMAGES THAT CONNECT PEOPLE

This chapter introduces vivid metaphors that enable us to connect with anyone from any generation. The metaphors are
- Chess or Checkers
- Quarterbacks or Referees
- Stethoscopes and Treatments
- Guard Dogs or Guide Dogs

- Surgeons or Vampires
- Bridges or Walls

How do we do this? Discussing and practicing these six meta-phors will at least begin the process of enabling generations to connect with and help each other. These are from our leadership courses I mentioned throughout this book called *Habitudes: Images That Form Leadership Habits and Attitudes®*. Each image represents a timeless principle that fosters both good conversation and good practice.

Roll the DICE

I have found that the ideal pedagogy to teach these images is to "roll the DICE":

- **D – Dilemma:** Begin with the challenge that needs to be addressed.
- **I – Image:** Next, introduce the image that teaches a principle that will address it.
- **C – Conversation:** Since pictures are worth a thousand words, it sparks discussion.
- **E – Experience:** Finally, all good conversations should lead to a practical application.

I will introduce each of these principles to spark your own conversations on generational diversity. These are only introductions.[71]

1. **Challenge:** We often assume others are like us and want to be treated as we do.
   Image: Chess or Checkers
   Wise leaders play chess, not checkers, in their relation-ships. Instead of assuming they should treat everyone alike (checkers pieces), they discover the strength and personality of each player (like chess pieces) and lead accordingly. Just like the two games, however, playing chess in relationships takes longer and is harder than playing checkers. Leaders

must take the time to get to know team members and explore their personality, style, and gifts before they lead them.

2. **Challenge:** We can suspect the worst in those who are different and focus on rules over relationships and on policies over people.

   Image: Quarterbacks or Referees

   All football games have referees who enforce rules, call fouls, and watch boundaries. Quarterbacks provide direction, inspire, and deploy their team. Life-giving leaders fight the temptation to become a referee. They are quarterbacks. Truth be told, when we suspect people may not be up to speed, when we suspect they don't "get it" or they're not like us, we frequently shift into "referee" mode, watching for wrong moves instead of believing the best about them. Effective leaders stay in quarterback mode.

3. **Challenge:** With diverse people, we can lack the insight or empathy to feel what they feel.

   Image: Stethoscopes or Treatments

   No doctor enters a patient's room and instantly offers a prescription. Physicians spend time examining patients and making a diagnosis before prescribing treatments. So it is with leaders. Empathy precedes direction. Before leading someone—especially from a different background or generation—we must invest the time, diagnosing the best approach to empower them. Good leaders perform like good doctors. Our direction follows careful interaction, understanding, and compassion.

4. **Challenge:** We're naturally self-protective, but to build trust we must become vulnerable.

   Image: Guard Dogs or Guide Dogs

   A guard dog's job is to protect. A guide dog's job is to partner. One is suspicious, growling, barking, and distrustful. The other initiates, trusts, guides, and is vulnerable. Good leaders are guide dogs who initiate vulnerability and create safety for teams. Belonging (inclusivity) works from the outside in. It happens when we initiate transparency, show trust, and ultimately become vulnerable. Because our inclination is to protect, leaders must take the lead in launching a culture of trust and openness.

5. **Challenge:** When frustrated with differences, we can offer feedback out of relief, not belief.

   Image: Surgeons or Vampires

   There is an art to giving helpful feedback. Unfortunately, it goes against our natural tendency. When criticizing or evaluating people, we often do it when we're frustrated, and we vent. We're like vampires, sneaking up on our victim and attacking them, and they often don't recover. Surgeons also draw blood, but their work leads to recovery. They prepare ahead of time and take great care to remove only what is necessary, and healing results. Vampires give feedback out of *relief*. Surgeons offer it out of *belief*.

6. **Challenge:** It's easy to build bridges to those in the same generation and walls that divide us from those who are not.

   Image: Bridges or Walls

   Each of us encounters different people as we lead. Our natural inclination is to see differences and put up a wall. We must consciously build bridges that can bear the weight of honest disclosure. Sadly, it's quicker and easier to build a wall than a bridge. Because we're human, we tend to like those who are like us; we spend time on those who are easier to relate to and avoid the tougher work of connecting with those who are different. We must be intentional to invest energy into people who are different.

Let me close with the obvious. These conversations are ideal for leaders to discuss with one another, but later, in smaller learning communities where various generations are represented, they can spark surprisingly transparent interactions along the way.

We must choose, however, to welcome a wider perspective.

DO DIFFERENT GENERATIONS TEND TO INFLUENCE DIFFERENTLY?

The Insights Research Team performed a gigantic global study that included over half a million people from sixty nations or regions of the world (561,507 to be exact).[72] An analysis was done by the researchers on the "style" of each age group as they played a role on a team. The results were interesting to me. The color types that indicate one's style include:

- Red – Director
- Purple – Reformer
- Dark Green – Supporter
- Blue – Observer
- Orange – Motivator
- Aqua – Coordinator
- Yellow – Inspirer
- Light Green – Helper

To be honest, when interacting with teammates, the generations were not dramatically different. In other words, all the styles existed in each generation. There were, however, patterns of behavior that can inform any team leader who manages multiple generations. The younger participants tended toward extroversion, while the older participants tended toward introversion. Most interesting to me, however, was the favorite *style of influence* each took when interacting with other team members.

1. The preference of those under 25 years old was Sunshine Yellow, Inspirer.
2. The preference of those 25–34 years old was Sunshine Yellow, Inspirer.

3. The preference of those 35–44 years old was Cool Blue, Observer.
4. The preference of those 45–59 years old was Earth Green, Supporter.
5. The preference of those over 60 years old was Earth Green, Supporter.

As I have said multiple times in this book, leaders must capitalize on who's on their team. We must play to the strengths of each individual, recognizing the style or preference they bring. The preceding analysis should remove any stereotype we have of assuming the older team members are strong directors, while the younger ones want to remain quiet and follow orders. It's easy to see only what we assume we'll see, then become guilty of confirmation bias. By this I mean when we already have an opinion or a suspicion about someone, we tend to see it confirmed by subsequent experiences. We find what we look for. Even more subtle and sinister, however, is survivorship bias. Too often, we fail to combat this blind spot.

Survivorship Bias

Organizations need diversity of thought and approach. Different perspectives move us closer to achieving a full view of what's happening. Individuals cannot be perfect, but teams can be.

In World War II, Allied airplanes were getting shot down by the Nazis in large quantities. In response, our forces decided to do an analysis to see whether they could strengthen the aircraft and increase their survivability. So they placed large red dots over the bullet holes in the planes to get a better look. Their immediate deduction was to reinforce the areas that were hit most often (indicated by the red dots) until Abraham Wald, a mathematician, came to a different conclusion: the red dots only represented the damage on planes that made it home. He suggested, instead, they should reinforce the places where there were *no dots*, because those are the places a plane traditionally wouldn't survive being hit.

This fresh perspective changed the Allied forces' approach to plane safety and survival. My uncle benefited from this change as an Air Force pilot who was shot down.

This phenomenon has been subsequently referred to as "survivorship bias." It occurs when we look at the items that *survived* when we should be focusing on the ones that *didn't*. There are at least two vivid lessons to be learned from it:

- Don't be so sure that your first deduction is the most correct.
- When you consider the problem to be solved, surround yourself with diversity of thought.

At times, the difference between blind spots and seeing the big picture is a matter of life and death. In the next chapter, I suggest a regular exercise that could be a game changer for your team and enable you to capitalize on the generations on it.

Talk It Over

(1) Can you see how these six conversations could benefit your team? How so?

(2) Which of the six would be most relevant?

(3) How could you set up these conversations so the images become a memorable language?

14

THE ART OF REVERSE MENTORING

ONE SIGNIFICANT REALITY GENERATION Z BRINGS WITH THEM INTO their careers is an intuition on where culture is heading and often how to capitalize on it. I've seen this time and again. Seasoned veterans can get locked into the way commerce used to work and not see some opportunities.

We need the vision of Beau Jessup.

Beau is a little like any other teenager from the United Kingdom except for one reality—she's making hundreds of thousands of dollars and funding her way through college by naming Chinese babies. She is just nineteen years old and has found a need she can meet—a hole she can fill.

It all started when Beau was fifteen and traveling with her father to China. When one of his business associates, Mrs. Wang, asked for help giving an English name to her three-year-old daughter, Beau felt honored and surprised. "It seemed like a really important thing to do," she recalls.

Wanting to choose an "appropriate" name, Beau asked Mrs. Wang to share a little more about her hopes for her daughter. Most of all, said Wang, she wanted people to be surprised by the things her daughter could achieve. So after careful thought, Jessup suggested Eliza, inspired by the fictional heroine from *My Fair Lady*, Eliza Doolittle. Wang was delighted, Beau said, and went on to explain the significance of having an English name for people who are Chinese.

That year, 2015, marked the end of the "one-child" policy in China, and the birth rate rose almost 8 percent. Almost 18 million new babies were born, and many families wanted an English name for their child. It was then that Beau decided to launch Special Name, a website to enable Chinese parents to upload five attributes or hopes for their child so that internal algorithms could help them select the perfect name. Six months later, she had made more than $60,000 naming 200,000 babies. Since then, she's named a total of 677,900 babies and has generated an estimated $400,000 that goes toward paying for college, investing in property, and, of course, paying back the loan her dad gave her, with interest.[73]

I believe this is a picture of the future.

Generation Z already feels empowered and entitled by that smartphone in their hands. It's given them a predisposition to make things happen and not wait for an adult to do something, or even wait wait for permission from an adult to do something. The organizations that can see this and capitalize on it will benefit.

This is why I recommend you begin a system that enables you to practice reverse mentoring.

WHAT IS REVERSE MENTORING?

When Angela Ahrendts (a Boomer) accepted the offer to become the CEO of Burberry in 2006, the luxury coat company's sales were in decline. They had been for years. Burberry had been around for a hundred and fifty years, and while the brand retained an elite reputation, it was a company known for its plaids and for selling coats to rich, older women.

Angela was asked to lead the company because of her past success and experience. No doubt, she arrived on the scene with ideas for turning that company around, which made her early moves curious. After meeting her direct reports, she scheduled a series of meetings with her youngest team members at Burberry. Beyond that, she began recruiting sharp, young professionals, even interns, whom she could meet with and listen to for insights into reaching Millennials (a population Burberry was failing to reach at the time). "Ahrendts also hired a young marketing team, most of whose members were under age 25. Burberry jumped onto Instagram, Pinterest, and Twitter, using bold photography to engage Millennials on their own turf."[74]

Probably the wisest move Angela made was to establish an in-house digital team led by a young Christopher Bailey (now Burberry's CEO), who served as chief creative officer, and John Douglas, who served as chief technology officer. This team brainstormed ideas to attract young shoppers. One of the team's most successful moves was to launch "a new website and innovative social media campaigns, including the Art of the Trench, a photo platform that allows visitors to upload photos of themselves in iconic Burberry trench coats."[75] And boy, did those Millennials post photos. Tons of them. I've been to the page on their site, and it is full of pictures of young, classy twenty- and thirtysomethings wearing Burberry coats on downtown streets.

In the end, it paid off big-time. In her seven years at Burberry, Angela raised the company's value from 2 billion pounds annually to more than 7 billion.

What I love most about her story is that Angela entered as both a *teacher* and a *learner*. She was an instructor to her executive team, insisting they make moves to go digital, update their marketing approach, and hire young team members. Indeed, she put on a clinic in how to turn a brand around. Yet among her wisest decisions was to become a student as well. One of her ongoing steps during her years at Burberry was to listen to young staff who intuitively knew how to reach their peers.[76]

Angela Ahrendts remained teachable as she moved into her next role as senior VP of retail at Apple in 2014. *Business Insider* reported,

Working in a senior leadership role at a technology company like Apple also showed Ahrendts the importance of moving quickly, especially in an age during which our attention is dominated by apps like Instagram, YouTube, and Uber. "I told the leaders very early on, move fast, fast," she said. "So, we got rid of all the manuals, got rid of everything and started doing three-minute YouTube videos. That's how we united and aligned 70,000 people around the world."[77]

Angela concluded, "Building a culture of trust frees people to act on their leadership intuition which results in innovation and the ability to move at a faster pace." She accomplished this at Burberry by practicing *reverse mentoring*.

Popularized by General Electric CEO Jack Welch in the 1990s, reverse mentoring is the secret to every generation adding and extracting value from one another. When veteran teammates and new team members add value to one another from their strengths, everyone wins. Here is a summary of the story.

In the 1990s, computers were going mainstream. Many of General Electric's managers and executives had developed their own methods for working—and those didn't include a laptop or personal computer. But Welch knew that computers were the future. So looking at his workforce, he recognized the team members who were most at-home with computers and technology were the youngest team members—some of them just out of college. The seasoned veterans would need to learn from the rookies. He matched up fifty-eight-year-old managers with twenty-three-year-old team members and requested they practice *reverse mentoring*. The managers could mentor the younger employees about the ways of General Electric. They were Builders and Boomers. They could offer tips on how things got done, the secrets and shortcuts that could accelerate productivity, and so on. However, the managers could also learn from their newest employees, Generation X, about those newfangled computers.

It worked.

Not only did both generations benefit from the other, but deeper relationships were formed. Many continued far beyond the need to learn about the company and the computers. The key was to recognize what each generation offered the other and create environments for growth and connection to take place.

They will understand the world of the future faster than we do.

WHY SHOULD WE LISTEN TO A YOUNGER GENERATION?

When Margaret Mead died in 1978, she was the most famous anthropologist in the world. She helped shape our understanding of culture and how all aspects of human life were connected. While controversial, she helped ordinary people grasp cultural anthropology during the twentieth century. During the latter part of her career, she wrote about modern society and how it was changing the very way we live. My friend Rob Hoskins reminded me of her conclusions a few years ago, and we discussed how prophetic Mead was in her evaluation of our world. She recognized that history has given us three distinct periods of cultural growth.

> When have you benefited from a reverse mentoring relationship?

The Postfigurative Society

For many centuries, people grew up in a *postfigurative society*. This period was marked by tradition. In this era, adults predetermined how life would be for their children. Not much changed. Parents and family prescribed almost everything—from whom the child would marry, to where they would work, to what they would do, to how they'd continue the customs and norms of their society. For millennia, society simply perpetuated the customs of the past. Previous generations dictated how life would look for new generations.

Some refer to this as the Agricultural Age. The primary way people made a living was out in the field with crops and livestock. While there were trades such as blacksmiths and shoe cobblers, most worked the land outdoors. The critical element that differentiated you was your muscles. It's how we got things done.

The Cofigurative Society

As modern times emerged, nations experienced the Renaissance and Enlightenment. Humankind began to question the simple perpetuation of customs, traditions, and ways of life. Gutenberg's printing press increased education levels. Reason ruled the day. This leveled the playing field for young and old. Both became involved in who the young would marry, where they'd live, and what they would do vocationally. Humanity moved to a *cofigurative society*. Because change was in the wind, everyone (adults and emerging adults) had to figure out life together. Everyone was getting used to new discoveries, communication, and characteristics that marked their day.

During this period, which lasted for centuries, the Industrial Age was born. People began to make their world more efficient. Both science and industry progressed as devices were introduced to increase proficiency. It was about speed and volume. The critical element that differentiated you was your machines. It's how we got things done.

The Prefigurative Society

Mead suggested we are currently living in a *prefigurative society*, when change is occurring so fast that adults have almost nothing to offer kids in terms of how to deal with new realities. In fact, the kids are figuring out life as it comes to them. Often, a young person understands the "new norm" sooner than adults do; they adapt to new technology, new patterns, and new paradigms that surface with the new technology and frequently march into new territory before their elders do. Sadly, this makes it difficult to lead young adults, which can make us feel irrelevant as leaders. Adults can feel ill-equipped to guide children since kids embrace the paradigm shifts more quickly than they do. Our time period is marked by innovation and adaptation.

In this period, which has been around for only a few decades, we entered the Information Age. We enjoy not only mass communication from radio and television but also personal interaction through computers and portable devices. Data is everywhere because it can be produced and shared by everyone. The critical element that differentiates us is our minds. That's how most of us make our living and get things done.

But wait, there's more.

I believe we've only begun to taste this prefigurative world. Over the next two decades, we'll experience an astonishing transformation of our lifestyles and expectations. In fact, I believe we are now entering what we might call the Intelligence Age. We not only have technology in our lives; it's now smart technology. The cell phone changed our lives, but the smartphone *transformed* them. Our phones have been smart for years now. Our homes are now smart; residents can communicate remotely to set alarms, lock doors, and turn lights on or off. Our cars are smart. Soon all our appliances and toys will be smart; then our clothes will be smart, communicating with the washer when to use hot or cold water. It will be stunning. So much so, that I believe the critical element to differentiate people will be their morals.

Yep, I just said that.

Our world will be so full of smart technology that we must be prepared ethically and morally for the technology that will be introduced so rapidly. We must harness it. It will be easier to merely be utilitarian instead of a good Samaritan.

In many ways, we're "building the bridge as we cross it." New realities are introduced every year, and the older we are, the more challenging it is to climb out of our ruts and master new habits. In her book *People and Places: A Book for Young Readers*, Mead wrote, "In the modern world we have invented ways of speeding up invention, and people's lives change so fast that a person is born into one kind of world, grows up in another, and by the time his children are growing up, lives in still a different world."[78]

My point in all of this is simple. Our young generations may need older generations to pass along the timeless values and virtues that make civilization work. But we may need them to envision where the future is taking us. As I have said, they have a natural intuition about it all. Just like Beau Jessup. We teach them the timeless. They teach us the timely.

Both older and younger generations need each other.

If this makes sense but sounds daunting, let me share some good news with you. Most people in all generations seem to want this kind of connection. According to a 2020 study by Barna Research Group, more than two-thirds of American adults report having intergenerational friendships—and these are most prevalent among the youngest adults. What's more, Morning Consult data shows (as I mentioned earlier) that Gen Z trusts older generations more than any other social institution.[79]

Where have you seen this reality illustrated in your life?

So, you don't think Generation Z wants to meet with older teammates for guidance?

Three out of four in Generation Z (75 percent) believe their authority figures have their best interests in mind; the same proportion (76 percent) feels valued by the older people in their lives, according to a 2020 Barna Poll. Almost half (44 percent) say they meet regularly with someone whom they consider to be a mentor. According to that same poll, older adults are also a source of support and guidance in tough situations, helping young adults to navigate hardships. Nearly three-fourths (73 percent) agree that when difficult decisions come up, they turn to older generations for advice, and just as many (75 percent) even welcome positive criticism from older adults.[80]

What's even more incredible, perhaps, is the fact that they want to be on the other side of such developmental relationships too. More than one-third (35 percent) of Gen Z respondents said they meet with someone whom they mentor. The challenge goes back to comfort levels. While Generation Z feels comfortable seeking wisdom from older generations, they tend to first go to their peers. A majority of them (64 percent) still say they mainly trust their peers for insights and advice.[81] Why? Gen Z's technology habits enable hyperconnectivity between them. They just text message or DM (direct message) a friend and speak in a convenient and comfortable way. Further, 71 percent of Gen Z members agree older generations don't fully understand the pressures Gen Z finds themselves under.[82] Consequently, if we can somehow communicate empathy and understanding for their plight, we become accessible to them.

The key will be to establish safe places where people from different generations not only interact but where this kind of mentoring and informal coaching can take place. It will require you to become an uncommon leader.

Becoming an Uncommon Leader

In my 2021 book *The Eight Paradoxes of Great Leadership: Embracing the Conflicting Demands of Today's Workplace*, I talk about the difference between common leaders and uncommon ones. I am inviting you to become an uncommon leader—one who is hungry to grow and learn from other generations. Here is a summary of the difference:

Common Leaders	Uncommon Leaders
1. Listen to me when I speak.	1. Speak to me and I'll listen.
2. I know the answer already.	2. I am seeking new alternatives.
3. Never question my judgment.	3. Let's always be asking questions.
4. I seek solutions from experts.	4. I seek answers from anyone.
5. I want your respect.	5. I want your input.
6. This is the way we've always done it.	6. I am looking for ways to make it better.
7. I'll figure it out myself.	7. Let's collaborate and the best idea wins.
8. Never let them see you sweat.	8. I am authentic and vulnerable.

Common Leaders	Uncommon Leaders
9. I have more experience, so I know best.	9. Since I am older, I'm working to adapt.
10. I am the only teacher on this team.	10. I am a lifelong learner.

Thanks to the rapidly changing, smart-tech, on-demand, instant-access world we live in today, younger generations will yearn for leaders who are uncommon. It must become our new normal.

HOW TO MAKE THE MOST OF YOUR BRAIN BASED ON YOUR GENERATION

I believe the key is to embrace the stage of life I am in and capitalize on it. For the first time in my life, I know people from seven sociological generations:

- My aunt and uncle are from the Senior generation (1902–1928).
- My mother and father-in-law are from the Builder generation (1929–1945).
- My wife and I are both from the Baby Boomer generation (1946–1964).
- My teammates Shawn and Nicole are both from Generation X (1965–1982).
- My children are from the Millennial generation (1983–2000).
- My spring intern, Hannah, is from Generation Z (2001–2015).
- My little buddies Wilson and Weston are from the Alpha generation (2016–2030).

Each of these individuals possesses a little different perspective on the world. Why? As I argue early in this book, they were shaped by different events in their early years. Our brains develop a little like wet cement. I recently began to feel a little despondent about this. Reviewing the research and knowing that I'm clearly past midlife, I wondered if I were washed up. I'm not kidding. Our world needs innovation, and at my age, most of that will come from the emerging generation, not the retiring generation. This is one of the reasons I'm committed to developing a new generation of leaders. Our hope lies in developing them. It doesn't lie in me.

Then I discovered some good news for my old brain.

Two Kinds of Intelligence

More than fifty years ago, a British psychologist named Raymond Cattell discovered some fascinating insights as he researched human intelligence. In 1971 he published a book titled *Abilities: Their Structure, Growth and Action*. In this book, he posited that all people possess two kinds of intelligence, but they ebb and flow at different points in life.

The first kind is *fluid intelligence*. We experience this most in our early years. Our brains are young and are best at thinking flexibly, reasoning and solving novel problems. These abilities are strongest in our young adult years and begin to diminish in our thirties and forties.

The second kind is *crystallized intelligence*. We experience this most in our second thirty years. It's defined as the ability to use a stock of knowledge learned from the past. It's the capacity to collate information, summarize it, and express it to others. We do this best past midlife.

Fluid Intelligence	Crystallized Intelligence
1. Strongest our first forty years	1. Strongest our second forty years
2. Adaptation and innovation	2. Clarification and summarization
3. I can see what's coming.	3. I can share what we've learned.
4. I tend to learn things quickly.	4. I tend to teach things quickly.
5. I'm a creator—I invent.	5. I'm a coach—I synthesize.

Arthur Brooks, a social scientist at Harvard Business School, says, "When you're young, you have raw smarts. When you are old, you have wisdom. When you are young, you can generate lots of facts. When you are old, you know what they mean and how to use them."[83]

Darwin and Bach

Two examples from history inform us. Charles Darwin is considered a brilliant scientist, but most people don't realize he made his initial discoveries in his twenties. When he was thirteen years old, he set up a science lab in his garden shed. When he was sixteen years old, Darwin was sent to Edinburgh to train to become a doctor, like his father and grandfather. He transitioned to biology and took a voyage aboard the HMS *Beagle* to study species around the world when he was twenty-two. Some of his best work happened as a result. Sadly, he died years later a very disappointed man. He grew despondent about not staying at the top of his field. The problem was that he expected himself to continue in fluid intelligence instead of learning to capitalize on his crystalized intelligence.

Johann Sebastian Bach may have managed his career better. He wrote groundbreaking music in his twenties and thirties. He grew famous for composing every major Baroque genre, including concertos, sonatas, cantatas, and numerous organ pieces. Along the way, he fathered twenty children. One of his sons, Carl Philipp Emmanuel, introduced the world to classical music. Bach's son was considered the most talented in the family. Instead of brooding over this, he celebrated his son's success and became his best teacher. Bach could have become embittered like Darwin, but instead he took pride in his son surpassing him. He shifted into crystalized intelligence. In his later years, he taught and multiplied his talent in others. He literally died while teaching.

Repurposing Your Life

If you've read this far, I'm sure you care deeply about the emerging generation. If you're like me, you want to make a difference, but you may feel a distance between your mindset and a younger person's mindset. You may even feel a little like a dinosaur. As I said earlier, I felt washed up for a while. But I am repurposing myself again. My career has a new spark to it. Why?

1. I am allowing the young to play to their strengths, and I welcome their new ideas.
2. I expect their innovation and ask them to help me adapt to it.
3. I am pushing myself to play to my strengths, which are mentoring and teaching.
4. I intend to put wind in their sails as they innovate and come up with new ideas.
5. I'll celebrate their success, helping them stand on my shoulders and surpass me.
6. I won't try to be "cool" or "hip." No one looks to me for those cues. I am who I am.

I came to realize that Johann S. Bach's career had two parts. At first, he was a music innovator. Later, as his musical creativity declined, he was a music instructor. He wrote a textbook that a century later was considered both a guide for students and a piece of literature. His best trait was his resiliency, transitioning from creator to coach. Far from frustration or depression, he finished his career a happy father and a marvelous teacher. Like him, we must change where we draw our fulfillment. Let's *pass* wisdom on to the young so they can *surpass us* by standing on our shoulders.

BECOMING A TEACHER AND LEARNER

Let me offer some practical steps you can take to practice the ideas in this chapter.

1. **Match up reverse mentoring relationships across your team.** This is essentially what Angela Ahrendts did at Burberry. She met with those different from her (younger, different skill sets, varied backgrounds) and sought their insight as well as offered hers. Why not match your seasoned veterans with your newest team members and have them swap stories? Then allow them to spot how they could add value and mutually coach one another. Peter Drucker said, "The most pressing task is to teach people how to learn."

2. **Offer them a sequence of questions to start the journey.**
   To avoid awkwardness, provide participants from each generation a set of questions to answer for one another. A helpful
   lineup could be as follows:
   a. Begin by sharing the highlights of your life story.
   b. Identify three elements of your life you have
      in common.
   c. What is most unique about your life or your
      characteristics?
   d. What are one or two areas in which you most need to
      learn or grow?
   e. If you were to help someone by sharing what you know
      best, what would it be?

3. **Make it a weekly (or monthly) goal to learn something new.**
   Each January, I determine five to six areas in which I want
   to grow. They vary from financial investments, to cultivating
   a better marriage, to the art of negotiation. Next, I choose
   specific people who can mentor me in each area. I don't
   assume one person can be a "Socrates" and coach me in all
   areas; I just need a specialist who's ahead of me in one area. I
   meet with them regularly, bring a pad of questions, and seek
   to learn. What if you identified a team of specialist mentors
   who can coach you in your goals?

4. **Add regular personal and professional growth times to your
   team's calendar.**
   To use a cliché, too often we only spend time working *in our
   business* instead of *on our business*. I've improved my personal
   and my team's growth curve by planning times for learning
   and development. We have weekly team growth times. I host
   an optional monthly leadership session and one-on-one
   coaching times too. The key is to be intentional, just like
   we are with our meals. I had a mentor who used to ask me,
   "When was the last time you did something for the *first time?*"

Good question. John Dewey put it this way: "Education is not a preparation for life. It is life itself."

I have an assignment for you. This week, practice "reverse mentoring." Start with yourself. Then, if you're in a position of influence on your team, match older executives who may be hesitant to learn new technology, apps, or paradigms with younger team members. Yet allow the older executives to add value on what they've learned about getting things done at your organization. Just like at General Electric, relationships can be deepened. Trust can be built. Value can be added. And both can receive dignity.

Everyone benefits.

Talk It Over

(**1**) How could reverse mentoring add value to your organization?

(**2**) What could you do to set these relationships up that isn't overscripted?

(**3**) Who could you meet with in a reverse mentoring relationship?

15

MY CHALLENGE FOR YOU

THE DIVERSITY WE FEEL AMONG OUR TEAMS IS NOT GOING AWAY anytime soon. Because people are living and working longer, we will experience multiple generations on our staff. Because people are traveling more often, we will experience multiple backgrounds on our staff. And because people are more approving of mixed marriages and partnerships, the types of races will continue to increase. To wish for a homogenous group of people to work alongside is wishing for a past that has long ago evaporated.

What we must do is learn to lead others who are different from us and who are from various generations. I've come to believe this will make our organizations stronger. Our teams will have intuition about reaching a variety of demographics (in our customer base) because we ourselves are from a variety of demographics.

GoodHire released a study uncovering how full-time American workers (really) felt about their jobs in 2021. They surveyed four thousand Americans—with an equal number of Baby Boomers, Gen Xers, Millennials, and Gen Zers—and found:

- 83 percent of all American workers prefer a four-day workweek.
- 57 percent of Millennials are very happy at work, making them the happiest generation.
- 22 percent of Gen Zers are either unhappy or hate work, making them the most unhappy generation.
- 60 percent of Millennials find great meaning and purpose at work—making them the most fulfilled generation.
- Gen Z is the least fulfilled, with just 41 percent finding great meaning and purpose.
- Gen Z is the least satisfied with work-life balance, while Millennials are the most satisfied.
- Only 30 percent of Baby Boomers are completely happy with their pay, followed by Gen Z (32 percent), Gen X (42 percent), and Millennials (47 percent).
- 68 percent of Millennials are happier working remotely, while Baby Boomers are the least happy with remote work (37 percent).
- Only 9 percent of all American workers surveyed are less engaged and satisfied when working remotely.
- Millennials lead the charge in searching for a new job in the next twelve months, with 46 percent of them planning to do so.
- Baby Boomers are the least likely to be on the job hunt the following year (19 percent).
- Gen Xers, Millennials, and Gen Zers are most bothered by their boss or manager, while Baby Boomers are most bothered by insufficient pay.[84]

Don't miss this: Millennials are the happiest with their work, but they are the most likely to be pursuing a new job. They find work (in general) fulfilling—but maybe not the job they currently have. Can we change that through connecting with them?

One of my favorite examples of a leader who made others feel he connected with them is President Franklin D. Roosevelt. He led our nation during the Great Depression and World War II, and he knew he had to communicate that he understood the fears and struggles that Americans felt. He delivered speeches over the radio, talks he called "fireside chats." They were meant to feel like conversations as families gathered around the radio in their family rooms to listen. He assured Americans that we would get through those difficult times.

Roosevelt passed away in 1945. As you can imagine, thousands of people lined the streets of Washington, DC, to pay their respects as his casket was carried through the city. People were seen wiping tears from their eyes, grieving this man who'd been elected as president four times. One man was overtaken by emotion and fell to his knees weeping over the loss of his leader. After a moment, another gentlemen next to him helped him to his feet. "Did you know the president?" the gentleman asked.

"No," the sobbing man replied. "But he knew me."

My hope is that everyone I lead can say that about me. And I wish that for you as well. Let's build bridges rather than walls to these various generations.

APPENDIX

AN EARLY INTRODUCTION TO THE ALPHA GENERATION

I'D LIKE YOU TO MEET THE MINI-MILLENNIALS: GENERATION ALPHA, the population of kids born after Generation Z. Like a mirror of their parents, this generation is on track to become the largest generation in history worldwide.

Although the findings are still early, there are signs the Alpha generation could end up looking like the Senior generation one century before them. News journalist Tom Brokaw called the Seniors the "Greatest Generation" as they survived a pandemic (Spanish Flu), grew up in the "Roaring Twenties," endured the Great Depression as young people, and then fought in World War II. They were more *doers* than *talkers* when it came to reaching their goals, and those Seniors achieved some mighty outcomes. We can hope the Alpha Gen responds much the same.

There's not yet a general consensus on the birth years of Generation Alpha. Some sources say Alpha Generation birth years begin in 2011. However, many definitions of Generation Z ending in

2012 or 2015 would indicate that the oldest members of Generation Alpha were born in 2013 or 2016. I suggest Generation Z was born between 2001 to 2015. This new generation of children were born into a very different world:

- Theirs was a politically polarized world, with the Trump administration taking office.
- A pandemic marked their early years, with infections, mask-wearing, and increased death rates.
- The mental health of their Millennial and Gen Z parents has been a problem their entire lives.
- The number of US mass shootings increased; in 2019 we had more shootings than days in the year.
- Conspiracy theories and distrust became common among millions of Americans.
- Smart technology has become ubiquitous. Alphas have used smart devices since preschool (90 percent).
- The economy and culture were especially volatile and uncertain, spiking then dropping in their early years.

Let's review some interesting facts about the Alpha Generation.

DO YOU KNOW THE ALPHAS?

While the Alpha generation is predicted to be the largest generation in the world, they're much less prevalent in the United States since Millennial parents have had fewer children, and those children, when ready to have babies, will be a smaller population of parents. Thanks to the impact of the pandemic, birth rates dropped dramatically as families felt they could not afford more kids. In addition, fertility rates have fallen due to higher standards of living and women prioritizing a career first, then having children later, according to Rachel Lopez in "Baby Monitor: See How Family Size Is Shrinking."[85] Provisional data from the Centers for Disease Control and Prevention reveals that US fertility rates have fallen below the replacement level of 2.1 since 1971. In 2017 it dropped to

1.765, the lowest in three decades. In short, we are not replacing our current population.

More than half of the human population (55 percent) now lives in urban areas. If the current trend continues, it will reach two-thirds by the middle of this century. A direct consequence of urbanization is falling fertility rates. In rural areas, children can be considered an asset—that is, additional labor. But in the cities, children are a burden. They are an additional expense.

The United Nations estimated in 2019 that the human population will reach about 9.7 billion by 2050, but this is lower than earlier projections. Already, eighty-three of the world's countries now have subreplacement fertility. In 2018 we witnessed the first time that the number of people above sixty-five years of age (705 million) exceeded those between the ages of zero and four (680 million). Education is one of the most important determinants of fertility. The more educated a woman is, the later she tends to have children, and fewer of them. That being said, here is what we know about Alphas:

- They will likely be the most educated generation ever.
- They will likely be the most technologically immersed generation ever.
- They will likely be the most materially endowed generation ever.
- They will likely be the most impatient generation ever.
- They will be the generation who experiences more virtual (Siri, Alexa) relationships.
- They will be the most likely generation to spend their childhood without both of their biological parents.

The title, Alpha Generation, is usually credited to Mark McCrindle, a generational researcher in Australia who leads a consulting agency. In 2008 his online survey revealed people felt that following Generation Z ought to be a return to "A," or alpha, the first letter in the Greek alphabet. According to McCrindle, "Gen Alpha will likely stay in education longer, start their earning years later and so stay at home with their parents later than even their predecessors, Gen Z and Gen Y. The role of parents, therefore, will span a longer age range—with many of these Gen Alphas likely to still be living at home later into their 20s."

Because the Alphas are exposed to the realities of the world at younger ages (90 percent of them were on a smart portable device in preschool), they will care about the world much sooner and much more than preceding generations. A branding agency recently polled a group of seven- to nine-year-olds on a wide range of mostly nondivisive issues (such as the importance of "making sure everyone has enough food to eat") and concluded that Generation Alpha "cares more about *all* issues than their Millennial and Baby Boomer [predecessors] did when they were kids, or even than they do now."[86] Child entertainment is increasingly dominated by smart technology and streaming services, with interest in traditional television concurrently declining. Studies show allergies, obesity, and health problems related to screen time have become increasingly prevalent among kids in recent years. Think of the changes to childhood this way:

- **The tablet is the new pacifier.** When my kids were toddlers, we gave them a pacifier if they became fussy or fidgety. Today nine out of ten preschool-aged children are on a tablet or portable device amusing themselves.[87] It tends to pacify them.
- **The baby monitor is the new babysitter.** These monitors have been around for decades, but now we use them to watch both the children and the babysitter we've hired while we're away from our home. Cameras are everywhere.
- **Netflix is the new playground.** Our kids were outside playing more than kids are today. Children now will spend hours vegging and binging on Netflix shows. They're sedentary but safe, secluded, and satisfied. Virtual is close enough.
- **Fortnite is the new pickup baseball game.** I recall playing outside for hours after school with whoever was available for a baseball or basketball game. Now, pickup games are played

with friends or strangers on a video screen. They can be anywhere in the world.

- **Instagram is the new photo album.** This one has made life easier. Instead of buying a physical photo album and storing it away in the attic, we now have our library of pics on social media sites we can access more simply and faster. We can filter them too!

- **Google is the new encyclopedia.** Move over dictionaries, textbooks, and encyclopedias—Google, Siri, and Alexa are here to answer all our questions. By default, kids will revert to Google over Wikipedia to find facts and news. The Internet's always accurate, right?

- **YouTube is the new TV.** In 2019 data revealed that kids spent more time watching YouTube videos than watching television shows. The videos are raw and, unlike TV, the videos are unregulated and unrated. This could be troublesome for parents.

- **TikTok is the new shopping mall.** In 2021 the social media app TikTok passed Google as the most popular platform in the world.[88] Kids spend more time on it than they do on visits to the mall to hang out. It provides hours of entertainment that feel raw and real.

- **Medication is the new time-out.** Over the years, kids have been given larger amounts of meds for a widening variety of allergies or diagnoses. We have to be careful that these meds don't replace the pain of disciplining them.

In our desire to make life convenient, quick, and easy, Generation Alpha members are the beneficiaries of our new brand of parenting and leadership. Unfortunately, unless we make changes, the Alphas could be the loneliest generation our world has seen. In our focus groups, kids reported higher levels of solitude than past generations and say they feel lonely almost every day. (A pandemic and quarantine in early childhood didn't help.) It is easier to make connections today but tougher to experience authentic and deep relationships. Research psychologist Jean Twenge notes there is a "link between the rise of smartphones and social media and the increase in depression, anxiety and loneliness in today's youth."

HOW SHOULD WE LEAD THEM?

In light of the early research on the Alpha Generation, these kids will need some discerning leadership in our homes, schools, teams, and workplaces as they enter the job market.

1. **Focus on developing their emotional intelligence.**
   They will naturally feel at home with screens, much like Generation Z before them. We must be intentional about helping them build interpersonal skills and teaching self-management.
2. **Nudge them to play with physical toys.**
   While Alphas will acquire new skills thanks to new tech, we must know that as the use of physical toys is reduced, the development of imagination and creativity will suffer.
3. **Help them cultivate deeper relationships.**
   Since our digital connections are often superficial and normal for children, we must enable them to develop meaningful interactions with friends and acquaintances.
4. **Promote time for physical activity and outdoor exercise.**
   Like Generation Z before, children are more sedentary and obese than past generations. Why not have them shoot some hoops as they review spelling words or take walks each day?
5. **Limit their screen time.**
   The data shows that a kid who spends less than two hours daily on portable devices is far less vulnerable to anxiety or depression. If it's over two hours, then their vulnerability climbs markedly.

Five Experiences That Can Be Rites of Passage for Generation Alpha

I read about a father, Paul Wallich, who built a camera-mounted drone helicopter to follow his young son to the bus stop. He wanted to ensure his son arrived at the bus stop safe and sound. There is no doubt that gizmo provided some entertainment for everyone. For me, Paul Wallich gives new meaning to "helicopter parent."

Today, I see not only a new generation of kids on our hands but a new generation of parents as well. While I applaud the engagement of these moms and dads, we've focused so much on safety, self-esteem, and status that our children can grow into adulthood unready for the hard knocks of life. Too often,

- we risk too little.
- we rescue too quicky.
- we rave too easily.

Over time, we fail to offer the rites of passages that former generations gave kids. I decided to do it differently. Since 1979 I've been committed to mentoring emerging leaders—both students and young professionals. I became a father in 1988 and now have two adult children. Over time, I identified the experiences that are the most meaningful to my mentees; they help kids mature as well as build grit and depth. Collectively, they serve as a sort of "rite of passage" for them. I invite you to consider inserting these experiences as you invest in your kids.

Do Something Scary

There is something about stepping out of our comfort zones to attempt a risky act that's unfamiliar and even a little frightening that makes us come alive. Our senses are heightened when we feel we are taking a risk; we don't know what we're doing; we have to trust and even rely on one another. Ideally, these initiatives are intentional and well-planned, but they should not be scripted. They must include the element of chance. As a mentor, I've taken my mentees downtown to spend the night with homeless people. Those students were wide-eyed as we interacted with an entirely different population of people and slept on trash bags with newspapers as a blanket. A small dose of "danger" mixed with a large dose of "unfamiliar" accelerate growth.

When my son was twelve, he and I took a father-and-son trip to a city he'd never visited before. We explored some new places, but the scariest part the four-day trip was when I traded places with him in our car and had him drive it around a parking lot. After explaining the gears and pedals, Jonathan overcame his panic and drove that big automobile. In moments, he was grinning from ear to ear. This sparked a remarkable conversation comparing his fear to what he'll experience becoming a man. Manhood is not for the fainthearted; it's about responsibility, about being "drivers," not "passengers" in life.

Facing fears is a rite of passage for kids. Doing something that's neither prescribed nor guaranteed unleashes adrenaline and other chemicals in our bodies that awaken us. Other "feel-good" chemicals also come into play with scary experiences, including dopamine, endorphins, serotonin, and oxytocin. Part of the reason more teens don't "come alive" is we've protected them from high stakes in the name of safety.

Meet Someone Influential

Another challenge for them to rise to is meeting someone they deem significant. Because children are less at home meeting adults face-to-face, the encounter itself stretches them. On top of that, meeting significant people invites them to prepare questions to ask and fosters listening skills as well. These can be famous people, but they don't have to be. The key is, they're people the students believe to be important due to what they've accomplished. I was invited to participate in a special meeting in Washington, DC, when my daughter, Bethany, was just nine years old. Since I would be meeting congresspeople, ambassadors, and other civic leaders,

I wanted her to experience it with me. Encountering noteworthy people can be intimidating, even to adults. It was fun to introduce her to these people and witness her interacting with them and eventually feeling quite at home.

For the first twenty years of my career, I worked for bestselling author John C. Maxwell. My kids were fortunate enough to build a relationship with John and his wife, Margaret. Interacting with the Maxwells enabled them to overcome social fears and to see noteworthy people as "human." Today my kids are not starstruck by celebrities and are comfortable interfacing with people of all ages and backgrounds.

Travel Someplace Different

We all know that travel is an education in itself. While classrooms are useful learning contexts, leaving the classroom and all that's familiar is better still. Travel not only pushes kids out of their comfort zones but also forces them to work at understanding others, at connecting with new environments, and at problem-solving because those new contexts are places where we cannot default to our subconscious. When we're in familiar situations, we can shift into "cruise control." We can become numb to reality since we're on our home turf. This doesn't occur in a foreign location. Cross-cultural service trips stir our curiosity, beg us to research, beckon us to learn, and invite us to grow up. We think new thoughts in new places. My friend Glen Jackson says, "A change of pace plus a change of place equal a change of perspective."

One of my favorite memories is of taking my daughter, Bethany, to Croatia during the Serbian-Bosnian War in 1993, when she was only five. My goal was to enable her to be comfortable in environments that were both foreign and struggling. Bethany helped serve clothes, food, and blankets to refugees who had relocated to the area. She saw poverty she'd never seen before and experienced the joy of providing for the needs of those who were displaced and suffering. It was life-changing.

Chase a Meaningful Goal

I believe teens need us to let them pursue an objective that has high stakes and give them full control. Past generations matured more effectively because they were given responsibility for jobs and goals that had genuine meaning at a young age. When we lower the stakes or give kids an artificial purpose to engage in, they end up with artificial maturity. While I believe in the value of academics, it's still a facsimile of a meaningful world, created by our current, contemporary structures. I meet too many students who master the skill of getting a good grade yet struggle to translate those grades into a career, a marriage, or a family. Information is meaningful as it becomes application.

When I speak of chasing a big goal, I mean aiming for a target that has deep meaning to your child, one that stretches their capacity and is important. As a teen, my son told us he wanted to pursue a career in the entertainment industry. My wife and I decided to let Jonathan step out at sixteen years old. As a homeschooler, he had more freedom with his time. He and his mom moved from Atlanta to Los Angeles for seven months so he could try his hand at acting. The experience was revealing, as you can imagine. Life in Burbank in an apartment competing with hundreds of other kid actors revealed the highly competitive world there. He soon recognized that the real influencers are the storytellers behind the camera. Returning home, Jonathan was a different person, clearer about his calling. He earned a degree in screenwriting and now writes scripts every week.

Wait and Work for Something You Want

One of the reasons teens and college students find "adulting" so challenging today is that they've grown up in a world where almost everything is "instant access" and "on demand." It can coerce us to expect instant gratification. The opposites of this trait are patience and work ethic. These signal maturity because the person is able to see a goal in their mind that is still invisible externally.

Consider what's happening in their brain. When a teen envisions an outcome before they actually experience it, it can cause the brain to release dopamine and endorphins, which signal pleasure and rewards. As teens experience *learned industriousness* ("I keep working because I know it will pay off"), acetylcholine kicks in. This chemical plays a vital role in learning and memory, and it deepens neuropathways as kids associate rewards with working for a goal. In our home, our kids paid for half of their first car, half of their smartphone, and half of a trip they each wanted to take in school.

My favorite outcome from all these experiences with my kids came years later. My daughter, Bethany, called me when she was twenty-five years old and living two thousand miles away. When I asked why she called, she replied, "I guess I just called to say *thanks*."

I said, "Well, every dad loves to hear that from his children—but what drove you to call me? Did something happen at work today?"

After collecting her thoughts, she blurted out, "I guess I just noticed that I work with a bunch of young professionals like me, but nobody sees the big picture around here. They act lazy, they're on their phones, and I don't see any work ethic. They're not ready to live on their own!" Then, she paused and concluded, "I guess I just realized that you and Mom did get me ready. And I just wanted to say *thanks*."

Through tears, I smiled and replied, "Bethany, you just made my year."

WHAT OUR KIDS NEED MOST FROM US EVERY DAY

Parents must remember they are leaders. Our families are our teams. We must remember first and foremost that our kids may have different reactions to disruptive times and be careful to not minimize the angst they are feeling, while at the same time remaining a source of steady hope. Kids need three items from their leader during a crisis, in this order: they spell the word *CAB*. I tell myself to jump in a CAB every day if I am going to reach my desired destination.

Context

It's easy for anyone to hear the news all day and get freaked out. We feel angst from all the bad news and the uncertainty this season. Good leaders provide context to problems: *This is not the worst crisis we have ever faced, yet it deserves our focused attention.* Context means you furnish perspective on what's happening, you stay knowledgeable on current details, and you become a source of wisdom, especially for those who fall on either end of the spectrum: those who feel it's no big deal and those who feel like the sky is falling. When kids see a calamity on social media and don't know what to think, you must be the one who offers perspective. Just as toddlers watch the reactions of adults to know whether they should cry when they fall down, our kids watch us to get a sense of context.

Applications

People usually need leaders to offer practical action steps in times such as these. Children will need them even more. If their minds are flooding and overwhelmed, our job is to turn the flood into a river. Sometimes adults need reminders of the applications we've been given to respond well to COVID-19: wash your hands many times a day, stay six feet apart from others in public, wear a mask outside, and shelter in place. The best leaders leave people with clear applications for their day. In fact, clarity is the greatest gift a leader can offer their team right now. It is true for parents as well. Be honest if you don't know the answers to all their questions, but be clear on the few actions you can be sure about. Clarity is king.

Belief

Napoleon Bonaparte said, "Leaders are dealers in hope." In uncertain times, I believe we owe it to people, and especially our children, to offer belief and hope for a better future. They need to hear a person they look up to speak words of belief and offer reasons why we believe: *This season will one day pass, and we may just return to a better normal.* Throughout history, many disease outbreaks have resulted in better vaccines, better job conditions, and better health practices. I believe we will improve due to COVID-19. Americans, once polarized in recent times, began to cooperate and focus on helping one another. We're applauding health-care professionals and essential workers. We will get through this and be better for it.

My friend Collin told me he got the greatest compliment from his teenage son during the pandemic in 2020. As the two were talking, his son said, "Dad, Mom's getting anxious about what's going on, isn't she?"

Collin paused, then agreed. "Yes, son, she's a little nervous right now." After a moment, the teen asked, "But you're not scared are you, Dad?"

Collin smiled and said, "No, son. I'm not scared."

His son replied, "Good. That's what I was hoping."

ACKNOWLEDGMENTS

I FEEL LIKE THE PROVERBIAL "TURTLE ON THE FENCE POST." YOU KNOW what I mean, don't you? That turtle only got there with the help of someone else. This book is a great example of a team effort and following are the people who were primarily involved. I am grateful.

I wish to thank...

Andrew McPeak, who's worked alongside me for seven years, helping me think through book ideas. We enjoy an iron-sharpens-iron relationship as colleagues, and I love you like family. Thanks for your tireless efforts, Andrew, to produce helpful resources.

Ben Wade, who took an early look at this manuscript and offered notes. Ben, you are a thinking person who has good input on ideas, always desiring to make them better. It showed up in this project. Thanks for our relationship and especially the relationship you have with my daughter.

Grace Hooley, who helped early on with some line edits and identifying sources. Grace is a person who wants to do things right, and I appreciate her for it. Thanks, Grace, for your help on this manuscript and your desire to tend to the details.

Matt Litton, who reviewed and edited my last four books and became a friend in the process. Matt, you are a like-minded writer who always makes my thoughts better and more logical before they become public. I always feel better about a book when you've been involved.

David Drury, whom I met thirty years ago when you were in college. I was impressed with you then, and I am even more so now. Thanks for helping to research data that I needed for this book. Your thoughts and advice make mine better than they were. I am grateful for you.

Allen Harris, who entered the journey in the spring of 2022 and became a godsend. Your edits and ideas were exactly what I still needed, and you provided them with grace. Thanks for taking the manuscript to a higher level. I hope to collaborate with you again in the future.

Andrea Callicot, who carved out writing days that we didn't plan on in the beginning. You have been with me now for many years and know the importance of sacred days to create. Thanks for believing in me and for helping to manage and "boss" my calendar.

Steve Moore and the Growing Leaders team. You are living examples of making good decisions out of faith in each other and believing the best when in doubt. You represent four generations and consistently find ways to collaborate and bring something unique to the table.

Jonathan Merkh and Jen Gingerich at Forefront Books, who "made it happen" as you oversaw the production of this project, including the cover design, editing, layout, and formatting. Thanks for your timely and empowering input as this manuscript became a book. You're outstanding.

Chad Johnson, who oversaw the branding and marketing of this book with the Maxwell Leadership team, including Chris, Heather, Jason, Becky, and so many others. Thanks for believing in the value of this resource and pushing to get the word out.

Mark Cole, CEO of Maxwell Leadership, who invited me to offer this book as the first resource released by Maxwell Publishing. My longtime friendship with Mark and my kinship with the Maxwell team made this decision a no-brainer. Thanks for your friendship and belief, Mark.

John Maxwell, who, as soon as he heard about this book, affirmed its value and encouraged me to pursue it. You have been a gigantic cheerleader for me since I was in college. I cannot put into words, John, how grateful I am for you. You'll have to imagine.

Finally, Pam, who said "yes" to my marriage proposal in 1980. I'd choose you all over again, as you've only gotten better and better with time. You have read this manuscript and helped me to improve the ideas in it since I began talking about them in 2001. I adore you.

NOTES

1 Paul Taylor and the Pew Research Center, *The Next America* (New York: Public Affairs, 2014), xx.

2 2 *Encyclopaedia Britannica*, s.v. "Great Depression," https://www.britannica.com/event/Great-Depression.

3 José A. Tapia Granados and Ana V. Diez Roux, "Life and Death during the Great Depression," *Proceedings of the National Academy of Sciences of the United States of America* 106, no. 41 (October 13, 2009): 17290–95.

4 Megan W. Gerhardt, Josephine Nachemson-Ekwall, and Brandon Fogel, "Harnessing the Power of Age Diversity," *Harvard Business Review*, March 8, 2022, https://hbr.org/2022/03/harnessing-the-power-of-age-diversity.

5 Amy Morin, "Parents, Please Don't Attend Your Adult Child's Job Interview," *Forbes*, August 29, 2017, https://www.forbes.com/sites/amymorin/2017/08/29/parents-please-dont-attend-your-adult-childs-job-interview/?sh=1d98afc72a31.

6 "Chapter 1: The Future of Jobs and Skills," World Economic Forum, https://reports.weforum.org/future-of-jobs-2016/chapter-1-the-future-of-jobs-and-skills/.

7 Neil Howe and William Strauss, *Generations: The History of America's Future, 1584 to 2069* (New York: Harper Perennial, 1991).

8 Emma Goldberg, "The 37-Year-Olds Are Afraid of the 23-Year-Olds Who Work for Them," *The New York Times*, October 28, 2021, https://www.nytimes.com/2021/10/28/business/gen-z-workplace-culture.html.

9 Pew Research Center, PewResearch.org, 2008.

10 Deborah Ancona, https://mitsloan.mit.edu/404.

11 Jean Twenge, *Generation Me* (New York: Simon and Schuster, 2006).

12 Veronica Zambon, "What Are Some Different Types of Gender Identity?" *Medical News Today*, November 5, 2020, https://www.medicalnewstoday.com/articles/types-of-gender-identity.

13 Joshua Q. Nelson, "Minnesota Fourth Graders Told to Hide 'Equity Survey' Questions from Parents," Fox News, July 26, 2021, https://www.foxnews.com/media/students-told-to-hide-equity-survey-questions-from-parents.

14 "The Great Generational Divide," Association for Talent Development, February 5, 2014, https://www.td.org/insights/the-great-generational-divide.

15 Taylor, *Next America*, xx.

16 *Global Demographic Report 2018*, Insights Group, pp. 9–10, https://www.insights.com/media/2205/insights-discovery-global-demographic-report.pdf.

17 Hilda K. Kabali et al., "Exposure and Use of Mobile Media Devices by Young Children," *Pediatrics* 136, no. 6 (2015): 1044–50, https://doi.org/10.1542/peds.2015-2151.

18 *Zero to Eight: Children's Media Use in America 2013*, Common Sense Media, 2013, https://www.commonsensemedia.org/sites/default/files/research/zero-to-eight-2013.pdf?utm_source=Master+List+%28Monthly%2C+Weekly%2C+Daily%2C+Events+%26+Offers%29&utm_campaign=f09cc79481-RSS_EMAIL_CAMPAIGN&utm_medium=email&utm_term=0_b8af65516c-f09cc79481-304149693.

19 Greg Toppo, "Techie Tykes: Kids Going Mobile at Much Earlier Age," *USA Today*, November 2, 2015, https://eu.usatoday.com/story/tech/2015/11/02/pediatrics-mobile-devices-study/75012604/.

20 "Improvements in Television Technology," Encyclopedia.com, https://www.encyclopedia.com/arts/news-wires-white-papers-and-books/improvements-television-technology.

21 Kelly Pledger Weeks and Caitlin Schaffert, "Generational Differences in Definitions of Meaningful Work: A Mixed Methods Study," *Journal of Business Ethics* 156, no. 4 (2019): 1045–61,
https://doi.org/10.1007/s10551-017-3621-4.

22 "The Baby Boom," Khan Academy, https://www.khanacademy.org/humanities/us-history/postwarera/postwar-era/a/the-baby-boom.

23 Zachary Wagenmaker, "The Baby Boom and the Suburbs," Course Hero, https://www.coursehero.com/file/82346019/Zachary-Wagenmaker-1-Baby-Boom-and-Suburbs-Reading-Digital-Versionpdf/.

24 Wagenmaker, "Baby Boom and the Suburbs."

25 D'Vera Cohn and Paul Taylor, "Baby Boomers Approach 65—Glumly," Pew Research Center, December 20, 2010, https://www.pewresearch.org/social-trends/2010/12/20/baby-boomers-approach-65-glumly/.

26 Tayor, *Next America*, xx.

27 "Quiz: Does Birth Order Affect Who You Are?" Grow by WebMD, https://www.webmd.com/parenting/rm-quiz-birth-order.

28 Isaac Maddow-Zimet and Katheryn Kost, "Pregnancies, Births and Abortions in the United States, 1973–2017: National and State Trends by Age," Guttmacher Institute, March 2021, https://www.guttmacher.org/report/pregnancies-births-

abortions-in-united-states-1973-2017.

29 Paul Taylor and George Gao, "Generation X: America's Neglected 'Middle Child,'" Pew Research Center, June 5, 2014, https://www.pewresearch.org/fact-tank/2014/06/05/generation-x-americas-neglected-middle-child/.

30 Taylor and Gao, "Generation X."

31 Lauren Strapagiel, "Gen Z Is Calling Gen X the 'Karen Generation,'" Buzz-Feed News, November 14, 2019, https://www.buzzfeednews.com/article/laurenstrapagiel/gen-z-is-calling-gen-x-the-karen-generation.

32 Kristina Byas, "3-Year Changes to Each Generation's Debt," LendingTree, July 10, 2019, https://www.lendingtree.com/personal/changes-to-each-generations-debt/.

33 "Millennials Became the Largest Generation in the Labor Force in 2016," Pew Research Center, April 10, 2018, https://www.pewresearch.org/ft_18-04-02_genworkforcerevised_feature1/.

34 Peter Gray, "The Many Shades of Fear-Based Parenting," *Psychology Today*, March 25, 2019, https://www.psychologytoday.com/us/blog/freedom-learn/201903/the-many-shades-fear-based-parenting.

35 Robert L. Leahy, "How Big a Problem Is Anxiety?" *Psychology Today*, April 30, 2008, https://www.psychologytoday.com/us/blog/anxiety-files/200804/how-big-problem-is-anxiety.

36 Kristenn Bialik and Richard Fry, "Millennial Life: How Young Adulthood Today Compares with Prior Generations," February 14, 2019, https://www.pewresearch.org/social-trends/2019/02/14/millennial-life-how-young-adulthood-today-compares-with-prior-generations-2/.

37 "Mental Health on College Campuses," MentalHelp.net, https://www.mentalhelp.net/aware/mental-health-on-campus/.

38 Dan Schawbel, "Why 'Gen Z' May Be More Entrepreneurial than 'Gen Y,'" *Entrepreneur*, February 3, 2014, https://www.entrepreneur.com/article/231048.

39 David Stillman and Jonah Stillman, "Move Over, Millennials; Generation Z Is Here," Society for Human Resource Management, April 11, 2017, https://www.shrm.org/resourcesandtools/hr-topics/behavioral-competencies/global-and-cultural-effectiveness/pages/move-over-millennials-generation-z-is-here.aspx.

40 "Generation Z in the Workforce," Concordia University–St. Paul, https://online.csp.edu/resources/infographic/generation-z-in-the-workforce/.

41 *What Gen Z Wants: How to Build an Organization That Attracts and Retains the Next Generation of Talent*, Ripplematch, https://f.hubspotusercontent20.net/hubfs/8139278/What%20Gen%20Z%20Wants%20-%20Building%20an%20Organization%20to%20Attract%20and%20Retain%20The%20Next%20Generation%20of%20Talent.pdf.

42 "Age Is Just a Number: The Truth behind Generational Stereotypes at Work,"

The Addison Group, https://addisongroup.com/insights/insight/age-is-just-a-number-the-truth-behind-generational-stereotypes-at-work/.

43 Arlene S. Hirsch, "How to Manage Intergenerational Conflict in the Workplace," Society for Human Resource Management, https://www.shrm.org/resourcesandtools/hr-topics/employee-relations/pages/how-to-manage-intergenerational-conflict-in-the-workplace.aspx.

44 Bialik and Fry, "Millennial Life."

45 *The Deloitte Global 2021 Millennial and Gen Z Survey*, Deloitte, accessed May 11, 2021, https://www2.deloitte.com/global/en/pages/about-deloitte/articles/millennial-survey.html.

46 *Deloitte Global 2021 Millennial and Gen Z Survey*.

47 Bialik and Fry, "Millennial Life."

48 Richard Fry, "Millennials Are the Largest Generation in the U.S. Labor Force," Pew Research Center, April 11, 2018, https://www.pewresearch.org/fact-tank/2018/04/11/millennials-largest-generation-us-labor-force/.

49 "Personal Histories Exercise," The Table Group, 2012, https://ttg-wp.s3.amazonaws.com/content/download/personal-histories-exercise,

50 Sue Shellenbarger, "The Office Rookies Who Ask for the World," *The Wall Street Journal*, April 8, 2019, https://www.wsj.com/articles/the-office-rookies-who-ask-for-the-world-11554730098.

51 Goldberg, "37-Year-Olds Are Afraid."

52 Sue Shellenbarger, "The Office Rookies Who Ask for the World."

53 Brené Brown, *Braving the Wilderness* (New York: Random House Publishers, 2017).

54 Jon Simpson, "Finding Brand Success in the Digital World," *Forbes*, August 25, 2017, https://www.forbes.com/sites/forbesagencycouncil/2017/08/25/finding-brand-success-in-the-digital-world/?sh=53d2d5e2626e.

55 Victoria Sakel, "Why Generation Z Isn't Interested in Your Statements, Promises and Commitments—Yet," Morning Consult, June 22, 2020, https://morningconsult.com/2020/06/22/why-gen-z-isnt-interested-in-your-statements-promises-and-commitments-yet/.

56 *Gen Z*, vol. 2, *Caring for Young Souls and Cultivating Resilience*, Barna Group and Impact 360, 2021, pp. 55–56.

57 Nick Davis, "Millennials Are More Likely to Oppose Racism," Data for Progress, January 29, 2019, https://www.dataforprogress.org/blog/2019/1/29/unpacking-millennials-racial-attitudes.

58 Rafael Gomez and Juan Gomez, *Workplace Democracy for the 21st Century: Towards a New Agenda for Employee Voice and Representation in Canada*, Broadbent Institute, June 2016, p. x, https://d3n8a8pro7vhmx.cloudfront.net/broadbent/pages/7736/attachments/original/1592501160/Workplace_Democracy.pdf?1592501160.

59 Jennifer Miller, "For Young Job Seekers, Diversity and Inclusion in the Work-

place Aren't a Preference, They're a Requirement," *Washington Post*, Feburay 18, 2021, https://www.washingtonpost.com/business/2021/02/18/millennial-genz-workplace-diversity-equity-inclusion/.

60 Miller, "For Young Job Seekers."

61 Kevin Gray, "Formal Diversity Recruity Efforts Climb among Employers," National Association of Colleges and Employers, March 7, 2022, https://www.naceweb.org/diversity-equity-and-inclusion/trends-and-predictions/formal-diversity-recruiting-efforts-climb-among-employers/.

62 Katherine Martinelli, "How Millennials Are Solving the Workplace Diversity Problem," Ozy, October 3, 2018, https://www.ozy.com/news-and-politics/how-millennials-are-solving-the-workplace-diversity-problem/89414/.

63 Cara Wong, *Boundaries of Obligation in American Politics* (Cambridge: Cambridge University Press, 2012), xx.

64 Chris Craddock, "Diversity and Inclusion: The Millennial Perspective," Projections, accessed May 2021, https://abetterleader.com/diversity-and-inclusion-the-millennial-perspective/.

65 Susan Page, Sarah Elbeshbishi, and Mabinty Quarshie, "Exclusive: Stark Divide on Race, Policing Emerges since George Floyd's Death, USA TODAY/Ipsos Poll Shows," *USA Today*, March 5, 2021, https://www.usatoday.com/story/news/politics/2021/03/05/americans-trust-black-lives-matter-declines-usa-today-ipsos-poll/6903470002/.

66 Dominic Price, "The Surprising, Science-Backed Value of Boredom at Work," *Atlassian*, September 27, 2021, https://www.atlassian.com/blog/productivity/boredom-at-work-creativity-neuroscience; Bryan Robinson, "Why Neuroscientists Say, 'Boredom Is Good for Your Brain's Health,'" *Forbes*, September 2, 2020, https://www.forbes.com/sites/bryanrobinson/2020/09/02/why-neuroscientists-say-boredom-is-good-for-your-brains-health/?sh=6f949be31842.

67 Christopher Mims, "For Teens, Romances Where the Couple Never Meets Are Now Normal," *Wall Street Journal*, May 18, 2019, https://www.wsj.com/articles/for-teens-romances-where-the-couple-never-meets-are-now-normal-11558152022?redirect=amp.

68 Ariel Scotti, "Teens Are Having Entire Relationships Online without Ever Meeting," InsideHook, May 22, 2019, https://www.insidehook.com/daily_brief/sex-and-dating/teens-are-having-entire-relationships-online-without-ever-meeting.

69 "Empathy: College Students Don't Have as Much as They Used To," University of Michigan, May 27, 2010, https://news.umich.edu/empathy-college-students-don-t-have-as-much-as-they-used-to/.

70 https://nationaljobs.washingtonpost.com/article-details/779/interpersonal-skills-a-necessity-in-personal-and-work-relationships/.

71 If you'd like to go deeper with this content, you can find discussion questions

and exercises at GrowingLeaders.com. You can also get more information on the origins of the content or speaking events at TimElmore.com.

72 *Global Demographic Report 2018*, Insights Group, https://www.insights.com/media/2205/insights-discovery-global-demographic-report.pdf.

73 Karen Gilchrist," This 19-Year-Old Is Paying Her Way through College by Naming over 677,000 Chinese Babies," CNBC, March 21, 2019, https://www.cnbc.com/2019/03/21/beau-jessup-teen-pays-college-fees-by-naming-chinese-babies.html.

74 Elizabeth Spaulding, "How Burberry Won Over Millennials," Bain & Company, December 7, 2015, https://www.bain.com/insights/how-burberry-won-over-millennials/.

75 Spaulding, "How Burberry Won Over Millennials."

76 "Chick-Fil-A Leadercast 2012," Integreat Leadership, accessed January 15, 2021, https://integreatleadership.com/development/chick-fil-a-leadercast-2012/.

77 Lisa Eadiciccio, Business Insider, May 12, 2019.

78 Margaret Mead, *People and Places: A Book for Young Readers* (New York: Bantam Publishers, 1959), xx.

79 Sakel, "Why Generation Z Isn't Interested."

80 *Gen Z*, vol. 2, *Caring for Young Souls and Cultivating Resilience*, p. 56.

81 Kim Parker and Ruth Igielnik, "On the Cusp of Adulthood and Facing an Uncertain Future: What We Know about Gen Z So Far," Pew Research Center, May 14, 2020, https://www.pewresearch.org/social-trends/2020/05/14/on-the-cusp-of-adulthood-and-facing-an-uncertain-future-what-we-know-about-gen-z-so-far-2/.

82 Parker and Igielnik, "On the Cusp of Adulthood."

83 Arthur Brooks, *From Strength to Strength: Finding Success, Happiness and Deep Purpose in the Second Half of Life* (New York: Portfolio, 2022), xx.

84 Sara Korolevich, "The Meaning of Work in 2021—A Generational Divide," GoodHire, November 9, 2021, https://www.goodhire.com/resources/articles/meaning-of-work-survey.

85 Rachel Lopez, "Baby Monitor: See How Family Size Is Shrinking," *Hindustan Times*, February 29, 2020, https://www.hindustantimes.com/more-lifestyle/baby-monitor-see-how-family-size-is-shrinking/story-UoCyWR2C4BPrmXGoSXi7II.html.

86 "Generation Alpha: New Study Shows How Being the Most Diverse Generation Yet Impacts Their Behaviors Now & in the Future," Business Wire, December 9, 2019, https://www.businesswire.com/news/home/20191209005093/en/Generation-Alpha-New-Study-Shows-Diverse-Generation.

87 Dimitri A. Christakis, "Interactive Media Use at Younger than the Age of 2 Years," *JAMA Pediatrics* 168, no. 5 (2014): 399–400, doi:10.1001/jamapediatrics.2013.5081.

88 Joseph Pisani, "TikTok Topped Google as the Most Visited Website in 2021," MarketWatch, December 22, 2021, https://www.marketwatch.com/story/tiktok-topped-google-as-the-most-visited-website-in-2021-11640205873.

ABOUT THE AUTHOR

DR. TIM ELMORE, FOUNDER AND CEO OF GROWING LEADERS, IS A world-renowned expert on leadership as well as on Generation Y and Generation Z. He equips executives, educators, coaches, youth workers, managers, and parents to impart practical life and leadership skills to today's emerging generations. His books addressing different generations include *Generation iY: Our Last Chance to Save Their Future*; *Marching Off the Map*; *Generation Z Unfiltered: Facing Nine Hidden Challenges of the Most Anxious Population*; and *The Pandemic Population*. Tim is also the founder of Tim Elmore Inc. and offers resources and events for leaders who serve in business and nonprofit organizations. You can learn more about his work, book him to speak, and purchase his resources at TimElmore.com, JohnMaxwell.com/Tim, and GrowingLeaders.com.

MAXWELL
LEADERSHIP

TIM ELMORE

ONLINE CLASS

LOOKING FOR MORE INSIGHTS INTO THE GENERATIONAL GAPS WE ARE ALL FACING?

IN THIS ONLINE COURSE WITH TIM ELMORE, YOU WILL:

- Get the most out of the strengths of each age group on your team.

- Build bridges rather than walls so that loneliness becomes connectedness.

- Connect people to learn how both veterans and rookies can mentor one another.

- THIS COURSE INCLUDES VIDEOS WITH **TIM ELMORE**,

- DOWNLOADABLE PDF GUIDES, AND

- APPLICATION QUESTIONS TO HELP YOU APPLY EACH LESSON.

Go to newdiversitybook.com/course to enroll now.

HABITUDES
FOR NEW
PROFESSIONALS:

THE ART OF LAUNCHING YOUR CAREER

HELPING BUSINESS LEADERS MOVE THEIR
NEW EMPLOYEES FROM BACKPACK TO
BRIEFCASE.

Today's workplace is a long-distance journey
from the school campus.

HABITUDES FOR NEW PROFESSIONALS
uses the power of images, conversations, and
experiences to help young employees and new
professionals:

- Overcome a sense of entitlement
  towards tasks that seem "beneath
  them."

- Persevere in a career when it may
  move slower than they wish.

- Learn to trust their supervisor, even
  when they don't completely agree
  with decisions.

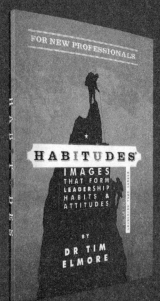

Growing Leaders bookstore
URL: https://growinglead-
ers.com/store/habi-
tudes-new-professionals/